PENGUIN

EARLY CHRIST..... .. . ..

CAROLINNE WHITE read Classics and Modern Languages at St Hugh's College, Oxford, and then wrote a doctoral thesis on Christian ideas of friendship in the fourth century, published in 1992. After two years spent in South Africa, teaching Latin at UNISA in Pretoria, she returned to Oxford, where she divides her time between research projects and tutoring in medieval and patristic Latin literature. She has worked on the supplement to the Liddell and Scott Greek Lexicon and the Bodleian Incunable catalogue, and she is now assistant editor on the Dictionary of Medieval Latin from British sources. She has also published translations of the correspondence between St Jerome and St Augustine, some of Gregory of Nazianzus' autobiographical poems, a selection of Early Christian Latin poetry and excerpts from Augustine's *Confessions*.

Early Christian Lives

Life of Antony by Athanasius
Life of Paul of Thebes by Jerome
Life of Hilarion by Jerome
Life of Malchus by Jerome
Life of Martin of Tours by Sulpicius Severus
Life of Benedict by Gregory the Great

Translated, edited and with Introductions by
CAROLINNE WHITE

PENGUIN BOOKS

PENGUIN BOOKS

Published by the Penguin Group
Penguin Books Ltd, 80 Strand, London WC2R ORL, England
Penguin Group (USA) Inc., 375 Hudson Street, New York, New York 10014, USA
Penguin Books Australia Ltd, 250 Camberwell Road, Camberwell, Victoria 3124, Australia
Penguin Books Canada Ltd, 10 Alcorn Avenue, Toronto, Ontario, Canada M4V 3B2
Penguin Books India (P) Ltd, 11 Community Centre, Panchsheel Park, New Delhi – 110 017, India
Penguin Group (NZ), cnr Airborne and Rosedale Roads, Albany, Auckland 1310, New Zealand
Penguin Books (South Africa) (Pty) Ltd, 24 Sturdee Avenue, Rosebank 2196, South Africa

Penguin Books Ltd, Registered Offices: 80 Strand, London WC2R ORL, England

www.penguin.com

This translation published in Penguin Classics 1998

038

Translation, notes and introduction copyright © Carolinne White, 1998
All rights reserved

The moral right of the translator has been asserted

Set in 10/12.5pt Monotype Bembo
Typeset by Rowland Phototypesetting Ltd, Bury St Edmunds, Suffolk
Printed and bound in Great Britain by Clays Ltd, Elcograf S.p.A.

ISBN-13: 978-0-140-43526-9

www.greenpenguin.co.uk

CONTENTS

AD 250   Paul withdraws to Egyptian desert   Persecutions under Decius and
                                                                      Valerian

————— ANTONY —————

AD 300   Hilarion settles as monk in   Persecutions under Diocletian and
         Palestine   Maximin
         Pachomius sets up ascetic   Constantine becomes emperor
         community in Egypt
         Malchus joins monastic
         community

————— ATHANASIUS —————

AD 350   Basil tours eastern monasteries
         Martin leaves army   Julian the Apostate becomes
                                                                      emperor
         Martin made Bishop of Tours   Theodosius the Great becomes
         Augustine's conversion   emperor

————— MARTIN —————

————— JEROME —————

————— SULPICIUS SEVERUS —————

AD 400   Cassian moves to Gaul and writes   Visigoths under Alaric sack Rome
         Conferences and Institutes

AD 450			
		BENEDICT	Theodoric the Ostrogoth becomes ruler of Italy
AD 500	Benedict retires to Subiaco		
			Boethius executed at Pavia
			Justinian becomes emperor
	Benedict moves to Monte Cassino		
		GREGORY	Totila king of the Ostrogoths overruns Italy
AD 550			
			Lombards move south into Italy
	Gregory becomes pope		
AD 600			

The World of Antony, Paul, Hilarion, Malchus, Martin and Benedict.

BLACK SEA

Constantinople •

Caesarea •

Nisibis •

Athens • • Antioch

Hilarion's Retreat •

CYPRUS

Jerusalem
• Bethlehem
Majuma •• • Gaza
Thabatha

MEDITERRANEAN SEA

Alexandria • • Pelusium

Paretonium

LIBYA

• Nitria

• Scetis

• Pispir • Antony's Cave

• Paul's Cave

RED
SEA

R. Nile

• Tabennisi
• Thebes

The Early Development of Monasticism

Martin Luther, looking back over the development of Christian monasticism during the Middle Ages,[1] praised Antony as the founder of a monastic way of life true to the spirit of the Gospels. Benedict was the author of a monastic Rule which became, as it were, the gold standard against which all later forms of western monasticism measured themselves. These two figures, Antony and Benedict, the Elijah and Elisha of Christian monasticism, stand at the chronological boundaries of this volume, for the eminent Christians whose lives are recorded here span the period from the mid third century when Antony was born to the mid sixth century when Benedict died, in other words, the period of Late Antiquity and the early Middle Ages. The six biographies of Antony, Paul, Hilarion, Malchus, Martin and Benedict have been selected for translation here primarily because of the enormous influence they were to have on the development of western spirituality and on many forms of literary composition throughout the Middle Ages. However, their interest lies not only in their *Nachleben*. They were written at various dates between the mid fourth century and the late sixth century, a period of crucial importance in history, and written by contemporaries or near-contemporaries of the people whose lives are the subject of these works: the authors are therefore in touch with the society, the places and concerns amidst which these lives were played out, and are in a good position to give us valuable information about them. Indeed, in most cases the authors were personally acquainted with the subjects of their biographies. For example, Athanasius, bishop of Alexandria, is likely to have met Antony, both in the Egyptian desert and at Alexandria,[2] and it was to Athanasius that Antony bequeathed his sheepskin tunic and worn-out cloak; Jerome claims to have heard the story of Malchus' life from Malchus himself while living in Syria in the 370s; Sulpicius Severus travelled from south-west France to visit Martin at Tours; while Pope Gregory the Great, although he was writing almost half a century after Benedict's death, acquired much of his information about Benedict's life and miracles from people who had known Benedict personally.

All these biographies share a monastic theme, providing information about the lives of men who were the founding fathers of monasticism in both the eastern and western areas of the Roman Empire. Nowadays, perhaps, the term monasticism primarily conjures up ideas of life in an enclosed community, lived according to a rigid pattern, often in magnificent buildings amidst beautiful countryside. However, such forms of monasticism developed only gradually, with Benedict in the sixth century playing an important role in the institutionalization of the monastic life in the west. It is true that the origins of Christian monasticism are obscure[3] but it seems certain that this movement really took off during the fourth century, developing as a result of the initial inspiration of a few men during the third and fourth centuries, each of whom made a decision to withdraw from the world of ordinary human affairs in order to be able to serve God in what they regarded as a more perfect way. Withdrawal from society with this particular aim appears to have occurred first in the desert regions of Egypt and the Middle East: according to Athanasius, Antony was the first to choose such a life of radical solitude, while Jerome, writing a few years later, expresses his belief that Paul of Thebes[4] was Antony's predecessor in the Egyptian desert. He also claims that Hilarion was the first in Palestine to adopt such a way of life.[5] And yet even within these early accounts there is evidence that certain people had already chosen various forms of life of chastity and withdrawal. Antony, when he started out on the ascetic life, is said by Athanasius to have entrusted his sister to the care of 'respected and trusted virgins' and taken as a model for his own life an old man in a neighbouring village who had from his youth practised the solitary life.[6] And Gregory of Nazianzus, in his funeral oration on his friend Basil of Caesarea, mentions the fact that Basil's paternal grandparents fled to the forested mountain regions of Pontus during Maximin Daia's terrible persecutions in the early years of the fourth century just before Constantine took over as emperor;[7] there they spent seven years, exposed to frost, wind and rain, avoiding all contact with the outside world and living off the spoils of hunting.

Why did people at this period opt for such a radical lifestyle? In the case of Basil's family, it was clearly a question of escaping the threat of martyrdom and maintaining their dedication to Christianity. As for the period after Constantine's conversion and his edict of toleration in 313 which promised religious freedom, the period when the ascetic life seems to have become increasingly popular, the principal theory for this sudden popularity is that many were driven by a desire to find a new means of proving their dedication to Christ at a time when the persecution had been replaced by tolerance and martyrdom by privilege. Certainly this may have been one motive, but it would be wrong to suppose that after 313 life as a Christian suddenly became a soft option. Christians could still be subjected to pagan attacks, particularly under the anti-Christian emperor Julian (361–3), but also to persecution by heretics, particularly the Arians,[8] a very powerful group who even had imperial backing under the emperors Constantius (337–61) and Valens (364–78). Such persecution could take the form of being compelled to do military service, being driven into exile, or falling victim to physical violence. Socrates' *Ecclesiastical History*, although written some hundred years later, provides a vivid picture of the kinds of 'Christian on Christian' violence raging throughout the fourth century, and Jerome mentions specifically the persecution by the Arians of Athanasius, whom they drove into exile on a number of occasions.[9] Orosius, who wrote his *History against the Pagans* in the early fifth century at Augustine's suggestion, mentions the monks as a particular target of the persecutors. He writes:

The vast solitudes of Egypt and its stretches of sand which were unfit for human use because of their aridity, barrenness and the extreme danger from numerous serpents, were then filled and inhabited by great numbers of monks. Officers and soldiers were sent on a new type of persecution to drag away to other places these saintly and true soldiers of God. Many companies of saints suffered death there. As for the measures taken against the Catholic churches and orthodox believers throughout the various provinces under these and similar orders, let my decision to remain silent be sufficient indication of their nature.[10]

It is clear from these early Christian biographies that there were in fact many different motives and circumstances that might impel people to adopt such a life. In the case of Antony, who was born in 251 just as a period of intense persecution was starting, Athanasius states that certain biblical texts were crucial in inspiring Antony to leave his home and sell his property. As a young Christian, recently orphaned, Antony was initially struck by the thought of how the apostles gave up everything to follow Christ and how others, as related in the Acts of the Apostles (4:34–5) had sold all their possessions and put the proceeds at the apostles' disposal for distribution to those in need. This thought was translated into a personal moral imperative when Antony shortly afterwards heard these words of Christ being read as the Gospel lesson in church: *If you would be perfect, go, sell what you possess and give to the poor, and you will have treasure in heaven* (Matthew 19:21). And so, in about 269, Antony sold the whole of his inheritance, gave the money to the poor, made arrangements for his sister's welfare and withdrew to a life of discipline and isolation, at first not far from his own village but later at increasingly greater distances from other people.

Paul of Thebes, Jerome tells us,[11] was a young man at the time of the persecutions carried out under the emperors Decius and Valerian.[12] In 250 Decius had ordered that everyone must have a certificate to prove that he had publicly sacrificed to the pagan gods: anyone who did not possess such a certificate was in serious trouble. Many Christians were put to death for not sacrificing, while others submitted and agreed to sacrifice or managed to buy certificates (such Christians were then regarded by the Church as 'lapsed'),[13] while yet others went into hiding.[14] At some moment during this period, at about the time when in another part of Egypt Antony was born, Paul decided to move to a remote spot until the persecutions should cease. But when he realized that his brother-in-law was about to betray him to the authorities he was forced to flee even further afield, this time right into the desert.

Hilarion heard about Antony in the Egyptian desert while studying at Alexandria: inspired by Antony's example he decided, after a two-month period spent learning with Antony, to settle as a hermit near Gaza in Palestine, probably during the first decade of the fourth century. This was at about the time of Diocletian's persecutions, though no mention is made of these in Jerome's biography of Hilarion. As in the cases of Antony, Paul and Hilarion, it was as an adolescent on the brink of adulthood that Malchus took the decision to leave the path of life his family expected him to take, but unlike them he was apparently motivated primarily by a desire to avoid marriage and to retain his virginity. It was for this reason that he moved away from home and joined a monastic community, probably around the year 320.

This was about the time of Martin's birth in what is now Hungary. Already as a young child Martin is said to have conceived a longing for a dedicated Christian life. Far from Egypt, Palestine or Syria as he was, by the age of twelve the future St Martin of Tours 'longed for the desert', though this longing for a life of withdrawal and service of God had to wait some years for fulfilment because of his father's determination that his son should have a military career. As for Benedict nearly two centuries later, he turned from the world on experiencing, as a student in Rome, how unsatisfying and treacherous were worldly pursuits and pleasures. In order to be able to please God alone, he decided that he must withdraw to a life of solitude. Solitude was a keystone in the early edifice of monasticism. In fact, the term 'monk' derives, via the word '*monachos*',[15] from the Greek word '*monos*' meaning 'alone'.

If solitude and withdrawal from the world were characteristic of early Christian monasticism, another element considered essential was celibacy, the commitment to a life of chastity. In fact it is this ideal, reflecting Jerome's own obsession with it, that is the focal point of the *Life of Malchus*. Having entered upon a life of detachment and chastity, the monk would practise a rigorous existence of self-scrutiny and discipline, involving manual labour as well as prayer largely based on meditation on Scripture.[16] If practised correctly and assiduously, it was believed, such a life would lead to spiritual liberation and an openness to love of God and of other people. In the words of Louis Bouyer, 'The love of God that would . . . drive Antony into solitude is in no way the desire for a lazy, aesthetic, egoistic kind of contemplation: it is the most realistic kind of Christian charity.'[17]

To those who would condemn these early monks for rigorous austerities which might seem purely negative, John Cassian, writing his works on eastern monasticism early in the fifth century, would reply, 'Our fastings, our vigils, meditation on Scripture, poverty and the privation of all things are not perfection, but the means of acquiring perfection.' This perfection, the aim of the monastic life, consists, according to Cassian, in 'the purity of heart which is love'.[18]

If such a life of austere routine might seem dull, it should be noticed that it is portrayed as being a constant battle against demonic attacks: the monk must always be on the watch, to guard against the temptation to sin. The life of withdrawal is regarded as in some sense an imitation of Christ's withdrawal into the desert after his baptism in order to face the devil's temptations. The Life of Antony in particular gives us a most vivid account of a life which is by no means dull, for Antony is kept on his toes by the devil who is constantly trying to catch him out, to surprise him by means of cunning and terrifying attacks.

If successful, such a life would produce a state of calmness and humility, at least periodically. In rare cases, the monk would also receive the grace of prophecy and the ability to perform miracles, as was the case with Antony, Hilarion, Martin and Benedict. Such spectacular spiritual gifts would inevitably lead to great fame: Antony received letters from the Roman emperors (to which he could hardly be bothered to reply) and Martin dined with (and gently snubbed) the emperor. The monk would generally be regarded as a spiritual father, attracting in particular those who wished to emulate him and those in search of healing. This might be regarded as a positive aspect of the monastic life, a way in which the monk could put his love into practice and be saved from becoming too self-absorbed. Is not a large portion of the Life of Antony devoted to Antony's speech of advice and encouragement given to those who came to visit him after he had spent twenty years in complete solitude in the deserted fort? And yet it is striking how often the monk, dedicated as he is to a life of solitude, far from seeing this as an opportunity, will complain that his peace is being disturbed by the crowds of people desperate for individual attention from him, and may even seek to escape. Antony said that like a fish out of water, so the monk cannot survive when taken out of the desert.[19] Similarly, it happens on occasion that the monk will, at least at first, refuse to heal a sick person, despite the entreaties of desperate relatives: for example, Hilarion tries to avoid curing the three sick boys until their mother's insistence forces him to yield and to go into Gaza to visit them; and Martin tries to avoid curing the paralysed girl at Trier until persuaded by the bishops to go to her house and see her.[20] Such incidents perhaps challenge our conception of the relation between love of God and love of neighbour.

The essential elements of the monastic life, then, are withdrawal from the world, chastity, abstinence, unceasing prayer and manual work. However, it is also true that from an early stage these ingredients were combined in various ways with the result that different forms of the ascetic life evolved. By the end of the fourth century there were already examples, in Egypt and elsewhere, not only of the eremitic or anchoritic life – the life of complete solitude in the style of Antony – but also of the coenobitic life – the life of communal monasticism – as well as of a form sharing characteristics of both the solitary and the communal.[21]

Antony's life was marked by progressive movements deeper and deeper into the desert, away from civilization. From his native village he moved to a tomb a short distance from his home, and later to the mountain fort, where he refused to speak to those who brought food. At the end of twenty years his peace was disturbed when a crowd of people arrived and forced him to come out to speak to them. The drama of this episode is conveyed by Athanasius in the fourteenth chapter of his *Life of Antony*. Deserting the fort in order to find somewhere he might regain the solitude he longed for, Antony ended up at the foot of the so-called Inner Mountain,[22] a place he fell in love with as soon as he saw it. Here he was to spend over forty years until his death at the age of 105, probably in the year 356. Antony did periodically return to the Outer Mountain at Pispir by the Nile, to visit his followers and admirers, and he did visit Alexandria, once to support the martyrs at the time of Maximin Daia's persecutions[23] and later at a time of particular crisis for the orthodox Christians in their struggle to survive in the face of Arian persecution.[24] Yet most of his life was spent in complete isolation, far from the volatile crowds of the Egyptian metropolis. For sustenance he depended on occasional deliveries of bread from the nomads travelling past or from his devoted followers, until he managed to grow some vegetables at the foot of the mountain so as to have something to offer the visitors who would arrive from time to time, exhausted by the difficult journey across the desert. Such an extreme way of life was perhaps rare, but Antony was not alone in adopting a life of solitude. Paul of Thebes, too, spent most of his long life in the Egyptian desert far from civilized society.[25]

Hilarion, too, is said to have spent twenty-two years in solitude in Palestine, though he did not build his hut quite so far from civilization as Antony. The rest of Hilarion's life was spent trying to escape from the effects of the fame he had acquired as a holy man. He was forced to move from Palestine to Sicily, from Sicily to the Dalmatian coast and then on to Cyprus, where he finally died in his remote and rugged hide-out up in the mountains.

However, even among Antony's followers, it became more common for those who sought solitude to live in their own cells but less distant from other anchorites. We must imagine large numbers of these monks covering a vast area of the desert, each keeping to his own tiny cell except when he goes out to gather spiritual wisdom from older monks. It is this sudden flowering of monasteries (in the sense of groups of monastic cells) in the desert that Athanasius describes with the striking paradox of the desert becoming a city.[26]

This was the kind of community, with the addition of a church where the monks would congregate at regular intervals, said to have been founded by Ammon at Nitria,[27] south of Alexandria and on the edge of the Western Desert, soon after 330. Ammon had withdrawn to that spot[28] after living a celibate life with his wife for eighteen years, by mutual agreement. As this semi-eremitic community expanded, Ammon felt the need to send out a colony so as to allow the monks sufficient solitude. It is said that at this point Antony intervened and advised Ammon that they should walk out into the desert from Nitria after the late-afternoon meal. They walked until sunset, and then Antony said, 'Let us pray and set up a cross here so that those who want to build may build here.'[29] This new settlement, to be known as Cellia (the Cells), was no more than twenty kilometres from Nitria, so that the monks could visit each other easily. Rufinus gives us the following eyewitness account of the life here:

Those who have already begun their training in Nitria and want to live a more remote life, stripped of external things, withdraw there. For this is the utter desert and the cells are divided from one another by so great a distance that no one can see his neighbour nor can any voice be heard. They live alone in their cells and there is a huge silence and a great quiet here. Only on Saturday and Sunday do they meet in church and then they see each other face to face as men restored to heaven.[30]

Under Ammon's direction the community at Cellia grew until there were about 600 anchorites living there. They had their own church, but were dependent on Nitria for their bread. Ammon seems to have lived for twenty-two years at Nitria, visiting his wife twice a year. When he died, Antony is said to have seen his soul being taken up to heaven by angels.[31] By the end of the fourth century, according to Palladius, the monks on the mountain at Nitria numbered 5,000.[32]

Further south, at Scetis among the natron lakes in the desert of Wadi-el-Natrun, another community of semi-eremitic monks sprang up around the deeply respected figure of Macarius,[33] a former camel driver. He had started out as a monk in his own village, but on being accused of fathering a child there he decided, even though proved innocent of the charge, to withdraw to greater solitude. But the solitude at Scetis did not last long after this: Macarius' fame spread and the desert at Scetis filled with those who wished to emulate his way of life or to learn from him. It is from the monks at Nitria, Cellia and Scetis that so much of the monastic wisdom was derived, often collected and written down by visitors. Such writings include the various collections of sayings of the desert fathers, known as the *Apophthegmata Patrum*, which provide a vivid and moving picture of the monks' austere routine but also of their astounding humility and psychological perceptiveness.

The third form of monasticism to develop during the fourth century was the life in an ascetic community, usually known as coenobitism from the Greek words for common life (*koinos bios*). This development is also associated with one individual, this time Pachomius,[34] the son of wealthy pagan parents. Conscripted into the army as a young man, he was being taken down the Nile with other soldiers. On the way they spent the night in the prison at Thebes[35] where they were brought food by some Christians. Impressed by their kindness, Pachomius asked what Christians were and when he was told, he decided on the spot to dedicate his life to Christ, if only he could get away from the army. This he did a few months later, probably in the year 313. After baptism he seems to have spent some time learning the austerities of the solitary life in the Antonian mould. One day, at a deserted village called Tabennisis, a voice came to him telling him to stay there and construct a monastery where many would come to be monks. In obedience to this voice, Pachomius began to build, and in this way the word for a single cell came to be applied to a community of monks. Gradually the disciples started arriving and the monastery came to life.

There were striking differences between this monastery and earlier groups of anchoritic cells. Pachomius' monastery was built not in the desert but on cultivated land near the Nile. It was a walled community with not only a hall for communal worship at certain times of the week, but also a refectory, guest-house, bakehouse, hospital and a number of houses in each of which there lived up to forty monks, in separate or shared cells. The community had a leader and each house had a 'house master'. It is easy to see how influential this pattern of communal life would become, far beyond the green belt of the Nile! It did not take long for the monastery at Tabennisis to become too full, and there came a need to expand.[36] Pachomius first established another monastery at Faou, some miles down the river, and by 352 there were some 600 monks here.[37] Expansion continued even after Pachomius' death, possibly in 346. The esteem in which he was held by this time is clear. Antony, when he learned of Pachomius' death, praised him highly. According to the *Lives of the Fathers*, Antony told two of Pachomius' disciples who visited him at the Outer Mountain, 'It was a good ministry he undertook in bringing together so many brothers.' When one of the disciples protests, 'But it is you, father, who are the light of all this world,' Antony rejects this, suggesting that Pachomius' hard work had resulted in a form of the monastic life that was a beneficial development from the earlier solitary asceticism practised by Antony himself. All the Pachomian monasteries were organized in accordance with the Rule, the set of precepts put together over the years by Pachomius,[38] which provided details of how the monks should dress, sleep, eat, work and worship. In 404 this work was translated into Latin – from a Greek translation of the Coptic original – by Jerome, now himself the head of a monastic community at Bethlehem. In this form Pachomius' Rule was to reach the west and make a contribution to the development of coenobitic monasticism, the form of monastic life that was to become fundamental to western society in the Middle Ages.

By the time that Jerome was translating Pachomius' work, his former friend Rufinus (by now his deadliest enemy) had already translated from the Greek the monastic rules composed by Basil of Caesarea during the years 358–64. Basil had travelled among the monks of Syria, Palestine and Egypt as a young man[39] and had come under the influence of Eustathius of Sebaste,[40] who had introduced the ascetic movement in eastern Asia Minor. Despite his early attraction to the solitary life in the desert, Basil eventually returned to his home city of Caesarea where he became bishop and established monastic communities. Here, too, he found time amidst the strains of ecclesiastical politics to write a collection of monastic rules in question-and-answer form. In these he demonstrated that he eschewed extreme asceticism, emphasizing instead the importance of practical charity. This work did contribute to the growing trend in favour of the coenobitic way of life, though it is arguable how influential it was in the long run for the eastern forms of monasticism. In the prologue to the Latin translation, Rufinus expressed his hope that Basil's Rule would become known in 'all the monasteries of the west'. A century and a half after Basil's death, in his own Rule Benedict mentions the

Rule 'of our holy father Basil' as a 'tool of virtue for good-living and obedient monks'.[41]

Under the influence of Church leaders such as Basil, Athanasius and Augustine the monastic life entered the cities. By the end of the fourth century we find people leading lives of asceticism and chastity in Caesarea, in Rome, in Trier.[42] Jerome relates how Marcella, a Roman aristocrat, decided to practise the ascetic life in her house in Rome as a result of meeting Athanasius during his exile there: he apparently told her about Antony and Pachomius and this inspired her decision at a time when 'no great lady in Rome knew anything of the monastic life'.[43] Jerome also writes of his friend Asella, who was living an ascetic life in Rome, that she considered solitude a delight and found for herself the desert of the monks in the centre of the busy city.[44] Even in Egypt there were monks not only in the desert areas but also in the towns and cities. The author of the *History of the Monks in Egypt*, visiting Oxyrhynchus on the Nile in 394, writes:

The city is so full of monasteries that the very walls resound with the voices of monks. Other monasteries encircle it outside so that the outer city forms another town alongside the inner. The temples and capitols were bursting with monks; every quarter of the city was inhabited by them.[45]

As in the case of Marcella, personal contact with those who had experience of desert monasticism was an important means by which enthusiasm for the ascetic life spread. That the Latin west came to know about the monastic way of life seems to have been to a large extent due to reports brought by eastern Christians who had direct experience of monasticism – men such as Athanasius and Evagrius of Antioch who both spent several years in the west – or by westerners who had visited the east, curious to witness the desert life at first hand.

As well as personal contacts, accounts at third hand of those who had adopted a life of asceticism, detached from careers and family responsibilities, could also be influential in others' decisions to adopt some form of monastic life. Augustine relates in the *Confessions*[46] how, at a critical moment on the long road towards conversion to a life of Christian dedication, he was told about the monks of Egypt and of how two men at Trier had been moved by a chance reading of

Athanasius' biography of Antony to renounce their civil-service careers in order to devote themselves fully to God. Their renunciation of the world inspired Augustine to do the same. What is perhaps surprising about this episode is that Augustine, in 385, had apparently never heard of Antony before. Augustine's experience is perhaps the most famous but certainly not the only example of the crucial importance of Athanasius' *Life of Antony* (addressed to the monks overseas) in its Latin translation in spreading knowledge of the desert way of life. Other works such as the *History of the Monks in Egypt*, translated into Latin and expanded by Rufinus, and the writings of John Cassian, continued to provide information and to inspire people to adopt a life of spiritual asceticism.

Despite the excitement aroused by reports of Antony's way of life, it is notable that in adopting and developing forms of monastic life, western ascetic enthusiasts tended to end up leading some form of coenobitic life. For example, Jerome began by attempting a harshly ascetic life in the Syrian desert[47] but he could only stand this for a few years; then, after periods at Constantinople and Rome, he chose to spend the last thirty-five years of his life in a monastic community at Bethlehem. When Augustine returned to North Africa after his conversion in Italy, he did not withdraw to a life of solitude. Instead he gathered a group of like-minded friends around him at Thagaste and later at Hippo and together they led a life of prayer and study even while Augustine was forced to accommodate the demands imposed on him as priest and bishop.

In the case of Martin, and later Benedict, it would seem that both were initially attracted to the solitary life but that as their reputation grew they became increasingly involved with others and drawn into positions of responsibility, Martin as bishop of Tours and Benedict as abbot at Monte Cassino. Sulpicius Severus tells us that Martin conceived a desire for the solitary life from his earliest boyhood and that as soon as he obtained his discharge from the army (probably in 356, the year of Antony's death), he established himself in a hermit's cell at Milan. When driven out by the Arian faction striving to take power within the Church, Martin and one other monk moved to the island of Gallinara off the Italian coast where they lived a life of utter simplicity and isolation.[48] Later he moved to Poitiers to be close to his mentor, bishop Hilary of Poitiers, who had returned from exile in the east. Even at Poitiers Martin lived on his own, about ten kilometres outside the city at Ligugé. His next move, forced upon him by his election to the bishopric, was to Tours. At first he lived not in a bishop's palace but in a simple cell next to the cathedral. Finding that life there was too noisy and distracting, Martin moved to another cell a few kilometres outside Tours, on the banks of the Loire. Of course, as bishop he was hardly likely to be able to lead a quiet life in obscurity: soon he was joined by many others wishing to lead an eremitic existence and in this way the regime here at Marmoutier quickly developed into something between the semi-eremitic and the coenobitic. The regime there may not have been as highly organized as in the Pachomian monasteries in Egypt, but the monks around Martin did apparently meet together for food and prayer at certain times of the day.

A feature of the western monastic settlements at this period seems to have been their relative proximity to civilization, in contrast to the usual Egyptian pattern. This was true, for instance, of Benedict's monastery at Monte Cassino, for although it was established on a mountain top, the mountain loomed over the main highway running between Rome and Naples. Benedict had in fact started out in a similar manner to Antony: having made the decision to cut himself off from the pleasures and responsibilities of the world, he withdrew from Rome to the village of Enfide together with his devoted nurse, and lived in or near the church there. At that stage, such a form of limited withdrawal clearly seemed to him adequate. According to Gregory's *Life of Benedict*, it was after Benedict's first miracle, as people's attention came to focus on this remarkable young man, that he felt the need to escape to complete peace and solitude at Subiaco,[49] in about the year 500. Here, some eighty kilometres east of Rome, he spent about three years living in a remote cave, his whereabouts known only to the monk Romanus who provided him with the little food he required. This was Benedict's equivalent of Antony's Inner Mountain and it was from this point of isolation that he was gradually drawn into a more coenobitic life, ending up as abbot of Monte

Cassino, and where he wrote the Rule which was to become the great authority for the monastic regime during the Middle Ages. A few years later, after Benedict's death, Monte Cassino was abandoned when the Lombards attacked it, and the monks fled to Rome. Benedict's monastery remained derelict until 717 when it was restored by Petronax of Brescia. In the meantime the abbot of Fleury in France had read Gregory's account of Benedict's life in the *Dialogues*. He was troubled to think of the relics of Benedict and his sister Scolastica lying abandoned at Monte Cassino, so he sent a monk to bring their relics to Fleury, from which time the monastery became known as Saint-Benoît-sur-Loire. This did not prevent the later monks at Monte Cassino from being adamant that they still possessed the relics of these two saints.

It would seem that particularly in the west the communal life won out eventually both in terms of many individuals' personal experience and of the overall development of the monastic life, and yet views on the relative merits of the eremitic and coenobitic ways of life differed throughout this period. Antony and Paul of Thebes were regarded as the great exponents of the eremitic existence. Although in later life Antony did return to the Outer Mountain on a regular basis[50] to give spiritual advice to his devotees, he clearly felt the need to live in increasingly rigorous solitude. Paul also gradually moved further into the desert until he found the mountain cave where he was to spend the rest of his life without any human contact, apart from at its very end when Antony came to visit him. But we have seen how Pachomius felt called from his life of solitude to create a community of monks, while Basil, after visiting the desert hermits in the years after Antony's death, decided that the communal life was more suitable as allowing for the practice of such virtues as charity, patience and obedience. Many also believed that the communal life most accurately reflected the life of the early Christians at Jerusalem as depicted in the Acts of the Apostles (4:32), where property was held in common and all shared 'one heart and one soul'. Cassian, in his *Conferences*, a work which takes the form of conversations on spiritual questions with a series of desert fathers, presents the view that the monastic community is preferable to the hermit's cave because it provides each monk with his everyday needs and thus permits him to take no thought for the morrow. The hermit, on the other hand, is likely to be prone to anxieties about his food supply, as well as to interruptions from visitors. However, in this same work we find expressed the idea that the solitary life was in fact superior, as being more difficult, though only suitable for one who had first been trained in the communal life.[51] Despite the fact that Jerome had been unable to endure the hardships of extreme asceticism in the desert, he too continued to believe that ascetic solitude was superior to life in common: for him, charity was less important than chastity. Benedict in his Rule for the communal life describes the anchorites or hermits as:

those who not in the first fervour of their conversion but after long probation in a monastery, having learnt in association with many brothers to fight against the devil, go out well-armed from the ranks of the community to the solitary combat of the desert. They are now able to live without the help of others, and by their own strength and God's assistance, to fight against the temptations of mind and body.[52]

On the other hand, the *Sayings of the Desert Fathers* adumbrates yet another view: Abba Matoes, aware of his own faults and the difficulties of living in harmony with other people, writes, 'It is not through virtue that I live in solitude. but through weakness: those who live in the midst of men are the strong ones.'[53]

What kind of people left their homes, their families[54] and careers for some form of ascetic existence, whether in solitude or within a monastic community? The usual view is that the desert monks of the east were all illiterate peasants, while the western ascetics were all educated aristocrats.[55] It is true that in the east there is the example of Antony, who was a Coptic speaker, ignorant both of Latin and Greek. And in the west we have, for example, Paulinus of Nola,[56] the close friend of Sulpicius Severus, the biographer of St Martin: Paulinus was a wealthy and educated aristocrat from Aquitaine who renounced his enormous wealth and settled with his wife to a life of chastity and strict but joyful asceticism south of Naples; or women such as Paula and Marcella, friends of Jerome, members of aristocratic and wealthy Roman families who chose to preserve their virginity or to reject a second marriage when they were widowed in order to devote themselves to prayer, biblical study and good works either at Rome or in the Holy Land. But such stereotypes will not hold, particularly for the eastern monks. We should not ignore the fact that the Roman aristocrat Arsenius, tutor to the emperor Theodosius' children, slipped away from the imperial palace and the lavish lifestyle to go and live at Scetis in the Egyptian desert as an anchorite renowned for his austerity and silence. Nor should we forget the desert father Ammonius, no peasant farmer but a learned scholar, or Apollonius the former businessman, or Moses, who had been a robber (there must have been as many of these robbers as monks in the desert, considering the frequency with which they crop up in the histories and biographies), or John of Lycopolis, whose change of profession transformed him from builder to ascetic recluse.

What was it about the early monks, in east and west, that drew others to them so powerfully? In the case of Antony, there seems something of Socrates about him in his rejection of the normal values of society, in the attraction his austerity had for others, as well as his intellectual humility combined with a devastating perceptiveness. The *Sayings of the Desert Fathers* contains the following anecdote which illustrates his rather Socratic attitude to knowledge:

One day some old men came to see Abba Antony. In the midst of them was Abba Joseph. Wanting to test them, the old man [Antony] suggested a text from the Scriptures, and, beginning with the youngest, he asked them what it meant. Each gave his opinion as he was able. But to each one the old man said, 'You have not understood it.' Last of all he said to Abba Joseph, 'How would you explain this saying?' and he replied, 'I do not know.' Then Abba Antony said, 'Indeed, Abba Joseph has found the way, for he has said, "I do not know."' [57]

Of course, Antony was not the only one to reject the normal values and aims of society in favour of humility and simplicity. The common attitude to property among the monks is exemplified in one story about Macarius the Great, the former camel-driver who visited Antony and won his praise. [58] One day Macarius came upon a man ransacking

Macarius' property and loading it on to his donkey. Instead of rushing to stop him, Macarius went up to the thief as if he were a stranger and helped him to load the animal. With complete calmness he watched the man depart, saying only, '*We have brought nothing into this world, and we cannot take anything out of this world.*' (I Timothy 6:7)

In their attitude to death, too, the monks often evinced an attitude reminiscent of Socrates' calmness when faced with execution by poison at the hands of the Athenian authorities.[59] In the biographies we find the monks foreseeing their own death and preparing for it with equanimity – even with impatience and joy – comforting their disciples and offering last-minute spiritual advice.[60] It is interesting that Antony and Hilarion make very specific requests before their death to avoid their bodies being preserved. In addition, Antony specifies that the place of his burial is to remain secret, and in fact when Hilarion later visited the place where Antony had spent his last days and asked to be shown his tomb, it would seem that its position was still a secret.[61] Even in death the monk seeks to avoid any kind of special treatment. But we see in these biographies how important the holy man's shrine[62] has already become as a place of pilgrimage and a focus of worship. Not only does Hilarion wish to visit Antony's tomb but in the *Life of Hilarion* it is said that the tomb had been kept secret to prevent a wealthy landowner in those parts from stealing the body and setting up a shrine for it on his land; and in the case of Hilarion's own body, his disciple Hesychius had it secretly moved from Cyprus, where Hilarion had died, to his original monastery in Palestine.

The historian Edward Gibbon recognized that similarities did exist between the early monks and the classical philosophers when he wrote that the monks 'rivalled the Stoics in the contempt of fortune, of pain and of death, revived in their servile discipline the Pythagorean silence and submission, and disdained as firmly as the Cynics themselves all the forms and decencies of civil society'. However, such similarities clearly did not inspire him with admiration for the monks: he also writes of them as 'a swarm of fanatics, incapable of fear or reason or humanity', invading the peace of the eastern Church.[63] However, this kind of attitude did not come in with the Enlightenment. There were plenty of people already in the fourth century, both pagans and

Christians, who were horrified by the craze, which was spreading like wildfire, for giving up everything and withdrawing from civilized society. Many evidently felt about those who adopted the ascetic life just as many nowadays feel about those who leave their families to join some religious sect demanding total devotion and a break with their past life. It is hardly surprising that the emperor Julian should have written in a letter to a fellow pagan:

There are some who leave the cities in order to take refuge in the deserts, although, by his very nature, man is a social and a civilized animal. But the perverse spirits to whom they have given themselves up impel them to this misanthropic way of life.[64]

Paulinus of Nola, though much admired by many for his dedication to the ascetic life, scandalized others, who were shocked that he should renounce all his wealth.[65] John Chrysostom also registered the fact that many Christians in his native Antioch were hostile to the growth of monasticism, and he felt moved to write a work in three books to defend the movement against such people.[66] Even in the fifth century Salvian of Marseilles can report that if some monk leaves the monasteries of Egypt, the holy places of Jerusalem or the retreats of the desert to venture into the cities, he will be greeted with jeering, whistles and insults.[67] Among the western ascetics, Jerome's friends Paula and Melania were subjected to a good deal of criticism from other Christian women for their decision to renounce the life of the world.[68] It is clear from the description of the poet Rutilius Namatianus, a former prefect of Rome, that he finds the monastic way of life not only incomprehensible but also reprehensible. In an account of a sea journey he made in 416, from Rome to Gaul, he describes how he sailed past the island of Capraria;[69]

which is filled with men who hate the light. They call themselves 'monks' (a word which comes from the Greek), because they desire to live alone and without anyone to see them. They are afraid of the favours of fortune, just as they fear the damage fortune does. How can it be that people should deliberately make themselves unhappy in this way, for fear of the future? . . . Fearing the evils of life, they refuse to accept its good things![70]

Furthermore, anxiety was sometimes expressed by Christians that the monastic movement might split from the Church, seeing that it could be regarded as a tacit criticism of the 'secular' Church for having become too involved in the things of this world.[71] The monks might also sometimes act as a disruptive force endangering the equilibrium of society. This was a particular danger on those occasions when a large number of monks descended on some city to intervene in some dispute or other[72] and it was not unheard of for groups of monks to behave like gangs of thugs. In 390 the emperors of both east and west jointly passed a law forbidding monks to stay in the cities.[73]

But despite the occasions for criticism, contempt and suspicion, the monastic movement survived and flourished. Running through Late Antiquity along various channels, and given fresh inspiration by great spiritual leaders such as Benedict, the movement remained an integral part of the Christian Church, serving to irrigate the culture of the Middle Ages in both east and west.

The Writing of Biography: Pagan Past and Christian Future

It was not the fate of the Christian ascetics alone to be reviled and mocked by some and lauded to the skies by others. Pagan philosophers who had adopted some form of eccentric or antisocial existence had long been the subject of both laudatory and critical accounts. Socrates' life, and particularly the end of it, had been described in such works as Xenophon's *Memoirs of Socrates* and Plato's *Apology* and *Phaedo*, thereby attracting much admiration through the subsequent centuries. A less favourable account of Socrates' life had been written by Aristoxenus of Tarentum.[74] Aristoxenus had also written a more complimentary biography of Pythagoras. The popularity of this philosopher had continued through antiquity: in the third century of the Christian era he became the subject of biographies by Porphyry and Iamblichus. Porphyry also wrote a biography of the Neoplatonist philosopher Plotinus, who died in 270, at about the time when Antony took his decision to withdraw from society. In Porphyry's biography Plotinus is portrayed as a kindly but decidedly unworldly figure whose life has certain features in common with the Christian ascetics:[75] he is not concerned about keeping himself clean,[76] the emperor himself pays homage to him as a later emperor did to Antony,[77] and like Antony he rejects any idea of physical preservation for posterity.[78] Another ascetic philosopher whose biography contains many elements which were to be found in Christian hagiography was Apollonius of Tyana. This Neopythagorean is said to have lived at the end of the first century AD, travelling not only around the Mediterranean but as far afield as India, dispensing wise and witty comments and narrowly escaping being put to death.[79]

Of course, philosophers were not the sole subjects of pagan biography. There was a long tradition of biographies of distinguished men – generals, literary men, emperors – as evidenced by the very popular works of Plutarch in Greek and Suetonius in Latin, each with his own individual method and style.

What of any Christian tradition of biography prior to the great masterpieces of the fourth century which were to be the models for so much later hagiography? The four Gospels, as well as the Acts of the Apostles, might be regarded as at least containing many features characteristic of biography.[80] But it was not only the lives of Christ and his disciples which were deemed worthy of commemoration. St Paul had indeed considered all Christians to be saints,[81] as witnesses of Christ who by baptism had been 'consecrated' to the service of God, but it later became accepted that the truest witness to Christ was provided by those who died for their faith:[82] it was these people who earned the name of martyrs from the Greek word for witness. A large number of the most famous saints achieved sanctity through martyrdom during the periods of pagan persecution, saints such as Katherine, Cecilia, Laurence. A need was felt to venerate and commemorate these people, not only because they were paragons of the Christian life but because they were thought to have the power to intercede with Christ on behalf of lesser mortals, to act as a kind of patron to other Christians. The tradition thus developed of celebrating the anniversary of the saint's death as a kind of birthday,[83] this being the day on which they were born to eternal life. Often, too, a record of the events leading up to the martyr's death was made, emphasizing the conflict between pagan and Christian and the triumph of faith in Christ. Alongside the numerous accounts of martyrdom, usually known as Acts or Passions, we find one account considered to be the earliest example of Christian biography. This is the brief *Life of Cyprian*, bishop of Carthage, who was beheaded in 258 during that period of persecution under the emperor Valerian mentioned by Jerome in his *Life of Paul of Thebes*. This eulogy was written by Pontius, who may have been Cyprian's deacon: he selected events from Cyprian's life to illustrate his virtues, but focused particularly on the events which took place on the day of his martyrdom.

But when, after the accession of Constantine, dying for the faith became less of an option, the creation of saints remained as popular as ever. Saints were now considered to be those whose lives had been of an exemplary holiness. We have already noted that in the early years of the monastic movement it was particularly those who chose this form of extreme ascetic life who were regarded as saints. During the fourth century, in fact, there were some who believed that the true saints were not the martyrs whose sufferings were usually brief, but the ascetics who suffered for a whole lifetime. At this time there was as yet no official procedure of canonization involving the pope, no necessity of proving that a certain number of miracles had been performed by the would-be saint during his lifetime or had occurred at his tomb. The term '*sanctus*' (holy one) was used also of living people who were clearly striving after perfection. But already in the saints' lives recorded in this volume we see evidence of the veneration accorded to the saint after his death, the importance attached to the site of the saint's burial and the determination to pay one's respect to the saint at his tomb on the anniversary of his death. These are attitudes which were to become increasingly dominant in medieval culture.

Gradually the writing of biographies[84] of such ideal men and women, whose lives were completely committed to the service of God and in whom God's grace could be seen to be working, became an essential part of the sanctification of an individual, serving to commemorate the special power they had from Christ, as expressed in their outstanding deeds. The lives of Antony, Martin and even

Benedict stand near the beginning of a long and fruitful tradition of hagiography stretching over the next millennium: not only did these biographies serve to spread knowledge of these particular saints far and wide but they were also to provide the literary models for so much later medieval hagiographical writing which was to be one of the areas of greatest literary productivity during the Middle Ages.[85]

Beside these early instances of hagiography in which the ascetic element is the most prominent, there are two further renowned biographies dating from the early fifth century which stand at the beginning of a slightly different strand of medieval hagiography, namely the *Life of Ambrose* by Paulinus of Milan and the *Life of Augustine of Hippo* by Possidius. Like the biography of Cyprian, mentioned above, and that of Martin of Tours, these give an account of men who were bishops, but whereas the life of Cyprian focuses on his martyrdom and that of Martin on his asceticism and missionary activity among the pagans, the biographies of Ambrose and Augustine are primarily concerned with these men's work as ecclesiastical administrators in North Italy and North Africa respectively. However, despite the difference of theme, Paulinus still claims in his preface that he took the Lives of Antony, Paul of Thebes and Martin as his models.[86]

Women, too, were recognized as worthy subjects of biographical works from an early stage, even though they could not gain distinction as bishops and were less likely to live dramatically eremitic lives in the desert. We know, for example, of St Macrina, the sister of Basil of Caesarea and Gregory of Nyssa, from the biography of her written by Gregory. Macrina comes across as a well-educated woman who turned the family home in the Pontus into a monastic community of which she was the head, and who inspired and guided her younger brothers in their spiritual development. It would seem in general that biographical writings about women at this period tended to be of a more personal nature than those about men: such works were often composed by someone who was a close relative or friend of the woman in question and written in the form of letters to friends. It was, for example, Jerome's closest female friends – Paula, Marcella, Fabiola – of whom he wrote biographical accounts in the form of long letters addressed to friends or relatives of the dead woman.[87]

These works are eulogistic while avoiding mention of extraordinary spiritual powers or miracles.

These early Christian biographies, which were the débutants in the tradition of saints' lives, the first links in the hagiographical chain, already manifest certain narrative elements which will recur later in the tradition. Examples of such hagiographical hallmarks are the theme of flight from an unwelcome marriage, as in the case of Malchus. Other themes that will be found time and time again, related to the special spiritual powers and superhuman status associated with saints, are the saint portrayed as a child of precocious wisdom, like Benedict, who 'from his very childhood possessed the wisdom of old age', the power of the sign of the cross, as demonstrated in the episode when Benedict is able to shatter a cup of poison merely by making the sign of the cross in front of it, the saint's ability to foresee events or to perceive what is happening far away, as we see in Athanasius' portrayal of Antony, and the fact that the saint's body is said to remain uncorrupted after his death, as in the case of Hilarion's body after his death on Cyprus. The extremely popular themes of encounters with wild beasts who prove unnaturally helpful or obedient occur particularly, but not exclusively, in the biographies composed by Jerome: the *Life of Paul* includes meetings with a centaur, a satyr, a raven and two lions who dig Paul's grave, while in the *Life of Malchus* we have the famous lioness who kills Malchus' master and the master's servant when they enter the cave where Malchus is hiding but does not harm Malchus or the woman who has lived as his companion in chastity and who is escaping with him from slavery. In the *Life of Antony* Athanasius shows us Antony speaking firmly to the donkeys who are ravaging his vegetable patch and as a result the animals caused no more damage, while in the *Life of Benedict* we see Benedict commanding the raven to fly away with the poisoned bread.

These are but a few of the themes that will recur again and again in medieval accounts of saints' lives, whose prime purpose was to edify rather than simply to record historical facts about a specific Christian life. Authors of later hagiographies would have been very familiar with these works of Athanasius, Jerome, Sulpicius Severus and Gregory the Great for they were read aloud during the celebration of the liturgy or at mealtimes in the monastery refectories. Paulinus of Milan may be unusual in referring explicitly to the influence of the earlier Lives but he was by no means the last to take these biographies as literary models: there is hardly any later example of hagiography in which echoes of their language cannot be heard or reflections of their structure seen. As a result, generation after generation was to hear and heed the words of St Antony when he said, 'Remember the deeds done by each of the saints so that the memory of their example will inspire your soul to virtue and restrain it from vices.'[88]

Principal Primary Sources relating to Early Monasticism

The biographies included in this volume are important sources of information about the lives of these six pioneers of monasticism. This is particularly true in the case of Jerome's *Life of Paul*, since his biography is the sole source of knowledge about Paul of Thebes. If Jerome made it all up, as this lack of corroborating evidence might lead one to believe, it was a story which was quickly accepted as genuine: Paul is soon to be found alongside Antony as an important model for the anchoritic life.

As for Malchus, he was more of personal interest to Jerome because of their shared preoccupation with chastity as the principal Christian virtue, rather than a person of widespread fame and veneration. Malchus' life is not portrayed by Jerome as being influential, and he does not appear to have attracted a cult: any influence he had would have come from the effect of Jerome's record of his life story. His example is therefore rather different from the others who became the subjects of biography.[89]

In the case of Benedict we are largely dependent on Gregory's account of his life in the *Dialogues*. No other mention is made of Benedict before Gregory's biography was written and the only other way of getting to know Benedict is to read his Rule.[90]

However, there are several texts from the fourth and fifth centuries which corroborate the information we gain from the Lives of Antony, Hilarion and Martin, or which provide additional (sometimes contradictory) details. Some of these texts have been mentioned already. As general accounts of the Christian Church at that period we have the *Ecclesiastical Histories* of Rufinus, Socrates, Sozomen and Theodoret. Rufinus' History is a translation into Latin of Eusebius of Caesarea's History, supplemented by Rufinus' account of the years 324–95, while Socrates, Sozomen[91] and Theodoret were all writing in Greek in the first half of the fifth century. More specifically focused on monasticism are Palladius' *Lausiac History*[92] and the *History of the Monks in Egypt*[93], both used as sources by the later historians. These were written in Greek, too, though the latter was soon translated into Latin by Rufinus who also added some material based on his own travels. Both works focus on asceticism in the east and contain many anecdotes about individual ascetics whom the authors had visited.[94] Through these anecdotes a striking and lively picture emerges of life in these remote regions.

With regard to Antony, we have seven letters[95] attributed to him by Jerome, as well as a number of sayings, contained in the *Sayings of the Desert Fathers* (also known as the *Apophthegmata Patrum* or *Verba Seniorum*). These are a collection of fragments of spiritual advice attributed to more than a hundred different desert fathers[96] from the fourth to the sixth centuries. These sayings are preserved mainly in two collections, the one arranged alphabetically according to the name of the monk to whom the sayings are attributed, the other arranged according to particular themes of ascetic life. These are usually referred to as the alphabetical and the systematic collections respectively. They appear originally to have been collected in Greek but translated into Latin within a few years, by about the year 560. Both collections open with sayings attributed to Antony. Further sources of knowledge about Antony, providing a rather different view of him from that in the *Life of Antony*, are the letter of Athanasius' friend Serapion of Thmuis to Antony's disciples, preserved in Syriac and Armenian, and the Lives of Pachomius.

Pachomius, the founder of coenobitism, had several biographies written about him in the years after his death, which can supplement

our understanding of early monasticism.[97] These are preserved (sometimes only in fragments) not only in Greek but also in Coptic, Arabic
and Syriac versions, in a complex textual tradition. As mentioned
earlier, we also possess the Rule of Pachomius, originally composed
in Coptic but soon translated into Greek, before Jerome translated it
into Latin!

Further information about the way of life of the desert monks and
their spiritual aims can be derived from the works of Evagrius of
Pontus and John Cassian. Evagrius was ordained a deacon by Gregory
of Nazianzus, then lived as an ascetic at Jerusalem in the monastery
of Rufinus and Melania. Later, perhaps in 382, he moved to Egypt,
living at Nitria and Cellia. His work of practical spirituality, the
so-called *Practicus*, was enormously influential. As regards information
which supplements what we learn from the biographies in this volume,
Evagrius records for example Antony's answer to a philosopher
who asked him how he could endure his long solitude without the
consolation of books: 'My book is the nature of created things,
which I have at hand so that I can read the words of God when I
want.'

It is not certain where Cassian was born, but as a young man he
seems to have spent some time in a monastery in Bethlehem, where
he was acquainted with Jerome, and then visited different monastic
settlements in Egypt. Later he moved on to Constantinople and Rome
before settling in Gaul, where he founded a monastery at Marseilles
and died in about 435. He wrote two Latin works of Christian
spirituality for which he is principally renowned, the *Institutes* and the
Conferences. Cassian's works, like those of Evagrius, provide detailed
advice, of a psychologically perceptive kind, for ascetic aspirants. He
follows Evagrius in distinguishing eight basic sins[98] (the ancestors of
the seven capital sins with which we are more familiar), which
hinder spiritual progress. The *Institutes* are concerned with patterns
of communal life as well as with sins, while the *Conferences*, in the
form of dialogues with Egyptian abbots, concentrate more on the
individual's encounter with God.

By the time of Cassian's death, the monastic movement would
have put down strong roots in Gaul in the century since Athanasius

had lived in exile at Trier and the seventy-five years or so since Martin set up his hermitage outside Poitiers. By the mid fifth century there were important monastic communities on the island of Lérins in the south, as well as at Marseilles and Tours. Our knowledge of the beginnings of monasticism in Gaul is however largely dependent on the writings of Sulpicius Severus, not only his *Life of Martin*, but also three letters written after Martin's death and the *Dialogues*, in which Martin's miracles are favourably compared to those of the monks of the Egyptian desert. Sulpicius' *Life of Martin* was rewritten in six books of hexametrical poetry by the fifth-century writer Paulinus of Périgueux.[99] A later writer who showed great interest in Martin of Tours was the sixth-century author Gregory of Tours, who wrote a work in four books on the miracles of St Martin. By this time the monastic movement had spread from Gaul to the Celtic regions of the British Isles, and the biographies translated here had found a new area of influence.

As we have seen, Augustine was another fourth-century figure who was interested in monasticism, a subject which he treats in a section of his work *On the Catholic Way of Life*,[100] composed in the early years after his conversion, and in that entitled *On the Work of the Monks* written in 401. He also composed a monastic Rule, apparently written for the religious community of which his sister was a member. This seems to have had a limited influence on early monasticism – traces of this Rule can be seen in the Rule composed by Caesarius of Arles, an important figure in the development of monasticism in Gaul after Martin and Cassian – but it was not until the late eleventh century that it gained a more widespread popularity, when it was adopted as their guiding document by several new monastic orders such as the Canons Regular, also known as the Augustinian Canons.

The Saints in Iconography

The importance of these saints is testified to also by their frequent appearance in works of art, particularly during the Middle Ages. Many of the biographical details contained in these works were represented in various media to illustrate significant episodes in the lives of these exemplary Christians, and indeed it may have been through visual representations that most people became familiar with them. However, of all those connected with this volume, it is actually St Jerome – the author rather than the subject of any of these biographies – who figures most prominently in late medieval art,[101] despite the fact that he had not worked any miracles nor been a great preacher and did not die a martyr to the faith. His great achievement lay in his translation work, in his production of the Vulgate, the Latin text of the Bible which was to be the standard version for many centuries, quoted and discussed by innumerable writers. In many paintings Jerome is depicted as a hermit in the desert (although he actually only spent about two years in the Syrian desert in the mid 370s), accompanied by a lion. This latter detail is due to a confusion between Jerome and St Gerasimus, a later hermit: it was in fact the latter who is said to have tamed a lion by removing a thorn from its paw.[102] In other pictures we see Jerome in his study, often with a red cardinal's hat to demonstrate his high standing in the church, although Jerome was never a cardinal – indeed, the office did not exist in his lifetime.

St Antony stands second to Jerome in iconographical popularity during the Middle Ages,[103] but he (or his temptations) comes into his own in the art and literature of the nineteenth and twentieth centuries. The two most common scenes depicted are his temptations by the devil in various guises,[104] and his visit to Paul of Thebes – the scene that is described solely by Jerome. The temptations take place either in front of Antony's cell, as on the Isenheim altar of Matthias Grünewald, or in the air, when the demons are striving to prevent Antony ascending to heaven, as on the Lisbon triptych by Hieronymus Bosch. With regard to his visit to Paul, Antony's meeting with the satyr and the centaur are occasionally depicted, but more common is the conversation between Paul and Antony and their breaking of the bread brought to them by the raven. Examples of this scene can be found, for example, on the Ruthwell Cross in Scotland, on a capital at Vézelay cathedral, on the Isenheim altar and in a painting by Velasquez, now in the Prado in Madrid. Both these scenes derive from the saints' lives translated here, but other of Antony's iconographical attributes (such as the bell, the tame pig and the Tau cross) depend on other sources.

Paul of Thebes is usually depicted as an old man – after all, he did live to the age of 113 – dressed in palm leaves. He is most often seen sharing a meal with Antony, but also appears as a corpse whose grave is being dug by two lions[105] while Antony looks on: both these scenes are based on Jerome's *Life of Paul*. Paul became particularly popular in Hungary after the Order of St Paul was founded there in the thirteenth century and his bones were removed to Buda.

Hilarion appears less often, though he does get into a mosaic in St Mark's cathedral at Venice. He is shown riding a donkey and facing a dragon. Malchus is even rarer, but in the Picture Gallery at Christ Church, Oxford, there is a fifteenth-century depiction of the scene in which he and his female companion are peeping out from their hiding place in the cave while his master is attacked by a lion.

Sulpicius Severus' *Life of Martin* served to make Martin an enormously popular figure. Depictions of him as soldier[106] or bishop were among the most frequent themes of medieval iconography, and not solely in France where his tomb at Tours became a place of pilgrimage on a par with Santiago de Compostela. Of the scenes from his life described by Sulpicius, the episode where he divides his cloak with the beggar was the most frequently depicted, with Martin either on horseback or, less often, on foot. Other popular scenes from the biography are that of the vision of Christ Martin has after he has divided his cloak,[107] the hewn pine tree which threatens to crush Martin, Martin as exorcist assisting Hilary of Poitiers, and Martin being healed by the angel after falling down stairs. The many stories found in Sulpicius Severus' biography were later supplemented by other episodes. For instance, in the *Dialogues* there is found the story known as the Second Charity, in which Martin gives his tunic to a pauper just before he is about to celebrate mass. As for other attributes, Martin is often depicted with a goose, presumably because goose was traditionally served on St Martin's Day rather than because of any connection between Martin and a particular goose.

Benedict, as the man to whom monks of the Benedictine order looked back as their founder, appears frequently in paintings, carvings and manuscript illuminations throughout the Middle Ages. Gregory's full account of his life provided ample material for lively representation. The most frequently depicted episodes were perhaps the scene of the devil breaking the bell used to signal the arrival of Benedict's bread supply, the raven carrying off the poisoned bread, the cup of poison shattering, the wine cask, with a snake sliding out of it, the young boy being crushed by the falling wall, and the deceit practised by Totila, king of the Goths.[108]

Translation Past and Present

It should be clear from what has been said that at the end of Late Antiquity, in particular, translations were regarded as an important means of reaching a large audience within the wide extent of the Roman Empire at a time of intense intellectual and spiritual activity. At this period the Roman Empire had not yet definitively split into two and there was still much contact and movement between east and west. Was not Athanasius forced to leave Alexandria to go into exile at Trier? Did not Hilary move from Poitiers to Asia Minor when driven into exile? And yet only a minority of the empire's inhabitants were bilingual in Latin and Greek and indeed many country people spoke another language exclusively, a language such as Celtic, Punic, Coptic,[109] Syriac or Armenian. It is therefore understandable that the people of Late Antiquity had no scruples about reading works in translation, even when the translation was not a literal one.[110] Two of the most famous and prolific translators of this period were Jerome and Rufinus. Jerome is renowned primarily for his translation of the Bible from Hebrew and Greek into Latin. However, he also translated writings of Origen and the work of Didymus on the Holy Spirit, as well as ascetic texts from the Greek. Rufinus, like Jerome, translated certain works of the Greek Church fathers, for example some of Origen's[111] as well as a selection from Gregory of Nazianzus' *Orations*, together with other ascetic writings.

But it would be wrong to suppose that all the effort of translation was in one direction: from Greek to Latin. It is true that as Latin took over from Greek as the language of the western Church, it took time for the west to catch up, to build up a body of theological writing of its own. A need was felt to know the Greek works in order to develop an orthodox Latin theology. Men like Hilary of Poitiers and Ambrose of Milan were largely instrumental in transmitting Greek theology to the west through works of their own. Yet there was movement in the other direction, too. Libanius of Antioch, in his autobiography, laments the fact that so many Greek speakers feel the need to travel to Italy to learn Latin because they believe that Latin is now the language which brings power and wealth, while Greek has lost some of its status.[112] But even among those who did not make the effort to learn Latin, there must have been a desire to read works of Christian culture from the Latin world. Not long after its composition, Jerome's *Life of Paul of Thebes* was translated into Greek, while later a translation of his *Life of Malchus* was made first into Greek and then into Syriac. According to Postumianus in the *Dialogues* of Sulpicius Severus, the *Life of Martin* had already, by the end of the fourth century, been read in Rome, Carthage and in Egypt:[113] it is not impossible that it had been translated in order to be read in Egypt, although no evidence of this survives.

It is against this background that I have decided to translate into English not the Greek version of Athanasius' *Life of Antony*, but the Latin translation made some fifteen years after its composition[114] by Jerome's friend Evagrius of Antioch.[115] Evagrius grew up in Syria with a knowledge of Greek but apparently learned Latin when he worked in Italy for a period of about ten years. It seems that his was probably not the first translation of the *Life of Antony* into Latin: at the beginning of the twentieth century a translation, on the whole more literal than Evagrius', was discovered in a manuscript of the tenth or eleventh century in the Vatican.[116] But it was the translation by Evagrius which became known to the west soon after its publication. This was the version read by Augustine and by innumerable readers throughout the Middle Ages, the version referred to or quoted by men such as Adomnan in his *Life of Columba*, by Peter the Venerable in his letters and by Abelard in the letter giving an account of the disasters that had befallen him.[117] This translation of the *Life of Antony* was a literary rather than a literal version, embellished with small pieces of additional material. I believe this is the first time Evagrius' *Life of Antony* has been translated into English, apart from the translation by William Caxton, made in 1495 from a French translation of the Latin version, as part of the collection known as the *Lives of the Fathers*.

In translating these works from Latin I have tried to avoid the freedom in translation adopted by Evagrius and have attempted to remain faithful to the original without offering a word-for-word translation. However, in all the saints' lives translated here there are certain problems of terminology which ought to be signalled at the outset. These problems are largely connected with the early development of Latin spiritual terminology, as words were taken over from classical Greek and Latin and infused with Christian connotations, or new words were formed to express specifically Christian concepts.

The first problem concerns the words 'monk' and 'monastery'. These words were originally used with reference to those who lived in solitude, in an individual dwelling far from others, or in one of a group of cells. But as monasticism developed from eremitism towards coenobitism, these words gradually widened their meanings. The word '*monachus*' (monk) came to refer to anyone living either on his own or in a monastery, while '*monasterion*' (monastery) was more often applied to any place where many monks lived together rather than to an individual cell. Evagrius is one of the first Latin writers to take over '*monasterium*' into Latin from the Greek, using it of Antony's hut. The translator of the earlier version of Athanasius' *Life of Antony* does not use this word. Jerome uses the word '*monasterium*' in both senses in his biographies of Hilarion and Malchus. Augustine, writing the *Confessions* at about the same time as Jerome wrote the above two biographies, applies the word '*monasterium*' to a coenobitic establishment.[118] In the *Life of Martin* we find the use of the word to apply to Martin's individual cell but also to a collection of many cells which sprang up around Martin at Marmoutier outside Tours.[119] Later the word 'cell' ('*cella*' or '*cellula*' in Latin) was used to refer specifically to a hermit's cell in contrast to a monastic community.

Then there is the word 'brother' which had been taken over in the early Christian period to refer to a fellow Christian. In the monastic writings this word can bear such a meaning when used in the context of the wider community of the Christian Church but can also be applied in a more restricted sense, as the equivalent of the word 'monk'.

A similar ambiguity is to be found with respect to two other Latin words. One is 'virtus', which in the monastic writings can retain its sense of 'virtue', but can also mean a kind of spiritual power or the performance of miracles. The other is 'habitus', meaning either a way of life or a garment which is the mark of a certain way of life. At times it is hard to decide which meaning the author has in mind, as both might fit the context in question.

As for the word which lies at the heart of all monasticism, the problem with the Greek word askesis, originally meaning 'training' and taken over from its use by Stoic and Neoplatonist philosophers, is that in Christian monastic writings it covers many different aspects of the ascetic life, its aims and practices. These include the practice of virtue, mortification and self-control, unrelenting endeavour and exertion, service of God in order to attain union with God, and the commitment to the monastic way of life. The earlier translator of the Life of Antony tends to use the Latin word 'studium', implying striving and commitment, which he then tries to make more precise by qualifying it by means of other epithets. Evagrius, on the other hand, translates it using a number of different words, depending on which aspect he considers to be uppermost in the intentions of Athanasius in a particular passage. It would certainly be difficult to find one word to translate it in every context, since the most succinct translation to convey its meaning accurately might be something like, 'a striving after moral perfection by means of mortification in order to serve God and grow closer to Him'! With regard to these words in particular, the technical terms of the monastic life, so to speak, the reader needs to be aware that different translations are possible and no one translation can claim to be definitive.

These translations are based on the following editions of the texts:

Athanasius, *Life of Antony*, translated from the Latin version of Evagrius, printed in *Patrologia Latina* (PL) 73 in the early seventeenth-century edition of H. Rosweyde but with a few emendations to the Latin text made by comparison with the edition of B. Montfaucon printed in *Patrologia Graeca* (PG) 26 at the foot of the page. The numbering of the chapters is given according to the edition in PG 26 since this is the numeration that is more generally referred to in other editions and secondary works. I give the numeration of the Rosweyde edition in brackets.

Jerome, *Life of Paul of Thebes*, *Life of Hilarion* and *Life of Malchus* are translated from the edition of D. Vallarsi printed in PL 23. This edition is in many ways unsatisfactory but despite the work of W. A. Oldfather and others,[120] it has not yet been definitively superseded. With the Vallarsi edition may be compared the *Life of Hilarion* edited by A. Bastiaensen in *Vite dei Santi* vol. 4 (Rome 1975) 72–142, and the *Life of Malchus* edited by C. C. Mierow in *Classical Essays Presented to J. A. Kleist* (St Louis, Missouri 1946) 31–60.

Sulpicius Severus, *Life of Martin*, translated from the text printed by J. Fontaine in his edition: Sulpice Sévère, *Vie de Saint Martin* vol. 1 (Sources Chrétiennes 133, Paris 1967).

Gregory the Great, *Life of Benedict (Dialogues* II), translated from the text printed by A. de Vogüé in his edition: Grégoire le Grand, *Dialogues* vol. 2 (Sources Chrétiennes 251, Paris 1979).

Notes

1. In his work *De Votis Monasticis*, published in 1522.
2. In the preface to the *Life of Antony* Athanasius claims to have visited Antony often. D. Brakke (*Athanasius and the Politics of Asceticism* (Oxford 1995) chapter 4) considers this to be an exaggeration and is even sceptical about the two specific indications in the *Life of Antony* of contact between Athanasius and Antony: in chapters 69–71 Athanasius speaks as if he had been present when

Antony visited Alexandria in 337 or 338, and in chapter 91 he mentions the cloak which he had presented to Antony. But despite the lack of evidence we cannot rule out the possibility that they did indeed meet often.

3. The fifth-century Church historian Sozomen points to the example of Elijah and John the Baptist, and refers to the Jewish writer Philo's claim that there were in his day Jews leading a monastic life near Lake Mareotis. Sozomen (*Ecclesiastical History*, I.12) (for full bibliographical details for each text cited, see Further Reading) also refers to the view that 'this way of life originated from the persecutions . . . by which many were compelled to flee to the mountains and deserts and forests and they became used to this kind of living.' For a brief summary of modern theories of the origins of monasticism, see C. H. Lawrence, *Medieval Monasticism*, pp. 1–3.

4. In his letter to Eustochium (22.36) Jerome sums up his view thus: 'Paul was the originator of this way of life, Antony made it famous and, going back further into the past, John the Baptist was the first example of it.' Paulinus, the biographer of St Ambrose, writing in the early fifth century, mentions Paul and Antony together as the founders of monasticism, as does Cassian in his *Conferences* (18.6). In the *Dialogues* of Sulpicius Severus, Postumianus says that he visited not only the two monasteries of Antony but also the place where the blessed Paul, the first of the eremites, lived. The author of the *Ancrene Wisse*, written around 1200, speaks of Paul as the first anchorite.

5. On the subject of early monasticism in Palestine, see John Binns, *Ascetics and Ambassadors of Christ: the monasteries of Palestine 314–631* (Oxford 1994).

6. If Antony adopted the ascetic life in about 270, this old man may have done so already in about 220.

7. Gregory of Nazianzus, *Oration*, 43.5–6.

8. The Arians were named after Arius, a priest at Alexandria. Regarding the question of the unity of the Trinity, he argued that if the Father begat the Son, there must have been a time when the Son did not exist and so He must have been created out of nothing. The Arians would not agree that the Son was of one substance with the Father, but only that He was of like substance.

9. Jerome, *Letter* 127.5. Athanasius spent about twenty years of his life, at different periods, in exile.

10. Orosius, *History against the Pagans*, 7.33.

11. Jerome is our only source for the life of Paul of Thebes, and some have doubted whether Paul really existed.

12. Decius was emperor from 249–51, Valerian from 253–60.

13. Disagreement over the treatment of such 'lapsed' Christians led to the

setting up of a separate sect, known as the Novatianist Church, which would not admit any who had lapsed during persecution.

14. Among these was Cyprian, bishop of Carthage, who was martyred a few years later under Valerian.

15. The earliest attested use of the word '*monachos*', meaning 'solitary one' is in an Egyptian papyrus document (*PColl. Youtie, 77*) dated to the year 324.

16. Silence is also occasionally specified as a monastic virtue: e.g., 'it was said of Abba Agathon that for three years he lived with a stone in his mouth, until he had learned to keep silence' (*The Sayings of the Desert Fathers*, p. 22).

17. L. Bouyer, *A History of Christian Spirituality*, trans. M. P. Ryan (London 1968) vol. 1, p. 309.

18. John Cassian, *Conferences*, I.7.

19. *Life of Antony*, 85; also quoted by Sozomen, *Ecclesiastical History*, I.13; *Apophthegmata Patrum* (*Patrologia Graeca* 65.77B–C; this series will henceforth be referred to as PG.)

20. *Life of Hilarion*, 14; *Life of Martin*, XVI.2–8.

21. The way of life which has characteristics of the solitary and the communal is usually referred to as the semi-eremitic life.

22. Three kilometres south-west of Antony's cave in the Inner Mountain, some thirty-five kilometres west of the Gulf of Suez and south-west of Zafaranah, there now stands a Coptic monastery known as St Antony's monastery (Deir al Qiddis Antun; map reference 28.56 N 32.21 E). Jerome gives a description of the site in his *Life of Hilarion*, 31.

23. Probably in 311.

24. In 337 or 338.

25. Paul's cave lay to the south-east of Antony's cell, beside a spring and tucked into the folds of the mountains, some seventeen kilometres from the Gulf of Suez. Later, over the site, a Coptic monastery was built, known as St Paul's monastery (Deir al Qiddis Bulus; map reference 28.51N 32.33 E).

26. *Life of Antony*, 14; in his Latin translation Evagrius phrases it slightly differently, speaking of 'the beginning of the desert's colonization'.

27. H. G. Evelyn White, *The History of the Monasteries of Nitria and Scetis* (New York 1932). For a fourth-century description of Nitria, see *The Lives of the Desert Fathers*, 20.5–7.

28. Palladius, *Lausiac History*, 8.

29. *Apophthegmata Patrum*, G Ant. 34.

30. *The Lives of the Desert Fathers*, 20.8.

31. *Life of Antony*, 60.

32. Palladius, *Lausiac History*, 7.2.

33. Often known as Macarius the Great or Macarius the Egyptian to distinguish him from Macarius of Alexandria.

34. Information (often contradictory) about Pachomius' life can be derived from a number of fourth-century sources, primarily the *Vita Prima*, written in Greek. For a modern account see P. Rousseau, *Pachomius: The making of a community in fourth-century Egypt* (Berkeley, California 1985).

35. *Life of Pachomius* (*Vita Prima*) 4.

36. Similarly, after St Bernard took over as abbot of Cîteaux in the early twelfth century, the Cistercian community expanded dramatically and was forced to create daughter houses to accommodate the influx of new recruits to this way of life.

37. *Letter of Ammon*, chapter 2.

38. According to the later accounts of Palladius and Sozomen, when Pachomius was told to found a community of monks, an angel presented him with a tablet on which the Rule was written. This tablet 'is still carefully preserved', says Sozomen (Palladius, *Lausiac History*, 32; Sozomen, *Ecclesiastical History*, III.14).

39. Basil, *Letter* 223.2, a letter written in 375 to Eustathius. Basil seems to have travelled among the desert monks during 357–8.

40. On Eustathius' ascetic innovations see Sozomen, *Ecclesiastical History*, III.14. Basil later broke with Eustathius because of his heretical views.

41. *Rule of Benedict*, chapter 73.

42. Although it lay more or less at the opposite end of the empire from the home of desert monasticism, the imperial city of Trier appears surprisingly often in the broad picture of the development of monasticism at this period. Athanasius spent several years in exile there, Jerome lived there for a while before going off to the desert near Antioch, and the incident between Martin and the emperor (*Life of Martin*, XX) took place here.

43. Jerome, *Letter* 127.5.

44. Jerome, *Letter* 24.4. However, Jerome also writes to Paulinus of Nola (*Letter* 58.4) warning him not to bother to visit Jerusalem: 'Keep out of cities and you will never lose your vocation.'

45. *The Lives of the Desert Fathers*, 5.1–2.

46. Augustine, *Confessions*, 8.6.15.

47. Jerome gives us an idea of how he suffered in the desert in a letter (22.7) addressed to Eustochium, a young girl to whom he is advocating a life of chastity.

48. Martin was not unusual in choosing an island as a monastic retreat. Jerome's friend Bonosus, for example, who had studied with him at Rome, went to live in solitude on an island off the coast of Croatia: Jerome describes him as sitting in the safe retreat of his island amid the threatening waves of the world (*Letter* 7.3). On his sea journey from Rome to Gaul, the poet Rutilius Namatianus saw a number of islands inhabited by monks.

49. Benedict established twelve small monasteries at Subiaco. Two monasteries still flourish there, one named after his sister Scolastica and one, known as Sacro Speco, is built around the cave where Benedict lived.

50. According to Palladius in the *Lausiac History* (21.2) Antony visited the Outer Mountain sometimes every ten days, sometimes every twenty, and sometimes as often as every five days.

51. Cassian, *Conferences*, 18.11.

52. *Rule of Benedict*, chapter 1.

53. *The Sayings of the Desert Fathers*, p. 145.

54. The monk's family often plays a prominent part in the accounts of the ascetic life, providing a tension between the responsibility felt towards one's parents and siblings and the desire to break free from such ties. Antony has to provide for his sister before he abandons his home, Malchus resists parental pressure to marry and provide grandchildren, Malchus and Martin, after adopting the monastic life, feel the need to return to visit their parents, and Benedict continues to meet his sister Scolastica once a year, and when he dies he is buried beside her.

55. See C. Stancliffe, *St Martin and his Hagiographer*, p. 21.

56. Paulinus of Nola also figures in the *Dialogues* of Gregory the Great, alongside Benedict.

57. *The Sayings of the Desert Fathers*, p. 4.

58. Ibid., p. 131.

59. See, for example, the final pages of Plato's *Phaedo* and Xenophon's *Memoirs of Socrates* IV.8.

60. *Life of Antony*, 91; *Life of Paul*, 11–12; *Life of Hilarion*, 44–5; *Life of Benedict*, XXXVII.

61. *Life of Hilarion*, 31.

62. See P. Brown, *The Cult of the Saints* (London 1981), although the author does not include the examples of Antony or Hilarion.

63. E. Gibbon, *The Decline and Fall of the Roman Empire*, 37 (Everyman Library, London 1910).

64. *The Works of the Emperor Julian* (Loeb Classical Library, 1913) vol. 2, p. 297.

65. Ambrose, *Letter* 58.5.

66. John Chrysostom, *Against the Critics of Those Who Adopt the Monastic Life* (PG 47).

67. Salvian, *On the Governance of God*, 8.4.19.

68. Jerome, *Letter* 45.4.

69. Capraria was a rocky volcanic island some thirty kilometres north-west of Elba, now known as Capraia.

70. Rutilius Namatianus, *On his Return*, 440–6.

71. For such criticism of the Church, see Jerome, *Life of Malchus*, 1.

72. For example, the monks of Nitria joined in the resistance at Alexandria to the installation of the Arian bishop Lucius as Athanasius' successor. A few years later, when a procession of monks at Callinicum was attacked by members of a Gnostic sect, the monks took revenge by setting fire to a Gnostic sanctuary, and in the ensuing disturbances, a Jewish synagogue was also burnt down; the emperor Theodosius and bishop Ambrose of Milan were forced to intervene.

73. *Theodosian Code*, XVI.3.1.

74. The Cynics, too, appear in the literature of antiquity, their way of life described with distaste: for example, in Lucian's satire entitled *The Cynic*, the Cynic is heckled in the following terms:

Why do you have a beard and long hair but no shirt? Why do you expose your body to view and go barefooted, adopting by choice this nomadic, antisocial and bestial life? Why unlike everyone else do you abuse your body by always inflicting on it what it least likes, wandering around and prepared to sleep on the hard ground?

75. It is interesting to note that Plotinus' philosophical work, the *Enneads*, ends with the statement, 'This is the life of the gods and of godlike and blessed men, deliverance from the things of this world, a life which takes no delight in the things of this world, escape in solitude to the solitary' (or, as it is often translated, 'the flight of the alone to the Alone').

76. Porphyry, *Life of Plotinus*, 2.

77. In the case of Plotinus, the emperor Gallienus is said to have honoured him: Ibid., 12.

78. Ibid., 1: Plotinus is said to have refused to have a portrait of himself made, exclaiming irritably, 'Is it not enough to carry the image which nature has encased us in? Must I agree to leave behind me a longer lasting image of the image as if it were something worth looking at?' Antony rejected the idea of his body being preserved by means of mummification.

79. Philostratus' account of the life of Apollonius of Tyana is translated in *Heroes and Gods: spiritual biographies in antiquity,* by M. Hadas and M. Smith (London 1965).

80. See R. A. Burridge, *What are the Gospels? A comparison with Graeco-Roman biography* (Cambridge 1992).

81. See, for example, 2 Corinthians 8:4 and 13:13.

1

82. By dying for their faith, martyrs were imitating Christ's sacrifice of His life, which was regarded as the supreme sacrifice. Ignatius of Antioch, who was martyred in the early second century, died as a martyr, 'so as not only to be called, but also to be found to be a Christian as well.' (Ignatius, *Letter to the Romans*, 2.1; 3.2.)

83. Note how Hilarion desires to mark the anniversary of Antony's death by spending it at the place where Antony died (*Life of Hilarion*, 30).

84. In applying the term 'biography' to saints' lives, I do not intend to imply that every detail recorded in these works is necessarily historically accurate, but neither do I believe we should be too eager to dismiss the miracles described in these hagiographies, as Charles Kingsley did in his book *The Hermits* (London 1868): in publishing a translation of the *Life of Hilarion* he omitted most of Hilarion's miracles, on the grounds that 'it is unnecessary to relate more wonders which the reader cannot be expected to believe' (p. 110). Biography is a flexible genre which is sometimes close to history, sometimes to eulogy, while hagiography is a special kind of biography with its own characteristics and aims, one of which is to show how the power of God manifests itself in human lives.

85. In fact, even among the authors included in this volume, there occurred a certain amount of imitation and cross-referencing to the earlier biographies.

86. Paulinus of Milan states that he has undertaken this work at Augustine's suggestion.

87. Jerome's *Letter* 108 was written after Paula's death in 404 to commemorate her holy life and is addressed to her daughter Eustochium. *Letter* 127 is a memoir of Marcella who died after the sack of Rome by the Visigoths in 410, addressed to her best friend, Principia. In *Letter* 77 Jerome consoles Oceanus on the death of Fabiola, praising her particularly for her assiduous study of Scripture. Other of Jerome's letters are more consolatory than biographical, for example, *Letter* 23 to Marcella on the death of Lea, *Letter* 39 to Paula on the death of her daughter Blesilla, and *Letter* 60 to Heliodorus on the death of his nephew Nepotian.

88. *Life of Antony*, 55.

89. It is interesting to note the similarities between episodes in Malchus' life and that of St Patrick, a century or so later: both men were captured and taken off into slavery in foreign parts; both worked as shepherds during their slavery and both managed eventually to escape; in both cases the period of slavery was crucial in creating or strengthening a commitment to a rigorously Christian life to which the rest of their lives would be devoted.

90. It is now regarded as likely that Benedict adapted a slightly earlier monastic rule, the so-called *Rule of the Master*, which is a much longer work. On

Benedict's Rule and its sources, see C. H. Lawrence, *Medieval Monasticism*, pp. 22–5.

91. Sozomen's *Ecclesiastical History* provides a few details about the life of Hilarion which are not to be found in Jerome's biography.

92. It is known as the *Lausiac History* because it was dedicated to Lausus, the chamberlain of the emperor Theodosius II.

93. Translated as *The Lives of the Desert Fathers*. The Latin text of the *History of the Monks in Egypt* given in volume 21 of Migne's *Patrologia Latina* (this series will henceforth be referred to as PL) is also referred to as *On the Lives of the Fathers* (*De Vitis Patrum*). The title *Vitae Patrum* is also given to the collection of saints' lives (including Evagrius' translation of Athanasius' *Life of Antony* and Jerome's three biographies) and other works on early monasticism contained in PL, volume 73.

94. Palladius seems to have spent the years 388–99 among the monks in Egypt.

95. *The Letters of St Antony the Great*, trans. D. Chitty (Fairacres, Oxford 1975).

96. As a result of the unsystematic way in which the material was collected and added to, it occasionally happens that a particular saying is attributed to more than one monk.

97. *Lives of Pachomius*.

98. Cassian, *Conferences*, 5.2; it was Gregory the Great who, in his work, *Moralia in Job*, reduced this to seven sins.

99. Printed in PL 61.1010–72.

100. Augustine, *On the Catholic Way of Life*, 1.31.65–8.

101. The National Gallery in London, for example, possesses thirty representations of St Jerome in its collection.

102. The lion story first attached to St Gerasimus is associated with Jerome in the Golden Legend, the thirteenth-century compendium of saints' tales which became immensely popular in the later Middle Ages.

103. Giovanni Bellini, for example, painted several pictures of St Jerome, but only one of St Antony.

104. On a twelfth-century capital at Chartres cathedral, for example, and in a painting by Cézanne from 1880, the devil is portrayed as a seductive woman.

105. As for example on a capital in Vézelay cathedral. Two other desert saints, Onuphrius and Mary the Egyptian, were also said to have had their graves dug by lions.

106. Simone Martini, at Assisi, depicted Martin as a knight in the Roman army in the emperor's presence, and later, leaving the army.

107. As for example on a capital in the cathedral at Moissac.

108. This last scene was painted by Rubens, in a work now in the museum at Brussels.

109. Fragments of Antony's letters survive in their original Coptic but more survives in the translations of them made into Latin, Syriac and Georgian. Athanasius knew Coptic as well as Greek, and presumably learnt Latin while he was in Trier and Rome.

110. Jerome, in his *Letter* 57 to Pammachius, expresses what seems to have been the commonly held view concerning the best method of translation when he says that in translating from Greek he aims to translate not word for word but in accordance with the general sense. He supports his view by pointing out that Cicero, in his work on the best kind of orator (section 14), and Horace, in his *Ars Poetica* (lines 133–4), had put forward similar principles. In this letter Jerome also quotes from Evagrius' prologue to his translation of the *Life of Antony* to prove that his method of translation was not unique among his contemporaries either. He does however concede that in translating Holy Scripture it is important to be more literal because 'the order of the words is a holy mystery'.

111. In fact much of Origen's work survives only in Rufinus' Latin translation.

112. Libanius, *Oration*, 1.214.

113. Sulpicius Severus, *Dialogues*, I.23.

114. Evagrius' version of the *Life of Antony* is addressed to his friend Innocentius, also a close friend of Jerome, who died at Antioch in 374: the translation is therefore presumably anterior to that date and may even have been written in Italy before Evagrius' return to the east.

115. For more information about Evagrius, see the introduction to the *Life of Antony*.

116. A. Wilmart was the first to indicate the existence of this text: see 'Une version latine inédite de la vie de saint Antoine par saint Athanase', in *Revue Bénédictine*, 31 (1914) 163–73.

117. See Adomnan of Iona, *Life of St Columba*, trans. R. Sharpe (Harmondsworth 1995) p. 58; Peter the Venerable, *Letter* 28.2; Abelard, *Historia Calamitatum*, trans. B. Radice (Harmondsworth 1974), p. 84.

118. Augustine, *Confessions*, 8.6.15.

119. *Life of Martin*, X.9.

120. *Studies in the Text Tradition of St Jerome's Vitae Patrum*, W. A. Oldfather, ed. (Urbana, Illinois 1943). In the volume entitled *Early Christian Biographies* in the Fathers of the Church series (Washington DC 1952), it was stated that a new edition of the Latin text of these three works, based on Oldfather's studies, would shortly be appearing in the Corpus Scriptorum Ecclesiasticorum Latinorum series, but there is no sign of it yet.

Early Sources

Life of Antony in the earliest surviving Latin translation, edited by G. J. M. Bartelink in *Vite dei Santi* vol. 1 (Milan 1974).

Basil: *Ascetical Works*, translated by M. M. Wagner in *The Fathers of the Church* vol. 9 (Washington D. C. 1962).

Benedict: *The Rule*, in *The Rule of Benedict: a guide to Christian living* (Dublin 1994).

John Cassian: *Conferences* (selections), translated by C. Luibheid with an introduction by O. Chadwick (The Classics of Western Spirituality, Paulist Press 1985).

Evagrius of Pontus: *Practicus*, translated by J. E. Bamberger in *Evagrius Pontius: the Praktikos and chapters on prayer* (Cistercian Studies 4, Kalamazoo 1978).

Gregory of Nyssa: *Life of Macrina*, translated by W. K. Lowther Clarke (London 1916).

Pachomius: *Rule*, translated by A. Veilleux in *Pachomian Chronicles and Rules* in *Pachomian Koinonia. The Lives, Rules and Other Writings of Saint Pachomius and his Disciples* vol. 2 (Cistercian Studies 46, Kalamazoo 1981).

Lives of Pachomius, translated by A. Veilleux in *The Life of Saint Pachomius and his Disciples* in *Pachomian Koinonia. The Lives, Rules and Other Writings of Saint Pachomius and his Disciples* vol. 1 (Cistercian Studies 45, Kalamazoo 1980).

Palladius: *The Lausiac History*, translated by R. T. Meyer in *Ancient Christian Writers* vol. 34 (London 1965).

Paulinus of Milan: *Life of Ambrose*, translated by J. A. Lacy in *The Fathers of the Church* vol. 15 (Washington D. C. 1964).

Pontius: *Life of Cyprian*, translated by M. M. Muller, R. J. Deferrari in *The Fathers of the Church* vol. 15 (Washington D. C. 1964).

Possidius: *Life of Augustine*, translated by M. M. Muller, R. J. Deferrari in *The Fathers of the Church* vol. 15 (Washington D. C. 1964).

Socrates: *Ecclesiastical History* 305–439.

Sozomen: *Ecclesiastical History* 323–425.

Both works translated in *A Select Library of Nicene and Post-Nicene Fathers of the Christian Church* vol. 2 (repr. Michigan 1989).

Sulpicius Severus: *Dialogues* and *Three Letters*, translated by B. M. Peebles in *The Fathers of the Church* vol. 7 (New York 1949).

The History of the Monks in Egypt, translated by Norman Russell as *The Lives of the Desert Fathers* (Oxford 1981).

The Sayings of the Desert Fathers: translated by Benedicta Ward (the Alphabetical Collection, Oxford 1981).

Later Works

Brown, Peter, *The Body in Society: men, women and sexual renunciation in early Christianity* (London 1989).

Chitty, D. J., *The Desert a City* (Oxford 1966).

Cox, Patricia, *Biography in Late Antiquity: A Quest for the Holy Man* (Berkeley, California 1983).

Donaldson, Christopher, *Martin of Tours. The Shaping of Celtic Spirituality* (Norwich 1997).

Head, Thomas & Noble, Thomas (eds.), *Soldiers of Christ, saints and saints' lives from late antiquity and the early middle ages* (London, 1995).

Kelly, J. N. D., *Jerome, His Life, Writings and Controversies* (London 1975).

Lawrence, C. H., *Medieval Monasticism* (2nd edition, London 1989).

Louth, Andrew, *The Wilderness of God* (London 1991).

Rousseau, Philip, *Ascetics, Authority and the Church in the Age of Jerome and Cassian* (Oxford 1978).

Rubenson, S., *The Letters of St Antony: monasticism and the making of a saint* (Minneapolis 1995).

Saint Martin et son temps (Rome 1961).

Stancliffe, Clare, *St Martin and his Hagiographer* (Oxford 1983).
Straw, Carole, *Gregory the Great. Perfection in Imperfection* (Berkeley, California 1988).
Waddell, Helen, *The Desert Fathers* (excerpts translated from the Latin) (London 1936).

Life of Antony by Athanasius

Athanasius probably[1] *wrote the* Life of Antony *during a period of exile in the desert when he was forced into hiding with the monks in the years following Antony's death in 356. Athanasius, who had attended the Council of Nicaea as a young deacon in 325 and had been bishop of Alexandria since 328, had already spent two periods of exile in Trier and Rome: in fact he was to spend about seventeen years of his episcopate in exile for he repeatedly fell victim to the hostilities and intrigues of the Arians, against whom he continued to fight in order to uphold the Christian beliefs worked out at Nicaea until his death in 373.*

Athanasius' portrait of Antony depicts the tension in the life of a man who desired solitude above all else but was forced to adopt the role of a spiritual adviser and healer by the people who were drawn to him because of the special status his extraordinary way of life gave him: Antony's determination to turn to the desert, away from people and from the things of this world, made him all the more attractive to them. Such tension does not however detract from the fact that the Antony we come to know in this biography is a 'holy hero',[2] *outstanding in his spiritual achievements but also in his humility and simplicity.*

In his preface to the Life of Antony *Athanasius indicates that he is responding to a request from ascetics overseas for information about Antony's life; at the end of the work he also expresses the view that it may be valuable to non-Christians, too, by showing them that Jesus Christ is God and that those beings whom they worship as gods are but demons and deceivers over whom the Christian God has power. But it has been suggested that Athanasius' portrait of Antony is not so much an accurate picture of the historical Antony but an expression of Athanasius' thought, based on earlier accounts of Antony, and intended as a 'tool for achieving political unity'.*[3] *It has also been claimed that the* Life of Antony *was intended as a piece of anti-Arian propaganda,*[4] like so many other of Athanasius' works: not only is Antony shown as an ally of the orthodox bishops in the struggle against heresy, but Athanasius insinuates aspects of Nicene theology at every possible opportunity. This may be the case, but it is nevertheless also true that later readers were less concerned with the niceties of Nicene theology than with the spiritual themes which are relevant to all those seeking to draw near to God by means of a life of asceticism.

Whatever the attractions, the Life of Antony certainly appears to have become an immediate bestseller, and to have remained one throughout the Middle Ages.[5] Translations were soon made and by the end of the fourth century the work had been mentioned by many contemporaries, both in the east and west.[6]

The most famous translation was that made into Latin by Evagrius, which provides the text for the translation in this volume. Evagrius of Antioch (not to be confused with his contemporary, the monk Evagrius of Pontus) came from a high-ranking family and started his career as a government administrator. By 362 he had left his secular career, was ordained and accompanied Eusebius, bishop of Vercelli, back to Italy,[7] where he spent about ten years. He seems to have been a man of some influence at the time: Jerome praises him for his success in combating Auxentius, the Arian bishop of Milan, who had driven Martin, later bishop of Tours, out of Milan;[8] Evagrius assisted Damasus[9] in becoming pope in 367 after a disputed papal election and successfully intervened with the emperor on behalf of a woman wrongly condemned for adultery.[10] Returning to Antioch in about 373, he was soon visited by Jerome, with whom he had struck up a close friendship while they were both in northern Italy. Jerome stayed with Evagrius at his estate called Maronia, some twenty-five kilometres outside Antioch,[11] before going off into the Syrian desert where Evagrius visited him regularly, bringing letters from friends.[12] It is possible that it was at this period that Evagrius undertook the translation of the Life of Antony. Certainly it is likely to have been written before 374 when Innocentius, the friend of Jerome and Evagrius to whom the work is addressed, died.

Meanwhile, Evagrius was forced to take sides in the Meletian dispute which had been rumbling on at Antioch since 360 and which would not be finally resolved until after Evagrius' death.[13] As a result of the extreme sensitivity regarding Arian doctrines at this time, it had happened that different factions in the church at Antioch had elected different bishops and neither faction would give way. Gradually the matter became an issue for the whole Church, with the east largely supporting bishop Meletius while the west – and Evagrius – supported bishop Paulinus. When Meletius died in 381 while chairman of the Council of Constantinople, it was hoped that everyone could be induced to support Paulinus, but unfortunately Meletius' supporters elected a successor, Flavianus. The same occurred in 388 at Paulinus' death: in fact the dying Paulinus took canon law into his own hands and on his own authority consecrated Evagrius as bishop of the old-Nicene minority which continued to refuse to accept Flavianus: in this way the schism was prolonged even further. We know nothing of what Evagrius achieved during his episcopate. Jerome mentions him as still living in 392,[14] but there is no mention of him later than that date.[15] It may be that he lived on until 398, for one of John Chrysostom's first acts when he became bishop of Constantinople in that year was to write to the pope at Rome to ensure that Flavianus would now be recognized as the sole bishop of Antioch.

Evagrius' later fame was to depend on his translation of the Life of Antony, although in fact his whole life was spent in the company of the great men of the fourth century, involved in important events, and he is mentioned in the writings of Libanius, Basil of Caesarea[16] and Ambrose of Milan as well as those of Jerome. Of him Jerome writes, 'If I were to suppose that I could give an account of all the work he has done on Christ's behalf, I should indeed be foolish.'[17]

The Life of Antony offers a chronological account of the whole of Antony's life from his infancy until his death. In chapter 3, after making provision for his sister, Antony withdraws to a place not far from his native village, where he leads a life of manual work and prayer, occasionally visiting other ascetics to learn from them. In chapter 8 he moves further afield, choosing to live enclosed in a tomb where he can continue his painful struggles with the devil. Here he stays until the age of thirty-five when he moves on into the desert (chapter 11) and finds a deserted fort (12) which is to be his home for the next twenty years. During this period he rarely leaves the fort and is seen by hardly anyone. It comes as a surprise to all when he comes out of the fort after twenty years of solitude and hardship and is seen to be as youthful and physically fit as before. Chapters 16–43 are devoted to Antony's speech of spiritual advice, given to those who come to visit him at the fort. Chapter 46 tells of Antony's visit to Alexandria during the persecutions of Maximin Daia. On returning to the fort he realizes that he can no longer find there the peace he desires. His decision to move to the Upper Thebaid is thwarted by a voice from heaven advising him to move further into the desert (49). In chapter 50 he reaches the Inner Mountain, which will be his home for the rest of his life. Athanasius then relates certain episodes in Antony's life which provide evidence of his spiritual power and wisdom and of his great fame. Chapters 89–93 tell of the end of his life and the manner of his death, while in the final chapter the author once more addresses the monks at whose prompting the work was written. Antony's struggles with the devil are principally described in the earlier part of the work, before his long speech, while those miracles which Athanasius mentions occur in the second half, miracles such as the healing of Martinianus' daughter (48), of Fronto (57) and the girl from Busiris (58). But it is not primarily Antony the wonder-worker whom we see in Athanasius' biography, unlike for example the Benedict of Gregory's biography: any miracles that occur are clearly depicted as the work of God. It is instead Antony's wisdom that is emphasized, together with his prophetic abilities, his calmness and spiritual strength – all of which are dependent on his close relationship with God. These are what set him apart and serve as an inspiration to all.

Evagrius' prologue to his translation

Evagrius the priest sends greetings in the Lord to Innocentius, his dearest son.

A literal translation made from one language to another conceals the meaning, like rampant grasses which suffocate the crops. As long as the text keeps to the cases and turns of phrase, it is forced to move in an indirect way by means of lengthy circumlocutions, and it finds it hard to give a clear account of something which could be succinctly expressed. I have tried to avoid this in translating, as you requested, the life of the blessed Antony, and I have translated in such a way that nothing should be lacking from the sense although something may be missing from the words. Some people try to capture the syllables and letters, but you must seek the meaning.

Preface

Bishop Athanasius to the monks abroad:

Brothers, you have entered the most noble contest, striving either to equal the monks of Egypt or to outdo them in striving after moral perfection by means of rigorous self-discipline. Indeed, there are already numerous monasteries in your part of the world, the word monk is very familiar, and everyone will rightly be impressed by this intention of yours: may God grant you the fulfilment you desire in your prayers. You asked me to write to you about the life of the blessed Antony, for you wish to know how he started out and what he was like before he made his holy commitment, as well as what the end of his life was like and whether those things are true which rumour has spread abroad concerning him, so that you might be able to undertake to emulate him and follow his example. It is therefore with great joy that I have undertaken what you asked. Indeed, the very act of remembering Antony is of enormous profit and benefit to me and I am sure that you, listening in wonder, will be keen to follow his commitment: for to know who Antony was offers us the perfect path to virtue.

In short, therefore, you should believe everything that those who talk about him claim, and consider that you have heard only the least remarkable of all the very remarkable things he did. For I am convinced that they cannot know everything, since even I, in answer to your request, will be unable to give an account which accurately conveys his merits, however much I reveal in my letter. You, too, must diligently question all those who sail from this country[1] so that by means of their individual reports of what they know, you may obtain a full account which is in keeping with such a great name and worthy of it. After reading your letter, I wanted to invite some monks to come here to me, in particular those who used to visit Antony frequently, so that I might gain more information and thus be able to send you greater gifts. But seeing that the sailing season was coming to an end and the letter-bearer was in a dreadful hurry, I have hastened to note down for you those things I myself know (for I visited him often) and those I learned from the person who spent a good deal of time with him for the purpose of supplying him with water.[2] In the case of both these sources, I am concerned about the truth: I do not want anyone to hear too many things in case this might make him sceptical of the miracles; on the other hand I do not want anyone to hear anything less than is warranted by Antony's merits, in case it would make him consider this man unworthy of a miracle despite his great reputation.

Life of Antony

1 (1) Antony, then, came from Egypt, the son of well-born and devout parents. He was brought up so carefully by his family that he knew nothing apart from his parents and his home. While he was still a boy

he refused to learn to read and write or to join in the silly games of the other little children; instead he burned with a desire for God and lived a life of simplicity at home, as it says of Jacob in the Bible.[3] He also often went with his parents to church but did not fool around as little children tend to nor did he show a lack of respect as young boys often do; instead he concentrated on what was being read and put the useful precepts into practice in his way of life. He was never a nuisance to his family, as children usually are because of their desire for a variety of dainty foods. He did not long for the pleasures of more delicate food: he was content with just what he was given and asked for nothing more.

2 (2) When he and his little sister were left completely on their own after the death of their parents (Antony being then about eighteen or twenty years old), he took good care both of his house and of his sister. But before six months had passed it happened that while he was on his way to church as usual, he came to think of how the apostles had rejected everything to follow the Saviour[4] and how many people, as it says in the Acts of the Apostles, had sold their possessions and brought the proceeds to lay at the apostles' feet for distribution to those in need.[5] What great hope was stored up for these people in heaven![6] Turning these things over in his mind, Antony entered the church. It happened that just at that moment the Gospel passage was being read in which the Lord says to the rich man, *If you wish to be perfect, go and sell everything you possess and give it to the poor and come, follow me and you will have treasure in heaven.*[7]

When he heard this, Antony applied the Lord's commandment to himself, believing that it was as a result of divine inspiration that he had first remembered that incident and that this passage of Scripture had been read out for his sake. He immediately went home and sold the possessions he owned. He possessed 300 fertile *arourae*[8] of the highest quality which he shared out among his neighbours to prevent anyone bearing a grudge against him or his sister. All the rest of his possessions, which were movable goods, he sold, and having made no small profit from them he gave it to the poor, keeping a little for the sake of his sister who seemed more vulnerable on account of her sex and age.

3 (3) On another occasion when Antony had gone to church and heard the Lord saying in the Gospel, *Take no thought for the morrow,*[9] he distributed also the rest of his wealth to the poor. He was not content to stay at home but entrusted his sister to some faithful virgins of good repute to be brought up according to their example, while he himself, now released from all worldly ties, eagerly entered upon a harsh and arduous way of life. But monasteries were not yet so numerous in Egypt and there was no one at all who was familiar with the remote desert: anyone who desired to benefit himself in the service of Christ would settle at no great distance from his own village. Now there was on a neighbouring estate an old man who from his earliest youth had led a solitary life. When Antony saw him, he was keen to emulate him in goodness. At first, when he started out, Antony lived in places which were at a relatively short distance from home but later on, if he heard of anyone engaging in this disciplined life, he would go out and search for him like a wise bee. He would not return to his own dwelling until he had set eyes on the one he longed for and then when he had, so to speak, obtained the gift of honey, he would go back home. After beginning in this way, his resolve grew stronger by the day until he reached the point where he no longer thought of his family wealth or of his relations but focused all his longing and attention on what he had undertaken and worked with his hands, for he was aware that it says in the Bible, *He who does not work, will not eat.*[10] The money he earned from his work he gave to the poor, apart from what he needed to buy bread, and he prayed often, for he had learned that one should pray to the Lord without ceasing.[11] He also listened attentively to the Scriptures so that nothing should slip from his mind. He preserved all the Lord's commandments, keeping them safe in his memory rather than in books.

4 He led his life in such a way that he was loved by all the brothers with pure affection. He obeyed all those whom he visited in his eagerness to learn and absorbed their various individual gifts – striving to imitate the self-restraint of one, the cheerfulness of another; emulating the gentleness of one, the nocturnal devotions of another, the assiduousness in reading of another; admiring one who fasted, another who slept on the bare ground and praising the endurance of one and

the compassion of another. He kept in mind the love they all showed one another and he would return to his own place refreshed by every aspect of their virtues. There he would think all these things over and strive to imitate the good points of each of them. He was never provoked to anger, not even against those of the same age: the only fire that burned in the heart of that exceptional man was that of his determination to appear second to none in the deeds I have mentioned. And he did this in such a way that although he surpassed all others in glory, he was nevertheless dear to them all. For when his neighbours and those monks whom he often visited saw Antony, they called him God's friend. To adopt the terms of a natural relationship one might say that some loved him as a son, others as a brother.

5 (4) While Antony was busy with these things which caused everyone to love him, the devil, an enemy of the word Christian, could not bear to see such outstanding virtues in a young man and so he attacked him with his old wiles. First of all he tried to see whether he could drag Antony away from the form of life to which he had committed himself: he made him remember his possessions, his sister's protection, his family's high status. He tried to awaken in him a desire for material things or for the fleeting honours of this world, for the pleasures of different kinds of food and all the other attractions which belong to a life of indulgence. Finally he reminded Antony of how difficult it is to attain the goal of virtue and the very hard work involved in achieving it; he also reminded him of the weakness of the body and the length of time needed. In short he created the greatest confusion in Antony's thoughts, hoping to call him back from his proper intention. But when, as a result of Antony's prayers to God, the devil realized that he had been driven out by Antony's faith in Christ's sufferings, he seized the weapons with which he normally attacks all young people, using seductive dreams to disturb him at night. First he tried to unsettle him at night by means of hostile hordes and terrifying sounds, and then he attacked him by day with weapons that were so obviously his that no one could doubt that it was against the devil that Antony was fighting. For the devil tried to implant dirty thoughts but Antony pushed them away by means of constant prayer. The devil tried to titillate his senses by means of natural carnal desires

but Antony defended his whole body by faith, by praying at night and by fasting. At night the devil would turn himself into the attractive form of a beautiful woman, omitting no detail that might provoke lascivious thoughts, but Antony called to mind the fiery punishment of hell and the torment inflicted by worms: in this way he resisted the onslaught of lust. The devil without hesitation set before him the slippery path of youth that leads to disaster but Antony concentrated on the everlasting torments of future judgement and kept his soul's purity untainted throughout these temptations. All these things served to confound the devil for he who thought that he could become God's equal was now being tricked by a young man, as if he were the most wretched creature, and he who exulted and boasted against flesh and blood[12] had been beaten by a man who was made of flesh. For the Lord was helping his servant, the Lord who took on flesh for our sake and granted the body victory over the devil so that any individual who became involved in this struggle could cite the words of the Apostle, *Not I, but the grace of Christ which is with me.*[13]

6 At last that most hideous serpent found he was unable to destroy Antony even by this means and saw that he was always being driven back by Antony's thoughts. So gnashing his teeth (as it says in the Bible)[14] and wailing, he appeared, as was fitting, in a form that revealed his true nature: an ugly black boy prostrated himself at Antony's feet, weeping loudly and saying in a human voice, 'Many have I led astray, many have I deceived, but now I have been defeated by your efforts as I was by other holy people.' When Antony asked him who it was who was saying this, he replied, 'I am the friend of fornication. I have used many different kinds of shameful weapon to attack young people and that is why I am called the spirit of fornication. How many of those who were determined to live chastely have I tricked! How many times have I persuaded those who were starting out hesitantly to return to their former foul ways. I am the one who caused the prophet to reproach the fallen, saying, *You have been led astray by the spirit of fornication,*[15] and in truth it was I who made them fall. I am the one who has often tempted you and always I have been driven away.' When the soldier of Christ heard this, he gave thanks to God and strengthened by greater confidence in the face of the enemy, he

said, 'You are utterly despicable and contemptible, for both your blackness and your age are signs of weaknesses. You do not worry me any longer. *The Lord is my helper and I will exult over my enemies.*'[16] And immediately, at the sound of Antony's singing, the apparition which had been visible vanished.

7 (5) This was Antony's first victory over the devil or rather the first sign of the Saviour's power in Antony, the Saviour *who had condemned sin in the flesh, so that the just requirement of the law should be fulfilled in us who walk not according to the flesh but according to the Spirit.*[17] But this one triumph did not give Antony a sense of security nor did the devil's powers fail completely, despite being shattered on this occasion. For the devil, like a roaring lion,[18] was on the look-out for some means of pouncing on him. And Antony, knowing from what the Bible says that the wiles of the devil are numerous,[19] maintained his commitment firm by means of skilful effort; reflecting that although Satan had been defeated in the struggles of the flesh, he could mobilize more deadly weapons against him and use new strategies. Consequently Antony subdued his body more and more, for fear that he who had been the winner in some contests should be the loser in others.[20] He decided therefore to impose upon himself the constraints of a more rigorous rule of life and even though everyone was amazed at this young man's untiring dedication, he patiently endured the holy endeavour, because the long-term exertion of voluntary servitude to God would transform habit into nature.

(6) Antony endured hunger and sleeplessness to such a degree that his powers were considered incredible. He very often spent the whole night in prayer and he ate only once a day, after sunset. Sometimes he continued fasting for two or three days at a time and only took refreshment on the fourth day. He ate bread and salt and drank a little water. Regarding meat and wine I think it is better to remain silent than to say anything, since this kind of thing is not found even among the majority of monks. When he allowed his limbs some rest, he would use a woven rush mat with a cover of goats' hair. Sometimes he would even lie on the bare earth and he utterly rejected the use of oil to anoint the body. For he used to say that it was hardly possible that the bodies of those who used such things, and especially young

men's bodies, should grow strong if they were to be softened by smooth oil. Instead they ought to use rigorous exercises to control the flesh, in accordance with the Apostle's claim, *When I am weak, then I am stronger.*[21] Antony also stated that wearing down the body's energies in this way could revive a person's mental powers. That was the reason why he did not measure the value of his tasks by the length of time spent, but with the love and willing servitude characteristic of a novice, he continued to maintain his desire to progress in the fear of God. Wishing new achievements to be added to old ones, he bore in mind the words of the learned man I mentioned earlier who said, *Forgetting the past and growing strong in the future.*[22] He remembered also what the prophet Elijah said: *The Lord lives, before whom I stand today,*[23] explaining that 'today' was added in that passage because Elijah was not reckoning past time but it was as if he was entering battle each day and wished to prove himself to be what he knew was worthy in the sight of God: pure of heart and ready to obey God's will.

8 (7) Then the holy Antony, considering that a servant of God ought to take as his model the way of life of the great Elijah and to use it as a mirror to organize his own life, moved away to some tombs situated not far from his settlement. He asked one of his friends to bring him food at regular intervals. And when this brother had shut him up in one of the tombs, Antony remained there alone. But the devil was afraid that, as time went on, Antony might cause the desert to become inhabited, so he gathered together his minions and tortured Antony by beating him all over. The intensity of the pain deprived Antony of his ability both to move and to speak, and later he himself would often tell how his injuries had been so serious that they were worse than all the tortures devised by men. But God's providence, which never fails those who put their hope in Him, saved him. The next day the brother whom I referred to earlier arrived with food as usual. He found Antony lying on the ground half-dead and the door smashed down. He lifted him on to his shoulders and carried him back to his house in the village. When people heard about this, a large number of neighbours and relatives came running and in grief they performed the funeral rites for Antony, who was laid out in their midst. But when half the night had passed, a heavy weariness overwhelmed those

who were keeping watch. Then Antony, his spirit gradually returning, drew a deep breath and lifted his head. When he saw that the man who had brought him there was awake while all the others were lying fast asleep, he beckoned to the man and begged him to carry him back, without waking anyone at all, to the place where he had been living.

9 (8) And so he was carried back and again he remained there alone as before. Since he was unable to stand as a result of the recent beatings, he prayed lying down and after praying he would say in a loud voice, 'Look, here I am, Antony. I do not run away from your fights: even if you arrange more difficult ones, no one will separate me from the love of Christ.'[24] And he would chant these words: *If they place an encampment against me, my heart will not fear.*[25] On hearing this, the devil, the enemy of the good, was amazed that after so many beatings Antony had dared to return. He gathered his dogs together and tearing himself to pieces in his fury, he said, 'You see how Antony is overcome neither by the spirit of fornication nor by physical pain, and on top of it all he challenges us insolently. Take up all your weapons; we must attack with greater force. Let him feel, let him feel; he must understand who it is that he is provoking.' He spoke and all those listening to him agreed with his exhortation, because the devil has countless ways of causing harm. Then there was a sudden noise which caused the place to shake violently: holes appeared in the walls and a horde of different kinds of demons poured out. They took on the shapes of wild animals and snakes and instantly filled the whole place with spectres in the form of lions, bulls, wolves, vipers, serpents, scorpions and even leopards and bears, too. They all made noises according to their individual nature: the lion roared, eager for the kill; the bull bellowed and made menacing movements with his horns; the serpent hissed; the wolves leaped forward to attack; the spotted leopard demonstrated all the different wiles of the one who controlled him.[26] The face of each of them bore a savage expression and the sound of their fierce voices was terrifying. Antony, beaten and mauled, experienced even more atrocious pains in his body but he remained unafraid, his mind alert. And though the wounds of his flesh made him groan, he maintained the same attitude and spoke as if mocking

his enemies. 'If you had any power, one of you would be enough for the fight; but since the Lord has robbed you of your strength, you are broken and so you attempt to use large numbers to terrify me, although the fact that you have taken on the shapes of unreasoning beasts is itself proof of your weakness.' And he went on confidently, 'If you have any influence, if the Lord has granted you power over me, look, here I am: devour me. But if you cannot, why do you expend so much useless effort? For the sign of the cross and faith in the Lord is for us a wall that no assault of yours can break down.' They made numerous threats against the holy Antony but gnashed their teeth because none of their attempts were successful – on the contrary they made fools of themselves rather than of him.

10 (9) Jesus did not fail to notice his servant's struggle but came to protect him. When at last Antony raised his eyes, he saw the roof opening above him and, as the darkness was dispelled, a ray of light poured in on him. As soon as this bright light appeared, all the demons vanished and the pain in Antony's body suddenly ceased. Furthermore, the building which had been destroyed a moment earlier was restored. Antony immediately understood that the Lord was present. Sighing deeply from the bottom of his heart, he addressed the light that had appeared to him, saying, 'Where were you, good Jesus? Where were you? Why were you not here from the beginning to heal my wounds?' And a voice came to him saying, 'Antony, I was here, but I was waiting to watch your struggle. But now, since you have bravely held your own in this fight, I will always help you and I will make you famous throughout the world.' When he heard this, Antony stood up and prayed; he felt so greatly strengthened that he realized he had received more strength now than he had had before he lost it. Antony was thirty-five years old at the time.

11 (10) Later, as his willing commitment caused him to grow in spiritual goodness, he went to the old man I mentioned earlier and begged that they should live together in the desert. When the old man refused, giving as his excuse his old age and the novelty of the plan, Antony went forth to the mountain alone, having lost all fear of that way of life, and attempted to open up the path to the desert which had hitherto been unknown to monks. However, not even

then did his tireless adversary give up. Determined to obstruct Antony's commitment to this way of life, the devil threw down a silver plate in his path. When Antony saw it, he recognized the cunning of that ingenious trickster. He stood still, fearless, and looking at the plate grimly, he rebuked the one who was trying to trick him with the illusion of silver, saying to himself, 'Why is this plate here in the desert? This track is remote and there are no traces of any travellers. If it had fallen out of someone's luggage, it could hardly have lain unnoticed – it is too large. If the person who lost it came back, he would certainly have found what had fallen out because this place is so empty. This is a product of your cunning, you devil, but you will not hinder my intention. May your silver plate go to hell with you.' As soon as he said this, the plate disappeared like smoke from the face of the fire.

12 (11) Next Antony noticed, not an illusion as before, but a large lump of real gold lying in his path. It is not clear whether the devil put it there to deceive him or whether the heavenly power revealed it to prove that Antony could not be seduced even by real riches. We are however convinced that what appeared really was gold. Antony marvelled at the size of this piece of shining metal and quickly ran all the way to the mountain, as if he were escaping from a fire. After crossing the river, he found there a deserted fort full of venomous animals (due to the length of time it had lain abandoned and because of its solitary location). There he settled, living as the fort's new tenant. Immediately on his arrival, a huge number of snakes fled as if they had been chased out. Antony then blocked up the entrance with stones and remained there all alone, storing up enough bread for six months (for it often lasts for a whole year without going mouldy), as is the custom among the Thebans, and with a small supply of water. He never went out and never received any visitors, even to the extent that when he took in his bread supply through the roof twice a year, he held no conversation with those who brought it to him.

13 (12) When many people, in their desire to see him and their eagerness to question him, spent the night outside his door, they heard noisy voices, as of a number of people saying to Antony, 'Why have you moved into our home? What have you got to do with the

desert? Leave other people's property alone. You cannot live here; you cannot endure our attacks.' At first those outside thought that some men had entered using ladders and were engaged in a dispute inside, but when they peeped in through the gaps, they saw no one and then they realized that demons were fighting Antony. They were terribly frightened and called to Antony for help. He came to the door to comfort the brothers: he begged them not to be afraid and asked them to go away. He assured them all in their terror that their fear was caused by the demons. 'Make the sign of the cross,' he said, 'and depart without fear. Leave them to mock themselves.' And so the people went back while Antony remained there unharmed, never tiring in his struggle, for the increase in his commitment and the weakness of his opponents accorded him the greatest relief in his fight and made him steadfast of mind. When there came again to the desert numbers of people who thought they would find him dead already, he sang forth from within, *Let God arise and let his enemies be scattered and let those who hate him flee before him. Let them disappear like smoke and as wax melts near the fire, so let the sinners perish before God.*[27] And he went on, *All the nations surrounded me and in the name of the Lord I have taken vengeance on them.*[28]

14 (13) Antony spent twenty years in the desert in this way, remaining cut off from the sight of men. But many came to him in their desire to imitate his commitment to that way of life, together with a large number of those who knew him, and there gathered there a great crowd of people who were suffering. When they had at last managed to tear down the doors by force, Antony appeared to them with an aura of holiness as if he had emerged from some divine sanctuary. They were all stunned at the beauty of his countenance and the dignified bearing of his body which had not grown flabby through lack of exercise; neither had his face grown pale as a result of fasting and fighting with demons. On the contrary, the handsomeness of his limbs remained as before, as if no time had passed. What a great miracle! What purity of mind was his! Never did excessive frivolity cause him to burst out laughing, never did the thought of past sins make him frown, nor did the high praise bestowed on him by his admirers make him conceited. The solitude had in no way made him

uncivilized and the daily battles with his enemies had not brutalized him. His mind was calm and he maintained a well-balanced attitude in all situations. Then the grace of God, through Antony, freed many people from unclean spirits and from various illnesses. His speech, seasoned with salt,[29] brought comfort to those who grieved, instructed the ignorant, reconciled those who were angry and persuaded everyone that nothing should be valued higher than the love of Christ. He would set before their eyes the great number of future rewards as well as the mercy of God, and he made known the benefits granted because God did not spare His own son but had given Him for the salvation of us all.[30] His words had the immediate effect of persuading many of those who heard him to reject human things: this marked the beginning of the desert's colonization.

15 (14) I will not fail to mention what happened in the region of Arsinoe. For when Antony planned to visit the brothers and it was necessary to cross the river Nile which was full of crocodiles and many dangerous river animals, he and his companions crossed it unharmed and returned safely, too. After that he continued resolutely in his ascetic efforts as before and inspired many of the brothers by his teaching, so that in a short space of time a large number of monastic cells came into existence. With fatherly affection he guided the monks, both old and new, according to their age and circumstances.

16 (15) One day, when the brothers who had gathered there were asking the holy Antony to provide some guidelines for their way of life, he raised his voice with a prophet's confidence and said[31] that the Scriptures were sufficient for all teaching of the rule but that it would also be an excellent idea for the brothers to support each other by means of mutual encouragement. 'And so,' he said, 'you should tell me, as if I were your father, what you have learned and I will reveal to you, as if you were my sons, what I have discovered as a result of my great age. But let this be the first rule, shared by all of you, that no one should weaken in the firmness of their commitment to the way of life he has chosen, but should always strive to increase his commitment to this undertaking as if he were just starting out, especially as the span of human life, compared to eternity, is very short.' After beginning in this way Antony was silent for a while.

Marvelling at God's great generosity, he then added, 'In this present life, things of equal value are exchanged: the seller does not receive more from the buyer. But the promise of eternal life is bought at a low price for it is written: *The days of our life are seventy years or if many, eighty years; whatever remains is hard work and suffering.*'[32] If we have lived in God's work for eighty or a hundred years, working hard, we will not reign for the same amount of time in the future; instead, in exchange for the years I mentioned, we shall be granted a reign lasting throughout all ages. It is not earth that we will inherit, but heaven. We shall leave this corrupt body and we shall receive it incorrupt.

17 'And so, my sons, do not allow yourselves to grow weary. Do not be seduced by pride in your achievement. *For the sufferings of this present time are not worth comparing with the glory to come that will be revealed to us.*[33] No one, once he has rejected the world, should think that he has left behind anything of importance, because the whole earth, compared to the infinity of the heavens, is small and limited. Even if we renounce the whole world, we cannot give anything in exchange which is of similar value to the heavenly dwellings. If each person considers this he will immediately realize that if he abandons a few acres of land or a small house or a moderate sum of gold, he ought not to feel proud of himself in the belief that he has given up a lot. Nor should he become despondent, thinking that he will receive only a little in return. For just as someone considers one bronze drachma of no value in comparison with winning one hundred gold drachmas, so too, anyone who renounces possession of the whole world will receive in heaven a hundred times as much in more valuable rewards. In short, we must realize that even if we want to retain our riches, we will be torn away from them against our will by the law of death, as it says in the book of Ecclesiastes.[34] Why then do we not make a virtue of necessity? Why do we not voluntarily abandon what must be destroyed when this light comes to an end, so that we might gain the kingdom of heaven? Let Christians care for nothing that they cannot take away with them. We ought rather to seek after that which will lead us to heaven, namely wisdom, chastity, justice, virtue, an ever watchful mind, care of the poor, firm faith in Christ, a mind that can control anger, hospitality. Striving after these things, we shall

prepare for ourselves a dwelling in the land of the peaceful, as it says in the Gospel.[35]

18 'Let us bear in mind the fact that we are servants of the Lord and that we owe a service to Him who created us. For a servant does not reject present or future authority on account of past service and does not dare to claim that because of his past work he ought to be released from the task in hand; instead, he continues to perform the same service with unbroken commitment (as it says in the Gospel)[36] so as to please his master and so that his wages will not be fear and beatings. In the same way it is right for us to obey the divine commandments, knowing that He who is a just judge will judge each person where He finds him, as testified by the words of the prophet Ezechiel.[37] For even the wretched Judas, on account of one night's wickedness, lost out on the rewards for all his past achievement.

19 'We must therefore maintain an unwavering firmness of commitment to this way of life with God as our helper, for it is written, *God works for good with everyone who chooses the good*.[38] In order to stamp on idleness, let us reflect upon the Apostle's words when he claims that he dies each day.[39] Similarly, if we bear in mind the unpredictability of our human condition, we will not sin. For when we wake from sleep, we must be doubtful as to whether we will reach evening and when we lie down to rest, we should not be confident that daylight will return. We should everywhere be mindful of the uncertainty of our nature and our life and understand that we are governed by God's providence. Not only will we not go astray nor be swept away by some flimsy desire, but neither will we be angry with anyone nor strive to accumulate earthly treasures. Instead, fearing death each day and always thinking of our separation from the body, we will trample upon all that is transitory. The desire for women will disappear, the fire of lust will be extinguished and we will pay our debts to each other, always holding before our eyes the coming of the final retribution. For a powerful fear of judgement and a terrible dread of punishment destroy the incentives of the lustful flesh and support the soul as it slips off the cliff edge, so to speak.

20 'I pray then that we should use every effort to press on towards this life's goal. Let no one look behind him like Lot's wife,[40] especially

since the Lord has said that no one who puts his hand upon the plough and looks back is fit for the kingdom of heaven.[41] To look back means to have second thoughts about your undertaking and to become entangled once more in worldly desires. I beg you not to fear the word "virtue" as if it were something unattainable. Do not think that such an endeavour which is dependent on our will is alien to you or something remote. Man has a natural inclination to this kind of effort and it is something that only awaits our willingness. Let the Greeks pursue their studies across the seas and go in search of teachers of useless literature in foreign lands. We however feel no compulsion to travel or cross the waves for the kingdom of heaven is to be found everywhere on earth: that is why the Lord says in the Gospel, *The kingdom of God is within you.*[42] The virtue that is within us only requires the human will. For who can doubt that the natural purity of the soul, were it not tainted by filth from outside, would be the fount and source of all virtues? A good creator must necessarily have made the soul good. But if perhaps we hesitate, let us listen to the words of Joshua, the son of Nun, who said, *Set your heart straight toward the Lord God of Israel.*[43] And John expresses a similar idea about virtue when he says, *Make straight your paths.*[44] For to have a straight soul means that its original soundness is not stained by the blemish of any vices. If it changes its nature, then it is said to have gone astray, but if it preserves its good nature, then that is virtue. The Lord has entrusted our soul to us: let us keep what has been entrusted in the same state as we received it. No one can put forward as an excuse that what is born in him is external to him. Let Him who made us recognize His own creation, and let Him find His own work as He created it. Our natural adornment is enough for us: you who are human must not disfigure what divine generosity has granted you. To wish to alter the works of God is to desecrate them.

21 'We ought to be careful to ensure that we control the tyrannical passion of anger, since it says in the Bible, *The anger of man does not work the righteousness of God,*[45] and also, *Covetous desire gives birth to sin and when sin is full grown it brings forth death.*[46] The divine voice has recommended that we should protect our soul with unceasing vigilance[47] and lead it towards perfection with all care and effort

because we have enemies who are trained to trip us up – I mean the demons whom we must fight without a truce, according to the testimony of the Apostle who says, *We are not contending against flesh and blood but against the principalities and the powers of this world, against the spiritual hosts of wickedness in the heavenly places.*[48] Huge numbers of them are flying through the air here; at no distance from us the enemy troops are rushing to and fro. I am not able to describe their diversity so I shall leave this task to those who are more competent than me. But I shall give a brief account, to the best of my ability, of what one needs to be aware of, namely the tricks the demons have devised against us.

22 'First of all we should hold firm in our minds the fact that God has made nothing that is evil and that the demons did not derive their origin from any arrangement on His part: their perversity is a fault not of nature but of the will. In fact they were good in that they were created by God, but they fell to earth from heaven by their own will. Wallowing there in the filthy mire, they introduced the wicked worship of paganism; now they are tortured by envy of us and never cease to devise every possible evil scheme to prevent us taking over the top positions they once held. But their wickedness is of various kinds and is shared out among them.[49] Some of them have reached the topmost summit of destructiveness while others seem less harmful in comparison with those who are more wicked. They have all undertaken different struggles against different causes according to the strength of their demonic powers. That is why it is necessary to ask the Lord to grant the ability to distinguish between spirits[50] so that we may see through their tricks and their efforts and raise the single banner of the Lord's cross in confronting the unequal battle. Paul showed that he had been granted this ability when he said, *For we are not ignorant of his designs.*[51] Following his example we too should use our own experiences to instruct each other in conversation.

23 'The demons are hostile to all Christians, but they especially hate those who are monks and virgins of Christ. They set traps along their paths and strive to undermine their commitment by means of irreverent and obscene thoughts, but let them not strike terror into you. For the prayers and fasting of those who have faith in the Lord

cause the demons to collapse immediately, but even if they are driven back a little way, do not think that you have gained complete victory. For they have a tendency, when wounded, to rise up with even greater violence and to change their method of attack: when they have no success with dirty thoughts, they use fears to terrify, transforming themselves into women one moment, wild animals the next moment and then serpents as well as huge bodies with a head reaching to the roof of the house, and finally turning into troops of soldiers and an infinite number of different shapes. All these vanish as soon as the sign of the cross is made. When these means of deception have also been recognized, the demons begin to prophesy and to try to predict future events, but when they have been thwarted in these efforts, too, they summon the leader of their wickedness, the culmination of all evil, to assist them in their fight.'

24 (16) Antony often claimed that he had seen the devil looking as he did when the Lord revealed him to blessed Job. *His eyes look like the morning star and from his mouth issue forth lamps of incense. His hair is sprinkled with flames and from his nostrils comes forth smoke, like a coal from the heat of a burning oven. His breath is like a glowing coal and a flame leaps forth from his mouth.*[52] 'It was in terrifying manifestations of this kind that the prince of demons appeared,' Antony explained, 'often making great claims, as I said, and raging with his boastful and godless tongue. But the Lord triumphed over him, saying to Job, *He counts iron as straw and bronze as rotten wood,*[53] the seas as land and the depths of hell as captive and the abyss as a gallery for walking. Through the prophet the devil boasts, saying, *I will pursue and overtake*[54] and I will hold the whole world in my hand like a nest and I shall take them away like eggs that have been abandoned.*[55] In this way the wicked one, by pouring forth deadly words, frequently ensnares some of those who live a good life, but we must not believe his promises or fear his threats for he always deceives and none of his promises are true. For if everything he says were not a lie, how is it that when he made such infinitely extravagant promises the Lord hooked him like a serpent using the hook of the cross and he was bound with a halter like a beast of burden, and tied up in chains like a runaway slave, his lips pierced by an iron ring,[56] and he was not given the chance to devour any of the faithful at all?

Now he is as miserable as a sparrow caught by Christ in the net to be mocked at; now he groans for his companions who have been trodden beneath the Christians' heel like scorpions and serpents.[57] He who took pride in the fact that he had destroyed all the seas, he who promised that he would hold the world in his hand, look at him! You have conquered him and look how he is unable to prevent me arguing with him. My dear sons, proud boastfulness must be completely rejected together with empty words. That brightness which pretends to shine is not the brightness of genuine light but is a sign of the flames with which he is to burn, for it disappears more swiftly than it can be told, taking with it the image of its own punishment.

25 'Often the demons sing the psalms while remaining invisible, shocking as it is to tell. In addition they recite the sacred words of Scripture with a foul mouth, for often when we are reading, they repeat the last words like an echo. They also awaken to prayer those who are asleep, so as to deprive them of sleep for the whole night. They disguise themselves as genuine monks and put pressure on many of the monks, accusing them of their former sins in which the demons themselves were their accomplices. But you must reject their accusations as well as their advice to fast and their suggestion that you should stay awake, for they are deceiving you. They assume shapes familiar to us so that they may harm us through their resemblance to virtue: they think they can more easily inject their poison and destroy innocent people by means of seemingly admirable behaviour. Finally, they claim that the monk's task is impossibly hard, hoping that the monks might come to regard what they have undertaken as too onerous and that despair might then lead to loss of enthusiasm and loss of enthusiasm to failure of effort.

26 'And so the Lord sent the prophet to denounce these wretched creatures: in a powerful voice he said, *Woe to him who gives his neighbour a troubled drink.*[58] By making suggestions of this kind the demons seduce people from the path which leads to heaven. And so, when the Lord came to earth and the demons spoke the truth about him against their will (for they said truly, *You are the Christ, the son of the living God,*[59]) He who freed the men who were tongue-tied shut their noisy mouths to prevent the demons mixing in the poison of error

with their announcement of the truth. The Lord also wanted us to follow Christ's example and to refuse to assent to the demons in any way, even if they persuade us of something that might be beneficial. For it is certainly not right for us, now that the Lord has granted freedom and the life-giving statements contained in the Scriptures, to accept advice on how to live from the devil who deserted his own post and feared Christ's holy authority. And so the Lord ordered the devil to be quiet even when he was quoting from Scripture because *God says to the sinner, Why do you declare my statutes and take up my covenant on your lips?*[60] The demons make all kinds of pretence: often they chat with the brothers, often a host of them produce strange noises, they grab the monks' hands, they hiss and cackle inanely, so that they might enter the Christian's heart at the moment of sin. But when they are driven back by everyone, their wailing at last proves their weakness.

27 'And indeed the Lord, in that He is God and conscious of His own authority, ordered them to fall silent. We, however, should follow closely in the footsteps of the saints and walk the same path as those who saw more clearly the tricks I have mentioned and used to sing, *When the sinner confronted me, I fell silent and was humiliated and refrained from saying good things* and *Like a deaf man I did not hear and like the dumb who opens not his mouth. And I was made like a man who does not hear.*[61] Christ commanded silence because he is the Lord; we must overcome the devil by not believing in him. If they force us to pray, if they persuade us to fast, we should do this not at their suggestion but because it is part of our way of life. Finally, even if they attack us and appear to threaten death, they ought to be laughed at rather than feared for they are weak and cannot carry out all their threats.

28 'I am aware that I have already spoken in passing about these matters, but now I must explain all this more fully because repetition brings greater security. When the Lord came, the enemy was destroyed and all his power was undermined. For this reason, when the devil sees that he has collapsed and remembers his former strength, like a tyrant who is now growing old, he attacks human wickedness. However, even when he uses thoughts and other tricks he still cannot

overturn a heart that stands firm for God. For it is clearer than day that since our adversaries are not clothed in human flesh they cannot give as an excuse for their inability to overcome us that they are unable to enter because we have closed the door against them. If they had been connected to this fragile body, when the entrance was blocked, access would have been denied to them. But although, as we said, they are free from this burden and are able to penetrate what has been blocked up and to fly all through the air without hindrance, it is obvious that because of their weakness the body of the Church remains unharmed. Finally, the evil thugs together with their leader, the devil, whom the Saviour in the Gospel confirms to have been from the beginning a murderer and the father of lies,[62] would never have been beaten despite our brave fight against them if their power had not been taken away. If I am lying, why do you spare us, Satan, you who rush around everywhere? Why are you, who are not imprisoned anywhere, unable to undermine the steadfastness of those who lead a life of virtue and who fight against you? But perhaps you love us, we whom you attempt each day to destroy? Is it credible that you are the master of goodness and that you help rather than harm those who are very good? And what can be so dear to you as to cause hurt, particularly to those who fight bravely against your evil deeds, as it says in the Bible: *For devotion to God is an abomination to the sinner.*[63] Who possesses a heart so prone to cunning? Who tries to carry out such practised wiles? We know that you are the most foul corpse; we know that we live as Christians and are safe when we clash with you because the Lord has deprived you of your strength. That is why you are pierced by your own darts because your threats have no effect. But if we are deceived, why do you attack our faith with terrifying phantoms and enormous shapes? If possibility were connected to willingness, the will alone would be enough for you. For it is a characteristic of power not to need outside assistance to deceive but to accomplish what it desires by means of its own strength. But now when you attempt to deceive, using changes of shape as in a theatre (as if you were trying to deceive naïve children by means of illusions on the stage), you prove more clearly that your strength is exhausted. Surely that true angel, sent by the Lord against the Assyrians, did not need the alliance of the peoples?[64] Surely he did not require noises or applause? Did he not rather wield his power in silence when he laid low one hundred and eighty five thousand of the enemy, more swiftly than it can be related, at the Lord's command? But as for you, because your strength is weak, everlasting destruction attends you.

29 (17) 'But someone may say, "Why did the devil go forth and destroy the whole house of the blessed Job? Why did he utterly destroy Job's belongings and knock down his walls to their very foundations and build one tomb for his numerous children? Why did he finally afflict Job with a strange and dreadful sore?" Anyone who makes such an objection must listen to the other side of the argument: it was not the devil who was able to do this, but the Lord, He who grants power against us twice over, either for our glory, if He approves of us or for our punishment, if we do wrong. In fact, anyone who objects ought to understand from this that the devil could have done nothing, not even against one man, if he had not received his power from the Lord, for no one begs someone else for something which is in his own power. But why do I mention Job whom the devil was unable to overcome even when he had got hold of him? Not even against Job's cattle nor against his sheep did he exercise his own strength without God's permission. Thus it is written in the Gospel, *The demons asked him, saying, If you cast us out from here, send us into the herd of pigs.*[65] How could those who seek the death of pigs be able by their own authority to overthrow man made in the image of God and a creature so dear to the Creator?

30 'My dearest friends, a pure life and fearless faith in God are powerful weapons against the demons. Believe me, for I have experience of this. Satan is terrified by the nocturnal devotions, the prayers, fasting, gentleness of those who live rightly; by their voluntary poverty, their contempt for vainglory, their humility, their compassion, their control over anger, and particularly by their pure love of Christ. That most foul serpent knows that it is at God's command that he lies beneath the footsteps of the just, for the Lord said, *Behold, I have given you authority to trample upon serpents and scorpions and upon all the power of the enemy.*[66]

31 'But if they pretend that they have the gift of divination, too, and

28

predict the arrival of some of the brothers, and if those whom they predicted would come do indeed arrive, even then you must not trust them for they are liars. That is why they anticipated those who were on their way, so that you might believe them when they made their announcement and then they could gain admittance to you when you were taken in by their deception. A Christian should definitely not think there is anything miraculous in this, since it is not only those who due to their insubstantial nature pass through everything that are able to arrive before those who are on their way: men who travel ahead with the speed of horses can also announce that others will soon arrive. They are not referring to things which have not yet begun to happen, (for God alone has knowledge of future events), but when they see the beginning of some action, they run like thieves and claim knowledge of it among those who are ignorant of it. For how many do you think there are now who could, if they were to run as fast as a boy, reveal to people far away our meeting here and our conversation directed against them, before anyone who is here has reported it? Let me use some examples to clarify what I mean. If someone sets out from the Thebaid or from a town in any other region and the demons see him walking on his journey, using that swiftness I mentioned, they are able to predict his arrival.

32 'It is the same with the annual flooding of the Nile: when they see plenty of rain in Ethiopia, which usually causes the river to become swollen and to burst its banks, they run on ahead to Egypt and announce that the river is on its way. But men, too, could easily predict this if they were able to run as fast. The blessed David's scout went up to the top of a hill and was able to see those who were coming before the people down on the plain saw them, and announced not some doubtful future events but something concerning people who were already on their way. In the same way the demons keep a close eye on everything and then rush to report them to one another. But if it were to happen that in accordance with God's will something that has been begun does not reach its conclusion, in other words, if a traveller turns back half-way along his journey or if the moisture hanging in the clouds is carried up to the height of heaven, then the

error both of those who deceived and of those who were taken in becomes apparent.

33 'This was how paganism started: by means of these prophets' tricks, the oracles spoken by the demons at the shrines used once to be believed. But at the coming of our Lord Jesus Christ they were silenced and became speechless and lost those they held captive. Who, I ask, thinks that a doctor has divine foreknowledge, when from his study of illnesses he gauges the fevers of a raging soul by means of light pressure of his fingers on the veins' pulse? Who would venerate with supreme honour a helmsman who uses the stars of heaven to find a way on his sea voyage? Who would not praise a farmer for his experience rather than sanctify him as a god if he makes predictions about the dry heat in summer or the amount of rain or the cold in winter? But if we admit for a moment that the demons do predict true things, tell me, what advantage is there in knowing what is to come? Surely no one ever wins praise for knowing these things or is punished for not knowing them? The question of whether each individual prepares for himself either torments or glory depends solely on whether he disregards the rules of Scripture or carries them out. None of us chose this way of life so as to have foreknowledge of the future but so that, obeying the Lord's commands, he might begin to be His friend rather than His servant.[67]

34 'We must not worry about knowing what is to come but about carrying out what we have been told to do, nor should we demand this as a reward for the ascetic life, for we ought instead to ask the Lord our helper for victory against the devil. But if it happens that anyone would like to acquire this skill, let him have a pure heart which will enable him to know the future, for I believe that the soul that serves God, if it continues steadfast in its original purity, can know more than the demons. Such was the soul of Elisha who witnessed powers unknown to others.

35 (18) 'Now I will reveal to you other means of deception practised by the demons. They often come at night, pretending to be angels of God and praising the monks' dedication, admiring their persever-ance and promising future rewards. When you see them, protect yourselves and your dwellings with the sign of the cross and immedi-

ately they will dissolve into nothing for they fear that sign of victory by which the Saviour, depriving them of their powers of the air, has shown them up. They also often leap around, twisting their limbs in various contortions and impudently present themselves to us so as to fill our minds with terror and make our bodies shudder in horror. But in this case, too, a firm faith in God will put them to flight as if they were merely feeble jokes. It is not difficult, with God's help, to distinguish between good and bad spirits. The holy angels are friendly and calm in appearance because they do not fight nor will they cry out nor will anyone hear their voice:[68] in fact they hurry on silently and smoothly, instilling joy, exultation and confidence in men's hearts, seeing that the Lord is with them, He who is the source and origin of happiness. Then our mind is no longer disturbed but becomes gentle and calm, illuminated by the angels' light; then the soul, aflame with desire for heavenly rewards, breaks out, if it is able, from its dwelling in the human body. Released from the burden of mortal limbs, it hastens towards heaven together with those whom it sees departing. Their kindness is so great that if anyone, due to human weakness, was terrified by their startling brightness, they would immediately dispel all fear from his heart. This was the case with Gabriel when he spoke to Zacharias in the temple,[69] as with the angels when they announced to the shepherds that the Virgin had given birth to God[70] and with those who kept watch over the Lord's body:[71] when these angels revealed themselves to the untroubled minds of those who saw them, they told them that they should not be afraid. For fear is not so much a product of mental terror: it is often caused by the sight of mighty beings.

36 'The ferocious expressions of these most wicked creatures, their terrifying sounds and vile thoughts, like the uproar and disturbances caused by lawless young men or robbers, immediately strike fear into the soul and numb the senses, producing hatred in Christians, depression and lethargy in monks, nostalgia for family, fear of death, desire for sin, lack of enthusiasm for virtue, dullness of the heart. If then the horror and trembling are replaced by joy and confidence in God and ineffable love, we know that help has arrived because calmness of the soul is proof of the presence of the holy power. For

thus did the patriarch Abraham rejoice when he saw God[72] and when John sensed that Mary had arrived (she who bore the progenitor of the universe in the guest-room of her holy womb[73]), he leapt for joy even before he was born.[74]

37 'But if the fear remains, it is the enemy who has appeared, since he does not know how to comfort as Gabriel did when he told the trembling Virgin not to fear and as the angels brought comfort to the shepherds. In fact he increases fear and drives people right down into the deep pit of impiety to make them bow down before him. That is why the miserable pagans, unaware of the Lord's prohibition, mistakenly believed that the demons were gods. But the Lord did not allow the Christian peoples to be ensnared in these deceptions, He who boldly repelled the devil in the Gospel when the devil claimed dominion over everything. The Lord said to him, *Get thee behind me, Satan; for it is written, You will worship the Lord your God and him alone will you serve.*[75] The power conveyed by these words has been granted to us, too, for the Lord spoke like this so that apparent temptations should be shattered by the words of our maker.

38 (19) 'I also advise you, my dearest friends, to be more concerned about your way of life than about miracles. If any of you performs miracles he must neither swell with pride nor look down on those who cannot manage it. Consider rather each individual's behaviour: in this life it is proper for you to imitate what is perfect and to supply what is lacking. It is not for our humble selves to perform miracles but for the power of the Lord, who in the Gospel said to the disciples when they were boasting, *Do not rejoice that the demons are subject to you but rather that your names are written in heaven.*[76] For the writing of names in the book of life is a testimony to virtue and merit, but the expulsion of Satan is a gift from the Saviour. That is why to those who take pride in prophetic signs rather than in the austerities of this life, and who say, *Did we not cast out demons in your name and in your name did many wonderful works?* the Lord will reply, *Amen, I say to you, I do not know you; go from me, you who work iniquity.*[77] For the Lord knows not the ways of the ungodly.[78] Let us therefore beg to deserve to receive the gift of distinguishing between spirits so that, in the words of Scripture, we may not trust every spirit.[79]

39 (20) 'I had wished to finish talking now and to be silent regarding things that have happened to my humble self. But in case you should think that I have wasted my time in mentioning things which could not possibly happen, I will tell you a few of the many things that have happened. Even if I am made to look foolish, yet the Lord who sees deep into my mind, knows that I am doing this not out of a desire to boast but for the sake of your progress. How many times have the demons tried to make me proud by praising me excessively although they received from me curses in the Lord's name! How often have they predicted the flooding of the river Nile although I said to them, "What has this got to do with you?" How many times did they threaten me like armed soldiers and surround me with scorpions, horses, huge beasts, and different kinds of snakes which filled the house where I was living! But I countered by singing, *Some are proud of their chariots and some of their horses but we take pride in the name of the Lord our God* [80] and at once Christ's compassion put them to flight. On one occasion they appeared with a great light and said, "Antony, we have come to bestow our brightness on you," but I closed my eyes because I refused to look upon the devil's light; I prayed, and before you could relate what happened, the light of those wicked creatures had gone out. A few months later, when they were singing in front of me and quoting to each other from the Scriptures, I pretended I was deaf and did not listen. Sometimes they shook my cell but I prayed to the Lord, my mind unmoved. Often they made loud noises, often they pranced around me and often they produced hissing sounds but I sang the psalms and then their sounds were turned to wailing.

40 'Do you believe, my sons, what I am telling you? Once I saw the devil standing very tall. He dared to claim that he was the power and providence of God and he said to me, "What do you want me to give you, Antony?" But I spat hard in his face and attacked him, protecting my whole self against him with the name of Christ: at once this tall figure of his disappeared just as I was about to get hold of him. While I was fasting he appeared to me as a monk and offered me bread, trying to persuade me in the following words to eat and to indulge this poor body of mine a little, "You, too, are human,"

he said, "and limited by human weakness. Cease your efforts for a while, otherwise illness may snatch you away." At once I recognized that serpent's ghastly face, and when I sought refuge as usual in the protection of Christ, he vanished like smoke wafting through an open window. In the desert he frequently tried to trap me with gold or to defile me by making me touch it. While I was being thrashed (for I admit that I was also often beaten by the demons), I would chant words such as these, *No one will separate me from the love of Christ.*[81] When they heard this, the demons turned on one another in their rage and were put to flight not at my command but at the Lord's, who said, *I saw Satan fall like lightning from heaven.*[82] And so, my children, mindful of the words of St Paul, *I have applied all these things to myself,*[83] so that neither fear of demons nor any weariness might weaken your commitment to this way of life.

41 'But since I have made myself look foolish by recalling many things for your benefit, I also want to tell you something I experienced, and no one who hears this can doubt that it is true. Once a demon knocked on the door of my cell. When I went out I saw a man of enormous height. I asked him who he was and he replied, "I am Satan." I asked him, "What do you want here?" and he answered, "Why do the monks make false accusations against me? Why do all the Christian people curse me?" And I said, "They are right to accuse you for they are often upset by your cunning tricks." But he answered, "I do not do anything – it is they who cause each other trouble. Rather, I am to be pitied. I ask you, have you not read, *The enemy's swords are broken for ever and you have destroyed their cities?*[84] Look, I have no place to be now; I possess no city; I have no weapons now. Throughout every nation and all the provinces the name of Christ rings out and even the desert is crammed full with monks. I beg you, let them look after themselves and let them not abuse me without cause." Then I marvelled and rejoiced at God's grace and addressed the demon in these words, "I cannot attribute such a strange and unheard of idea to your truth which is non-existent. For although you are the master of deceit, you have been forced to admit this without lying. Truly Jesus has utterly destroyed your powers: stripped of your honours as an angel, you lie rolling in the mud." I had hardly

finished speaking when his tall figure collapsed at the mention of the Saviour's name.

42 'What room for hesitation can now remain, my children? What fear can there be any longer? What whirlwind of theirs could snatch us away? The soul of each individual should now feel secure; let not idle thoughts imagine non-existent dangers. No one should fear that he could be carried off by the devil and dropped down a steep cliff. May all anxiety be dispelled, for the Lord, who has destroyed our enemies, remains in us as He promised[85] and has protected us from all Satan's various attacks. Look how the devil himself, who tries with his henchman to practise deceit of this kind, admits that he can do nothing against Christians. Now Christians and monks ought to be concerned in case their idleness give the demons power, for the way they present themselves to us usually depends on the state in which they find us and our thoughts, and if they find in our hearts some seed of dissatisfaction and fear, like thieves who take over abandoned places, they pile up more fears and punish the unfortunate soul by making cruel threats. But if we are eager in the Lord and are inspired by a desire for future rewards, if we always entrust everything to God's hands, not a single demon will be able to come close to try and take us by storm; instead, when they see that our hearts are fortified in Christ, they turn back in confusion. Thus the devil ran away from Job who was strengthened in the Lord but he robbed the most unfortunate Judas of his faith and shackled him with the chains of captivity. There is, then, only one means of overcoming the enemy – spiritual joy and the constant recollection of a soul that is always thinking of the Lord. The soul that drives out the demons' tricks like smoke will attack its adversaries instead of fearing them. For Satan is well aware of the fires to come and knows of the huge conflagration burning in hell.

43 'But to bring my speech to a conclusion I will just mention one final thing. When a vision appears to you, demand boldly of it who it is and where it comes from; if it is a holy apparition, the angel's comfort will immediately turn your fear into joy. But if it is really a temptation offered by the devil, it will vanish when the faithful soul interrogates him, because to ask who he is and where he is from offers the best guarantee of safety. In this way the son of Nun recognized

the one who was helping him by questioning him,[86] and the enemy, when he was questioned, was unable to hide from Daniel.'[87]

44 When Antony had finished speaking, everyone was in a joyful mood: in some a desire for virtue flared up, in others their flagging faith revived; false opinions were driven from the minds of some while from others the groundless fears besieging them were driven out. At the same time, now that they felt contempt for the demons' insidious attacks, they all marvelled at Antony's great gift of distinguishing between spirits, granted to him by the Lord. (21) And so there were on the mountain monastic cells like tents, filled with divine choirs of people singing psalms, reading and praying. Antony's speech had inspired them all with such an eagerness to fast and to stay awake to pray that in their desire for the future fulfilment of their hope, they devoted themselves unremittingly to showing mutual love and compassion to those in need. They appeared to inhabit an infinitely large area, a town removed from worldly matters, full of piety and justice. Anyone who set eyes on that multitude of ascetics, anyone who saw that heroic and harmonious community where no one caused any harm, where there was no slander from tale-bearers, but a crowd of people leading lives of restraint, competing with each other in the performance of their duties, would immediately burst out with these words, *How beautiful are your dwellings, Jacob! Your tents, O Israel, are like shady groves, like a garden by the river, like tents that have been pitched by the Lord, like cedars growing beside the waters.*[88]

45 (22) While these things were happening, causing the monks' commitment to a life of blessedness to increase each day, Antony was remembering the mansions set in heaven.[89] He rejected the pointlessness of the present life as if what he had already achieved was of little value and established himself at a distance from the other brothers. When his human condition forced him to allow his poor body some food or sleep or any other necessities of nature, he was overcome by an extraordinary sense of shame because the physical limitations of his poor body restricted his spiritual freedom. For it often happened that while sitting with the brothers, he would think of his spiritual food and withdraw from the meal set before him. Being human, however, he would eat, sometimes by himself, sometimes with

the brothers. And while he acted in this strange way, as I said before, he would persuade them with some embarrassment that great care must be shown, for the body must not be completely starved nor should it be overfed in case it should lose its ability to work, contrary to the Creator's will. For that reason every care must be taken to prevent the soul succumbing to bodily vices and being pushed into hell's everlasting darkness; instead the soul should claim the authority granted to it in the flesh and raise its dwelling up to the third heaven, like the apostle Paul.[90] Antony claimed that this was what the Saviour meant when he said, *Do not be anxious about your life, about what you shall eat or what you shall drink, nor about your body or what you shall wear, for this is what the Gentiles worry about. But your father knows that you need all these things. Seek therefore first the kingdom of God and his righteousness and all these things will be given you in addition.*[91]

46 (23)After these events, at the time when Maximin's most cruel persecution was raging out of control, devastating the Church,[92] and when the holy martyrs had been taken to Alexandria, Antony left his cell and followed those who were to become victims of Christ, saying, 'Let us go and be present at the glorious triumphs of our brothers; we shall either take part in the fight ourselves or we shall watch the others in battle.' And indeed, in his love he was already a martyr but since he could not give himself up of his own accord and as he was ministering to the confessors in the mines and in the prisons, he exhorted with great frankness and concern those entering the lawcourt for he hoped to prevent them being driven to deny Christ by fear of their wicked persecutors. Rejoicing that the sentence given meant that they received the martyr's crown, as if he himself was the victor, he accompanied them as far as the place where their blessed blood was to be shed. The judge was disturbed by the steadfastness of Antony and his friends and gave the order that no monk should watch the trial or stay in the city. And on that day everyone else thought it a good idea to hide, but Antony had no fear; disregarding the persecutor's order he washed his overgarment. The next day he took up a prominent position, dressed in white, to catch the judge's attention as he walked past, for Antony was burning with a desire for martyrdom. He demonstrated to us that Christians ought to persist in an attitude

that scorns punishment and death, in that he was saddened by the fact that despite his wish to suffer for the name of God, martyrdom was not granted him. But the Lord who was preparing a leader for his flock, saved Antony so that the monastic way of life, as it developed, should be strengthened not only by his words but also by his personal example. And yet he always followed so closely in the footsteps of the holy confessors that, bound by anxious concern for them and by the bonds of love, he suffered more than they did from imprisonment even though he was locked out.

47 But when the storm of persecution had died away and the blessed bishop Peter had now been crowned with a martyr's glory,[93] Antony returned to his former cell and achieved a daily martyrdom of faith and conscience, wearing himself out by means of more rigorous fasting and nightly devotions. He wore a hair-shirt next to his skin and a garment of animal skin on top, never washed his body, and never wiped the dirt from his feet except when necessity compelled him to cross through water. In fact, no one ever saw Antony's body naked until his death.

48 (24) At one time, when Antony had withdrawn from everyone's eyes and had closed his cell, refusing to receive a single visitor, a military officer called Martinianus, whose daughter was possessed by an evil spirit that tormented her, knocked at the door. He begged Antony to help his dear child and to come out and pray to God for his daughter. Antony had not the slightest wish to open up but he looked down from above and said, 'Why do you ask me for help, you who are a mortal man? I too am mortal and share your weakness. But if you believe in Christ whose servant I am, go and pray to God according to your faith and your daughter will be healed.' Immediately Martinianus believed and went away; and when he had called on Jesus, he took his daughter home, now restored to health. The Lord also worked many other miracles through Antony, and justly so, for He who promised in the Gospel, *Ask and it will be given to you*,[94] did not deny His power to the man He found worthy to receive it. For many suffering people came and slept in front of the closed entrance to Antony's cell and were cured through him by means of their faithful prayers to Christ.

49 However, the arrival of so many people was a nuisance to him for they deprived him of the solitude he desired. As a result he feared that all the miracles granted to him might either make him proud or induce others to have a higher estimation of him than was warranted, and so he decided to move to the upper Thebaid where no one would know him. When the brothers had given him some bread, he sat on the bank of the river watching for a boat to come by. As he sat there, his thoughts absorbed in these matters, a voice came to him from above, saying, 'Antony, where are you going and why?' And he answered without fear, as though the speaker's voice was familiar to him, 'Since the people do not leave me in peace, I thought it best to go to the upper Thebaid, especially since things are being demanded of me which exceed my feeble power.' And the voice said to him, 'If you go to the Thebaid and move to the Bucolia[95] as you are planning, you will endure a greater burden, one twice as heavy as the present one. If, however, you really wish to live in peace, go now further into the desert.' When Antony asked, 'Who can show me that remote place, for I do not know the area?' the speaker immediately pointed out to him some Saracens who often used to travel to Egypt for the purpose of trade. Antony approached them and asked them to take him with them into the desert. As no one had any objection they welcomed his company, accepting him as their companion as if he had been sent by God. After a journey lasting three days and nights he came to a very high mountain[96] at the foot of which there flowed a spring of sweet water; on a small strip of flat land encircling the mountain there grew a few untended palm trees.

50 Antony fell in love with this spot as if it had been offered to him by God (for this was the place indicated to him by the one who spoke to him as he sat on the river bank). He accepted some bread from his fellow travellers and he remained alone on the mountain, without any companion. He lived there as if he recognized that place as his own home. The Saracens, seeing his joyful determination, chose to travel that way to visit him and gladly brought him loaves of bread; the palm trees also offered him some, admittedly meagre, sustenance. (25) Later, when the brothers discovered where he was, out of solicitude for him they sent him food, like sons to their father. Then

Antony realized that for the sake of his comfort, many were being forced to carry out onerous tasks; and so, wishing to spare the monks in this, too, he asked one of those who were coming, to bring him a two-pronged hoe and some grain. When these were brought to him he went round the mountain and found a small area suitable for cultivation which he could irrigate from the mountain spring. There he sowed some seed and then produced a crop large enough for a year's supply of bread. He was pleased to be able to live in the desert by the work of his own hands, without troubling anyone else. But when some people again began to arrive there, he took pity on their exhaustion and grew vegetables on a small patch of earth so that the visitors might be somewhat restored when they arrived after their difficult journey. But the animals who came there to drink the water ate that small crop which was intended for the monks' refreshment. Catching hold of one of them, Antony said to them all, 'Why do you harm me when I have done you no harm? Go away, and in the Lord's name do not come near here any more.' Who would believe that as a result of this command the animals, as if they were afraid, never came near the place?

51 When Antony took possession of the impenetrable mountainous areas and the interior regions of the desert in this manner, devoting himself to prayer, the brothers who came to see him could only with difficulty persuade him, by earnest entreaty, to agree to accept the olives, pulses and oil which they brought for him after some months, and to make some concessions to his old age.

It was shocking to see what terrible struggles he underwent while he was living there. Indeed, we learned from those who visited him that he was *not contending against flesh and blood but against principalities and powers,*[97] as it says in the Bible, for they reported hearing loud noises and people's voices and the clash of weapons and said they saw the mountain filled with hordes of demons, while Antony stood firm and bravely wrestled with them as if with visible enemies. But he also comforted his visitors and encouraged them, at the same time as he destroyed the whole army of Satan on bended knee, using prayers as his weapons. It is certainly remarkable that one man, living in such great solitude, should not have been terrified out of his wits by these daily clashes with the demons nor overwhelmed by the ferocity of so many different beasts, whether four-legged creatures or reptiles. Rightly did David sing, *Those who trust in the Lord are like Mount Sion*.[98] Antony maintained his resolve, calm and unshaken: in this way he managed to put the demons to flight and to make the wild beasts be at peace with him, as it is written in Scripture.[99]

52 But the devil, as was said by the prophet I mentioned earlier,[100] gnashed his teeth as he watched him, but with the Saviour's help Antony remained safe from all attacks. So one night when Antony was staying awake to pray to the Lord, the devil gathered so many packs of wild animals outside his cell that Antony saw that he was surrounded by all the creatures[101] of the desert. When they snarled at him, threatening to tear his body with their teeth, he understood the cunning of the enemy and said, 'If the Lord has given you permission to attack me, I will give myself up to you for you to devour me; but if you are sent here by demons, go away as fast as you can for I am a servant of Christ.' And so it was: at the sound of his command, all the beasts ran away as if they had been whipped by the lash of God's power.

53 (26) A few days later another struggle took place with the same enemy. While Antony was busy (for he was always working so that he could present his visitors with some small gift in repayment for the things they brought him), someone pulled the plait or reed of the basket he was weaving. This movement made Antony stand up and he saw a creature with a human form down to the groin but whose lower body was in the shape of an ass. Seeing this, Antony made the sign of the cross on his own forehead and just said, 'I am a servant of Christ: if you have been sent to me, I shall not run away.' There was not a moment's delay: at once the hideous monster fled with its attendant evil spirits, more swiftly than you could relate it, and as it rushed in headlong flight it was destroyed. The death of the monster which had been scared off and killed marked the destruction of all the demons who despite all their efforts were unable to drive Antony from the desert. These marvellous deeds were followed by many more.

54 (27) Not long after these events Antony went out and he who had

won such great victories was forced to yield to the brothers' entreaties. For he was asked by the monks to agree to visit them and so he set off with them, after packing a supply of bread and water on to a camel, seeing that nowhere along the desert route could drinking water be found except in the place where his cell was, and so they had drawn their supply of water from this spring. But half-way along their journey the water supply ran out. The excessive blazing of the sun, the unbearable heat, everything threatened death. They went around searching for at least a pool of rain water, but found no relief, nothing to save them. Even the camel looked as if it was about to die of thirst, so they let it go, its throat burning with the heat and desperate with thirst. The old man was moved by the danger staring them all in the face, the brothers and himself equally, and in his distress he sighed deeply. Then taking refuge in prayer, his usual source of assistance, he withdrew from them for a short while. He knelt down and stretched out his hands in supplication to the Lord. Without delay, as soon as the tears fell from his eyes, there burst forth a bubbling spring in the exact spot where he was praying and when they had quenched their thirst and cooled their burning limbs, they filled their waterskins and then found the camel and let it drink. For it happened that as the camel wandered through the desert with the rope dragging along, the rope had got caught on a rock and the camel was held fast.

At last, his journey over, Antony reached the monks who had invited him. They all ran to meet him as if he were their father, vying with each other in their eagerness to greet him respectfully with kisses and embraces. Antony was glad to see how fervent they were in their commitment to the monastic way of life, and they were all happy at his arrival, for he brought gifts of spiritual nourishment, presents from the mountain, so to speak. He praised the rigorous self-discipline of the old monks and encouraged the new ones. When he saw his sister who had grown old as a virgin and was now in charge of other girls, he embraced her with great joy. Then he hurried back to the mountain, as if he had been away from the desert for a long time.

55 (28) There came to him now many people troubled by demons, driven by harsh necessity to dare to penetrate the desert regions. He consoled these people, while to all the monks he gave the same

message, saying, 'Have faith in Jesus; keep your mind pure from wicked thoughts and your body free from all sordidness. In accordance with the divine sayings, do not be seduced by the fullness of the stomach.[102] Detest pride, pray frequently, recite the psalms in the evening and in the morning and at noon, and meditate on the commands of the Scriptures. Remember the deeds done by each of the saints so that the memory of their example will inspire your soul to virtue and restrain it from vices.' He also used to persuade them constantly to bear in mind the words of the Apostle, when he says, *Let not the sun set upon your anger.*[103] Antony interpreted this as meaning that the sun should not set not only upon your anger but neither upon any human sin, in case the moon at night or the sun by day, which are witnesses of our sins, should ever disappear. He also warned us to remember that commandment which St Paul gave regarding these matters, *Examine yourselves and test yourselves,*[104] so that by keeping an account night and day, if they should discover any sin in themselves, they might cease to sin; but if no error was found, they should stand firm in their commitment to their undertaking instead of becoming swollen with pride and contemptuous of others or claiming righteousness for themselves, in accordance with the saying of the teacher I mentioned earlier who said, *Do not judge before the time.*[105] Rather they must await the judgement of Christ, to whom alone things hidden are revealed.[106] Many are the ways (as it says in the Bible) that seem just to men but they end with a view into the depths of hell;[107] often we cannot see our own sins, often we are deceived by ignorance of our deeds. The judgement of God who sees everything is different, for He judges not from outward appearances but according to the secrets of the mind. It is right for us to show compassion to one another and to bear one another's burdens,[108] so that leaving judgement to the Saviour we might keep a watch on our own consciences by examining ourselves.

Antony also used to say that the path to virtue is a wide one, if each person were either to watch what he was doing or to report all his thoughts to the brothers. For no one can sin when he has to report all his sins to someone else and endure the shame of revealing his wicked deeds in public. Finally no sinner dares to sin in front of someone else; even if he does sin, he wishes to avoid a witness to his sin and prefers to lie and deny it, thereby increasing his original error by adding the error of denial. 'And so,' Antony used to say, 'we are put to shame before our own eyes, as it were, in thought and in deed if we do everything with a view to giving a report of it, but much more so if we write down our sins in an orderly fashion, describing them faithfully. Then the account of our sins will be set clearly before the brothers' eyes. If we fear that the wax tablets will know of our sins, the letters themselves prove our guilt. And just as those who have intercourse with prostitutes are embarrassed by the presence of others, so we too blush at the writing, if we do this. Let us walk this path of virtue and keeping our bodies under the mind's control, let us wreck the devil's destructive plans.'

56 With encouraging words of this kind he inspired those monks who came to him to pursue their life of rigorous self-discipline and sympathized with those who were suffering. Through Antony the Lord freed many of them from their sufferings, but the healing of those he cured never made him arrogant nor did he become depressed and grumble at the fact that some bodies were still possessed by the demons. Instead he gave thanks to God, maintaining always the same attitude and the same look and persuading those who were possessed to bear with greater patience the attacks tormenting them. 'For this medicine,' he said, 'does not belong to me or to any other human being but to God alone who grants healing to those He chooses and at the time He chooses.' And so by means of his advice he taught those who were tormented to bear their trials with equanimity and those who were already freed to give thanks not to Antony but to God alone.

57 (29) A man from Palestine by the name of Fronto, who was tormented by a most violent demon – it caused him to lacerate his tongue with his teeth and tried to blind him – arrived at the mountain and asked the blessed old man to pray to the Lord on his behalf. Antony prayed and said to Fronto, 'Go, and you will be healed.' But the man did not believe this: violently refusing to heed Antony he stayed where he was. So Antony repeated the same message to him, saying, 'You cannot be cured here. Go away, and when you reach

Egypt, Christ's mercy will be upon you immediately.' At last Fronto was persuaded and set off, and as soon as he saw Egypt, the devil's possession ceased, just as the old man had promised in accordance with the Lord's revelation to him while he prayed.

58 (30) There was a young girl from Busiris, a city in the region of Tripolitana, who was suffering from an unknown and pitiable disease: when the mucus from her nose, the tears from her eyes and the pus from her ears dripped to the ground, they immediately turned into worms. Her suffering was increased by the fact that her body was paralysed and she was unnaturally cross-eyed. When her parents heard that monks were going to Antony, they took her (for they had faith in the Lord who in the Gospel had commanded the haemorrhage to cease when the woman touched His hem) and asked the monks to let their poor daughter accompany them, but the monks refused. So the parents carried her to Antony and waited outside with their sick daughter in the company of Paphnutius, the blessed confessor and monk, whose eyes had been gouged out because of his Christian belief during the persecution of Maximin[109] but who took pride in this physical disfigurement. And so the monks came to Antony but when they began to tell him about the girl's illness, the old man anticipated their account and related the whole story of her illness and the journey to St Paphnutius, as if he himself had been present. When the monks asked him to permit the parents to enter with their daughter, Antony would not allow it, but said, 'Go, and you will find the girl healed, if she is not dead,' adding, 'No one should come to me, insignificant creature that I am, for the bestowal of cures is not a matter for human wretchedness, but for the mercy of Jesus Christ who always gives assistance to those who believe in Him wherever they are. That is why this girl, too, for whom you ask my help, has been released as a result of her own prayers; when I prayed to the Lord, I was granted foreknowledge of her cure.' He spoke and his words were followed by the girl's restoration to health, for when they went out to the blessed Paphnutius the monks found the girl healthy and her parents overjoyed.

59 (31) A few days later when two brothers were travelling to see Antony, their water supply ran out on their journey: one of them

died of thirst while the other lay on the ground awaiting death. Antony, who was at the mountain, quickly called to him two monks who happened to be there and told them to grab a bottle of water and to hurry along the route leading to Egypt. He told them, 'One of the brothers who is on his way here has just passed away to the Lord; the other will do so, too, unless you help him. This was revealed to me just now as I was praying.' Thus he spoke and the monks, following his instructions, hurried off. They found the dead body and covered it with earth; they revived the other monk and carried him back (it was about a day's journey away). Perhaps someone may ask, 'Why did Antony not speak before the monk died?' but this question is utterly inappropriate for Christians to ask, because the judgement did not come from Antony but from God who passed the sentence He wished on the dying man and who was kind enough to give a revelation concerning the one who was thirsty. The only remarkable thing is that Antony who was living at a mountain far away became aware of everything happening at a great distance because the Lord made it known to his ever watchful heart.

60 (32) Again on another occasion while he was living at the mountain, Antony suddenly raised his eyes to the sky and saw something that appeared to be a soul moving towards heaven, while angels rejoiced at its approach. He was amazed at this strange sight: blessing the choir of holy beings he prayed that some understanding of this matter might be revealed to him. Immediately there came to him a voice, saying that this was the soul of the monk Ammon who lived at Nitria.[110] Ammon was a very old man who had continued in a life of holiness from his childhood to old age.[111] The place where Antony lived was a thirteen-day journey from Nitria. When the monks who had come saw Antony in a state of wonder, they asked him to explain the cause of his joy. He told them that Ammon – whom they knew very well because he had often made the journey to visit Antony and because he was famous for the miracles granted to him by the Lord – had just died.

I must just mention one of Ammon's miracles: at one point it was necessary for Ammon to cross a river called the Lycus[112] which had suddenly flooded; so he asked Theodore, who was with him, to withdraw from his sight a short distance so that neither of them should see each other's naked body. Theodore moved away but when Ammon was about to undress, he was still embarrassed by the thought of his own nakedness. While he was wondering what to do, the divine power carried him across to the opposite side of the river. Then Theodore, a man who was also devoted to God, crossed over to the old man and was amazed that Ammon had crossed the river so quickly. When he saw that Ammon's feet were not wet and that there was no sign of water on his clothes, he asked him to explain, as a father to his son, such an incredible crossing. But when Ammon refused to say what had happened, Theodore embraced his feet and swore that he would not let him go until he revealed his secret. And so the old man, seeing that the brother was obstinately determined to get his own way, demanded in turn from him that he should not reveal this to anyone before Ammon's death. Then he admitted that he had suddenly been carried across on to the opposite bank and that his feet had not touched the water at all. He claimed that this was just a privilege belonging to the Lord's body and to those – like the apostle Peter – to whom the Lord granted that the human body should be able to stand on the waters that lacked solidity.[113] Theodore kept quiet about this incident for the promised period of time but he made it known after Ammon's death.

The monks whom Antony had told about the death of Ammon made a note of the day and when the brothers came from Nitria after thirty days, the monks inquired of them and found that Ammon had died on the very day and at the very hour when the old man had seen his soul being carried up. They were amazed at the purity of Antony's mind, in that knowledge of something happening so far away had reached him without delay.

61 (33) When count Archelaus found Antony at the Outer Mountain, he asked him to pray for Polycratia, a virgin whose dedication to Christ was remarkable. She was in Laodicea at the time, suffering from the most terrible pains in her stomach and her side; as a result of excessive fasting and lack of sleep, her body was completely worn out. Antony prayed and Archelaus noted the day on which the prayer had been made. Then he returned to Laodicea and found the virgin

healed. When he asked her on which day she had been cured, he found that the time of healing corresponded to the time he had noted. Everyone was amazed for they realized that the Lord had released her from her pains at the moment when Antony, in his prayer for her, was appealing to the Saviour's goodness.

62 (34) He also often foretold, days and months in advance, the times of arrival of the many people who came to him, as well as their reason for coming. For some were drawn there by their great desire to see him, others by illness and some because their body was possessed by demons. But no one ever complained of any trouble or loss resulting from the difficult journey and they all went home filled with spiritual food. But Antony used to tell them that they should not praise him for this marvel: rather they should praise the Lord, who grants a knowledge of Himself to men according to their mortal capacity.

63 (35) On one occasion when he had gone out to the outer cells and was asked by the brothers to pray in a boat with some monks who were setting off, he climbed on board and was the only one among them to notice a most revolting smell. Everyone assured him that it was the stink of the salted and pickled fish lying in the boat. But he told them he was sure he could smell the stench of something else. While he was still speaking, a young man in the grip of a demon, who had slipped ahead beside the hull and hidden himself in the boat, suddenly cried out. Antony immediately cured him in the name of our Lord Jesus Christ and all the people realized that it was the devil who had given off that foul smell.

64 (36) Another man was brought to him, a nobleman possessed by an evil spirit. He was afflicted with such a degree of madness that he did not realize he was in Antony's presence and he was even eating his own bodily excrement. And so when the old man was asked by those who had brought him there to pray to the Lord on his behalf, he felt such compassion for the young man's wretched state that he stayed awake all night with him, striving to overcome the sufferer's madness. But when dawn came, the possessed man attacked Antony and gave him a hard push. Those who had brought him there became angry and began to ask him why he had hurt the old man. But Antony said to them, 'Do not blame the poor young man. This madness is

caused by the one who possesses him, not by the possessed. The enemy, who was offended because the Lord ordered him to come to this dry region, attacked me in this presumptuous way. This attack on me was a sign that Satan had been driven out.' No sooner had he spoken than the young man returned to his senses and gave thanks to God; he now recognized where he was and filled with love, he embraced Antony and kissed him.

65 (37) There are countless other miracles of this kind which we have learned about from the monks' frequent accounts, all of which agree. But one should not be amazed by these as much as by the following ones which far exceed the weakness of our human condition. At about the ninth hour, when Antony had begun to pray before the meal, he felt himself caught up in the spirit and being carried on high by angels. But when the demons prevented them from passing through the air, the angels began to ask their opponents what the reason was for holding Antony back, when he had no faults. The demons tried to set forth his sins, going right back to the time of his birth, but the angels shut the demons' slanderous mouths, saying that they should not recount his sins from his birth, for his sins had already been laid to rest through Christ's goodness. But if they knew of any from the period after he had become a monk and had devoted himself to God, they might mention those. The demons, lying shamelessly, accused him of many things, but since they could not prove their lies, Antony's way up to heaven lay open and unobstructed. Immediately returning to himself, he saw himself once more as he had been, in the very place where he had been standing. Then he forgot all about his meal and from that hour he spent the whole night groaning and lamenting, reflecting on the great number of enemies that humans have and the struggles they must endure against such a great army and their difficult journey through the air to heaven, as well as the saying of the Apostle where he states, *Our struggle is not against flesh and blood but against the prince of the power of this air.*[114] Paul knew that the powers of the air are always trying, by wrestling and fighting, to prevent us gaining an unobstructed passage to heaven and so he encouraged us with this advice, '*Put on the armour of God*[115] *so that your enemy, having nothing evil to say about you, might be put to shame.*'[116] Let us remember the

Apostle's words when he said, *Whether in the body or outside the body, I know not, but God knows*.[117] And in fact Paul was swept up as far as the third heaven, and after he had heard there words that cannot be uttered,[118] he came down again, whereas Antony was raised right up to the heavens and after his struggle he appeared unhindered.

66 (38) Antony also possessed the following kind of gift: if, while he was living alone on the mountain, there was something he did not know and he was wondering about it, the Lord would reveal it to him as he prayed; and he was, as it says in Scripture, taught by God.[119] Later, the brothers were holding a discussion and were earnestly questioning him as to what happened to the soul after the burden of the body had been laid down and where the soul was allowed to go after death. The following night a voice from on high was heard calling his name. It said, 'Antony, get up. Go and look outside.' So he got up and went out (for he knew whom he had to obey) and raising his eyes to heaven, he saw someone tall and terrifying, his head reaching as far as the clouds; he also saw some winged creatures attempting to fly up to heaven, but the tall being stretched out his arms to prevent them getting through. Some of these creatures the tall being caught hold of and threw back to the ground; others he tried unsuccessfully to hold back and seemed annoyed when they managed to fly past him up towards heaven. Those who got the better of him caused him grief but those who were beaten back gave him the greatest joy. At once a voice came to Antony, saying, 'Pay attention to what you see.' Then his heart was illuminated and he began to understand that these were souls that the devil was obstructing in their ascent. He realized that the devil took hold of those who were subject to him, but he was tormented by the flight of the holy ones whom he was unable to catch. Inspired by the examples offered in these visions, Antony advanced each day to better things.[120] (39) He did not tell the brothers what had been revealed to him for he did not wish to boast; but as he used constantly in his prayers to praise God for his assistance, he was forced to explain to the brothers when they asked. He did not want to conceal anything from his spiritual sons for his soul was pure in Christ, especially since the recounting of miracles of this kind was likely to stimulate their passion for that

way of life and show them what the fruit of their labours might be. 67 Never was he provoked to impatience by sudden anger nor did he allow his humility to become puffed up into pride. For he urged all the clerics right down to the lowest rank to pray before he did and he also bent his head for the bishops and priests to give him their blessing, as if he were their disciple in humility. Even when deacons came to him for their own benefit he would speak to them in order to help them but when it came to praying to the Lord, he put them before himself for he was not ashamed to learn from them. In fact he frequently questioned those who were with him and if they told him something useful, he admitted that they had helped him. (40) His face bore a look of exceptional grace and he also possessed the following wonderful gift from the Saviour: if anyone who did not know him wished to see him when he was surrounded by a large number of monks, he would go past all the others and run up to Antony without anyone having to point him out. He could recognize Antony's spiritual purity from his face and through the mirror of Antony's body he would perceive the grace of his holy mind. For Antony always had a cheerful look which showed that his mind was on heavenly matters, as it says in Scripture: *When the heart rejoices, the countenance is cheerful, but when it is in sorrow the countenance is sad.*[121] This was how Jacob recognized that Laban his brother-in-law was devising some plot against him and so he said to his daughters, *Your father's face is not the same as it was yesterday and the day before.*[122] This was how Samuel recognized David, for he had eyes that brought joy, and teeth as white as milk.[123] In the same way people recognized Antony because he always maintained the same expression in good times and in bad and was neither elated by his successes nor shattered by disasters. For his countenance made people love him and the purity of his faith made them marvel at him.

68 (41) Never did he associate with the schismatic party,[124] being aware of their long-standing wickedness and apostasy. Never did he even go so far as to bestow friendly words on the Manichees or other heretics, apart from such words alone which might serve to call them back from the error of their iniquity, for he spoke out against friendship with them and he would denounce what they said, believing that

these things led to spiritual ruin. He loathed the Arians, too, warning everyone not to go anywhere near them. For when some of the Ariomaniacs[125] came to him, he questioned them carefully and found that their sect was utterly sacrilegious: so he sent them away from the mountain, saying that their utterances were far more poisonous than serpents.

69 Once when the Arians falsely claimed that Antony held the same beliefs as they did, he was amazed at their audacity and was moved to righteous indignation. He was then asked by the bishops and by all the brothers to come down to Alexandria[126] where he publicly condemned the Ariomaniacs, declaring that this was the final heresy that would herald the arrival of Antichrist. He stated openly to the people that the Son of God is not a creature, that He was not brought into existence out of non-being, but is eternal, of one substance with the Father. He must not be regarded as something created or adopted or a mere name. He said that it was sacrilegious even to think that there was a time when He was not, since God, the Word of God who is eternal, is coeternal with the Father, for He was born from the Father who exists for ever. And so he used to say, 'You must have nothing to do with the Arians. *For what fellowship can there be between light and darkness?*[127] You who hold orthodox beliefs are Christians, but they teach that the Word, that is, the Son who comes from God the Father, is a creature, and so they are no different from the pagans who worship the creature instead of the Creator, who is blessed for ever.[128] Believe me, the very elements are angry and the whole of creation groans, to use the words of the Apostle,[129] in the face of the Arians' madness, because it sees its Lord, through whom and in whom all things were made,[130] being numbered among the creatures.'

70 (42) It is impossible to convey the degree to which this great man's words strengthened the people's faith. They rejoiced that this dangerous heresy, hostile to Christ, was being anathematized by a pillar of the church. At that time no one, of any age or either sex, remained at home. I am not speaking just of the Christians: the pagans, too, and even the priests of the idols came rushing to church, saying, 'We beg to see the man of God' (for this was what everyone called

Antony). They crowded round him, eager just to touch the hem of his garment, in the belief that merely touching it would benefit them greatly. How many people were freed from the devil's grip and from many different illnesses at that time! How many spoils were snatched from the idols! How many people were retrieved from pagan error and added to our flock! The number of those converted from the superstition of the idols in the space of a few days would no doubt be greater than the number of converts one would normally see in a year. And what is more, when his attendants turned the crowd away as it surged forward, because they thought that he would find this number of people a nuisance, he said calmly, 'Surely this gathering is no larger than the hosts of demons? Surely this crowd of followers is no more numerous than the army of those with whom I wrestled on the mountain?'

71 (43) It happened that while we[131] were escorting him on his way back, as we reached the gate a woman called out from behind, saying, 'Wait, you man of God. My daughter is tormented by the most hideous demon. Wait, I beg you. Wait, for otherwise I may die in my hurry to reach you.' On hearing this the wonderful old man stopped for a while – we did ask him to do so, but he himself also wished to. When the woman came up to him, the girl was hurled to the ground and lay there, while Antony prayed silently to the Lord Jesus: at his threats the unclean spirit immediately departed. The girl was restored to health, the people praised God and the mother was overjoyed. Antony, too, was pleased because he was returning to the solitude he longed for.

72 He was also remarkably wise: considering that he had no education it was amazing how very clever and shrewd he was. (44) On one occasion while he was at the Outer Mountain, two pagan philosophers came to see him, thinking that they could outwit him. When he saw them, he understood from their appearance that they were pagan, and going out to them he began to speak through an interpreter in the following way: why did these wise men want to put themselves to the trouble of such a long journey to visit a stupid man? When they said that he was not stupid but rather exceedingly wise, he replied pointedly, 'If you have come to see a stupid man, your effort is wasted;

but if you think I am wise and that I possess wisdom, it would be a good idea for you to imitate what you approve of, for it is right to imitate good things. If I had come to you, I would imitate you, but since you have come to me in the belief that I am wise, you should be Christians like me.' The philosophers went away, amazed at his mental acuteness and at his ability to drive out demons.

73 (45) He used this kind of argument to check others, too, who were similarly full of worldly wisdom, people who wished to mock him because he was uneducated. He would say to such people, 'Answer me: what comes first, mind or letters? And which is the cause of which? Does mind come from letters or letters from the mind?' When they declared that mind was the author and inventor of letters, he said, 'So if anyone's mind is sound, he has no need of letters.' Was there anyone present who did not exclaim in astonishment after this verbal contest, when even those whom he got the better of were astounded, marvelling at such great sagacity of mind in one who was uneducated? Even though he had spent his whole life living in the desert and the mountains, Antony was not boorish and lacking in grace; rather, he was pleasant and friendly and offered conversation that was seasoned with divine salt, according to the words of the Apostle,[132] with the result that no one felt any ill will towards him and he gained the affection of all.

74 (46) Meanwhile, as if it was not enough for paganism to be routed[133] twice, there came to him a third time men who were blinded by the fog of all secular wisdom and who, in their own estimation, were the most learned in all branches of philosophy. When they demanded from Antony an explanation of the faith which we have in Christ and tried to trick him by means of sophisms and cunning questions concerning the divine cross, he remained silent for a while, at first pitying their error. Then he began to speak through an interpreter who used to translate his words with great care into the Greek language. He said, 'What is more honourable, what is more proper – to worship the cross or to attribute adultery, parricide or incest to those whom you worship? In the one case, contempt for death is a sign of virtue but in the other a shameful religion is the teacher of obscenity. What is better – to say that the Word of God, remaining

what He was, took a human body for the sake of our salvation, so that by sharing our mortal condition He might take us up to heaven, allowing us to share in the heavenly nature; or, as you claim, that the breath of the divine mind bows His head to worship earthly things and confines the heavenly name within the forms of cattle and serpents? How do you dare to mock the credulity of Christians because they claim that Christ the Son of God, without suffering any harm, began to be what He was not while remaining what He had been, when you yourselves derive the soul from heavenly beings but then envelop it not only in human bodies but in those of serpents and cattle? Christian belief states that its God has come for the salvation of the world, but you, while proclaiming that the soul is unborn, change from one side to another. Christian faith, respecting God's omnipotence and mercy as it does, says that consequently the Incarnation was possible for God, but in such a way that this condescension did not cause Him to lose dignity. But you who proudly claim that the soul, issuing from the purest source of God, has shamefully fallen, and who dare to state that it is subject to change after its fall, you desecrate this nature, too, the mistress of the ages, by means of your wicked tongue and insults to the soul. For the image which according to you retains the natural likeness of its maker who has the same substance as that which flows from it, consequently sends back its own humiliation and injuries to its origin. So watch out: your insults to the soul will, as a result of your blasphemy, redound to their father, as you call him.

75 'At this point let us bring the cross of Christ, the Lord our God, into the argument. I ask, how is this an obscenity of religion? Is it not better to endure the cross or a death of this kind inflicted by wicked men than to bewail the unsettled and dubious travels of Isis in search of Osiris? Are you not embarrassed, I ask, by the plots of Typhon, the flight of Saturn and his most cruel devouring of his children? Blush at Jupiter's murder of his father and his incest, blush at the rape he committed and his intercourse with women and boys. According to your poets' stories, Jupiter gave out gentle moans of love in order to fulfil his lustful passion which was of the grossest kind: he flowed into Danae's lap, he who was both lover and reward; he sought the embraces of Leda, singing as a swan; he violated his

own sex, corrupting the royal boy with birds as his accomplices. These are what you believe, these are what you worship, these are the ornaments adorning your temples. Weigh our words with impartial justice, I beg you, for the sake of your salvation. Is all or nothing to be believed in the Christian books? If nothing, you should not acknowledge the name of the cross which you disparage. If on the other hand it is all to be believed, why do you tear apart the divine passion with your stupid arguments, when in the same books the resurrection is connected to the cross? Why do you not at once add the sight of the blind, the hearing of the deaf, the walking of the lame, the cleansing of the leprous, the sea obeying its God who walked upon it, the putting to flight of demons, the resurrection of the dead and the return from the underworld of those who were dead? All these things are included in the divine Scriptures which you falsify, and these same volumes contain the proclamations of divine power and the disgrace inflicted upon death. For this reason cast off the hatred with which you are imbued and you will immediately discover that Jesus is true God and that He took our weak nature upon Himself for the sake of human salvation.

76 (47) 'Now tell us about your religion – if you are not ashamed to do so. But how could wretched error call such disgraceful and foolish things religious practices? Unless perhaps (as I hear) you claim that the obscene and cruel behaviour of your gods, their deceptions and their deaths are but myths and so you veil them in allegory: according to your interpretation, the rape of Libera[134] represents the earth, the half-lame and weak Vulcan represents fire; Juno, the air; Apollo, the sun; Diana, the moon; Neptune, the seas; while Jupiter, the foremost lecher, represents the sky. But after this bold attempt at a cover-up, you disregard the Creator and acknowledge the created beings, not God. But if the beauty of the elements has drawn you to worship them, you should have limited yourselves to admiring not worshipping them for otherwise the veneration of created things might imply an insult to the Creator. For according to the kind of distorted logic you use, the honour due to the architect is transferred to the building, and the doctor's skill is attributed to the cures and the rewards and praises due to all craftsmen are bestowed instead on the products

themselves. What do you say to this? We wish to know what disgraceful belief you hold concerning the cross which you consider worthy of ridicule.'

77 (48) This argument caused the philosophers to look round at one another and mutter. Then Antony smiled and spoke once again through the interpreter. 'It seems very hard in the case of any task whenever a reasonable attitude to something is scorned and the reward for the task is accorded to the deeds rather than to the doers. Indeed sight itself proves that the elements, as I have mentioned, are in servitude. But since you are collecting all these things which are necessary, in your opinion, for dialectical proof, you force us, too, to use this ploy to affirm our religion. Answer me: how is knowledge of God proved more clearly? By means of intricate arguments or by the working of faith? And which comes first: the working of faith or debate proceeding by means of arguments?' When they answered that the working of faith was more effective than discussion and that this offered an accurate knowledge of God, he agreed that they had spoken well, for the working which derives from faith is produced by feelings in the mind, while dialectical argument depends on the skill of those who are setting it forth. 'And so,' he said, 'anyone who has faith working in his mind, will find superfluous the composition of words which you use to try and tear out the credulity rooted in our minds. Yet often you are unable to explain what we understand. Therefore the products of the mind are more reliable than the deceptive conclusions derived from sophisms.

78 (49) 'We Christians keep the mystery of our life stored up, not in worldly wisdom, but in the power of faith which God has granted us through Christ. The daily order of events proves the truth of what I say. For us, being ignorant and lacking your learning, God's words alone are sufficient to attain the knowledge of God. Look at all of us, we who have been taken from pagan flocks: each day we increase in number and are spreading throughout the whole world. It is undeniable that since the coming of the Lord, your complicated and cunning sophistries have failed you. Look at us, we who teach the simple faith of Christ: we have completely crushed the worship of idols. The preaching of the cross, which is despised, has caused golden

temples to collapse. Show us, if you can, those who have been persuaded by your intricate arguments to value paganism above Christ. Throughout the whole world Christ has now been acknowledged as the true Son of God. Sophistical eloquence and philosophical arguments can do nothing to halt the growing number of believers. When we call on the name of Him who was crucified, all the demons roar, yet you worship them as gods; as soon as the sign of the Lord's cross is made they flee from the bodies in which they were dwelling.

79 'Where are those legendary oracles now? What has become of the Egyptians' incantations? What good did the magicians' spells do? Everything was destroyed when Christ thundered forth to the world from His cross, and yet you fail to mention the hordes of those whose strength is broken. Instead you try to pour scorn on Jesus' glorious death. How is it that paganism which has never been shaken by the persecutions of tyrants – indeed it was beloved by the world and was given the support of human assistance – now comes crashing down? In contrast, the more they attempt to suppress us, we who are servants of Christ, the more we rise up and flourish. Your statues were once surrounded by decorated walls, but now the passing of time has caused them to collapse. The teachings of Christ which appear to you to be foolish and trivial despite the fact that they have endured the tyrannical attempts at persecution on the part of the emperors and have been attacked by various terrifying means, are not restricted to any one area and not confined within the boundaries of any barbarian peoples. When did a brightness as great as that of the divine knowledge shine forth? When did so many virtues appear at the same time? Chastity in marriage, virginity in the Church. The martyrs' glorious steadfastness on their Lord's behalf shines forth: for all of them the cross of Christ provides the foundation for their life.

80 'While you, amidst such great companies of virtues, spread the nets of your syllogisms and try to blot out the true light of things with your obscure arguments, look how we convince not by means of the pagans' attempts at persuasion but through the clearest faith which always precedes verbal affirmation, as our teacher said.[135] There are some here suffering from the torments of demons' – Antony brought them forward and repeated his words, saying – 'Now come on, use

your syllogisms and any wicked spells you wish, to drive out those whom you think of as your gods. But if you are unable to do so, hold out your conquered hands in supplication and take refuge in the signs of Christ's victory: the power of the divine majesty will immediately follow upon belief in the one who was crucified.' He spoke and, calling on the name of Jesus, he made the life-giving mark on their foreheads three times, corresponding to the number of the holy Trinity: as a result, the demons were driven out and the foolish wisdom of those philosophers present was refuted. They were shocked and terrified by Antony to whom God was granting, in addition to such wisdom, the ability to perform miracles. But he attributed everything to Christ who heals, for he answered with these words, saying, 'Do not think that it is I who have given these people health. It is Christ who performs these miracles through His servants. You too should believe and you will see that it is devout faith in God, rather than the empty pride that comes of clever talk, that is rewarded by such miracles. Take refuge in the law of Him who was crucified and imitate us who are His servants; content with this faith, you should not seek further arguments based on worldly ignorance.' Antony stopped speaking and the philosophers, struck with wonder and amazement, departed from him after saying a respectful farewell, admitting to each other that their meeting with him had been of great benefit to them.

81 (50) The remarkable thing about this man was that he who lived in obscurity on the furthest edge of the world found favour with the emperors and was honoured by the whole imperial court. For the emperor Constantine and his sons Constans and Constantius,[136] on learning of these things, sent him frequent letters as if he was their father, begging him to make them happy by writing back to them. But Antony remained exactly the same as he had been before the letters arrived, and showed no excitement at receiving greetings from the emperors. He called the monks together as if he had not received any letters and said, 'The rulers of this world have sent us letters – why should Christians be impressed by this? For although we are different in rank, yet our mortal condition is the same. What should be honoured with all due reverence, what should be held firmly and

positively in mind, is the fact that God wrote the law for men and that through His Son He enriched the churches with His own words. What business do monks have with the letters of emperors? Why should I receive letters, to which I do not know how to reply with the customary formalities?' But when all the brothers asked him to bring comfort to the Christian rulers by writing to them (for they were afraid the rulers might perhaps be annoyed at his silence), he wrote a suitable reply to the letters he had received. First of all he praised them for worshipping Christ and then gave them advice concerning their salvation to prevent them thinking that imperial power was anything wonderful and allowing the authority of the present flesh to make them swell with pride. He did not want them to forget that they were human and that they would have to be judged by Christ. Finally he strongly advised them to show compassion and justice to those who were subject to them as well as concern for the poor. In his letter he also declared that Jesus Christ is the one everlasting king of all ages. The rulers were extremely pleased to receive this letter. All people were inspired with such holy love for Antony that they wished to be called his sons, for his great kindness to those who came to see him made them all devoted to him.

82 (51) After he had confuted the pagans, advised the rulers and brought comfort to the brothers, he returned to the Inner Mountain and to the life of discipline to which he was accustomed. There, while walking around and sitting with his visitors, it happened that he would suddenly go quiet, as it is written in Daniel,[137] and after an interval of several hours he would continue with his answer: people understood from this that he had witnessed some secret revelation. For while he was at the mountain, he saw what was happening far away in Egypt and he related it to bishop Serapion[138] who was with him there. On another occasion a very sad vision appeared which caused him to weep floods of tears. For while he was working with the brothers seated around him, he began to stare intently at the sky, groaning and sighing, and after a time he began to shake with deep sorrow at the revelation: he immediately knelt down before God's face and prayed that His mercy might avert the terrible event which was to occur. His prayer was followed by tears and a great fear gripped those present:

they beseeched him to tell them what he had seen. His voice was racked by sobs, his tongue tied by tears and his attempts to speak were interrupted by groans. With a loud cry of grief he just managed to utter these words, 'It would be better, my dear children, to die quickly to avoid the impending disaster.' Beginning thus, he was again overcome by tears; amidst sighs of sorrow he was at last able to get these words out: 'A great disaster threatens, one which no previous age has known. The Catholic faith will be destroyed by a great whirlwind; men, like irrational beasts, will tear apart Christ's holy things. For I saw the altar of the Lord surrounded by a pack of asses who scattered everything by kicking repeatedly with their hoofs. This is the reason for those sighs of mine you heard: I heard the Lord's voice, saying, "My altar will be defiled."' The events warned of in the vision took place only a short while afterwards, for two years later the savage madness of the Arians erupted. Then the churches were ransacked, the divine vessels were profaned, the sacred ministries were defiled by the pagans' foul hands, and when the support of the pagan workers had been gained against Christ, the Christians were forced to go to church carrying palms (which is a mark of idolatry in Alexandria), so that they would be thought to belong to the Arians. What wickedness! The mind recoils from repeating what happened: virgins and married women were raped; the blood of Christ's sheep was shed in Christ's temple and spattered over the holy altars; the pagans defiled the baptistery by doing what they liked there. Antony's vision had been accurate in every detail as later events proved, for the wild trampling of the mules represented the Arians' wicked behaviour.

But Antony comforted them in their grief by giving the following positive revelation. He said, 'My dear sons, do not give yourselves up completely to grief. For just as the Lord was angered, so He will again have pity. The Church will soon regain her beauty and you will see those who preserved the faith of the Lord during the times of persecution, shining once more with their former brightness. The serpents will return to their holes and our religion will spread further. Just watch that the Arian filth does not stain the purity of your faith. Their teachings do not derive from the apostles but from the demons and their father, the devil. That is why their mind, resembling that of beasts, is represented by the foolishness of asses.'

83 (52) Such were Antony's words. We should not find it hard to believe that such a great miracle could be performed by a man. For the Saviour promised this when He said, *If you have faith like a grain of mustard seed, you will say to this mountain, 'Move,' and it will move, and nothing will be impossible for you.*[139] And another time He said, *Truly, truly, I say to you, everything that you ask for from the Father in my name, he will grant to you. Ask and you will receive.*[140] For He himself, promising His disciples and all those who believed in Him that the demons would be overcome and that many different diseases would be cured, used to say, *You received freely, give freely.*[141]

84 Was it by the authority of his own virtue that Antony healed? Did he think that what he had done was due to his own ability? The demons and illnesses were dispelled by his prayers, not by his commands and everything was always accomplished by calling on the name of Christ, our God.[142] No one who is wise attributes the miracle of healing to Antony, but to the Lord Jesus who was displaying His usual benevolence to His creatures when He behaved kindly at that time, too, through His chosen servant. Antony merely prayed and the Lord granted everything as a reward for Antony's virtuous life.

(53) Often – though against his will – he was taken by the brothers to the Outer Mountain. And when judges arrived who were unable to reach the inner stronghold or the harsh desert regions on account of the difficult journey and because of the large number of people accompanying them, and they asked to be allowed to see him, they were unable to get what they wanted as Antony found the disturbance caused by conversations very annoying. So they sent to him the men in chains (those who had been put in fetters as a result of some crime or by public force), knowing that Antony was unable to reject such people. Overcome by their weeping, he allowed himself to be taken to the Outer Mountain for he realized that by his efforts he could help these poor people; and he persuaded the judges who had invited him to come that they should put fear of God before hatred and favour in giving sentence. He said that they should bear in mind the

words of Scripture, *By whatever justice you judge, you will be judged.*[143] But even while he was speaking, he was thinking of his beloved solitude.

85 And so, forced to go there by the commander's entreaties and, to be more accurate, by the tears of the wretched prisoners, Antony gave advice which was beneficial for salvation and commended the prisoners, acquitting some of them. The commander then asked him to favour them with his presence a little longer. Antony replied that he was unable to stay there any longer, using this pleasing analogy: just as fish taken out of the water soon die on dry land, so too, monks who stay with people from the world are soon weakened by human conversations. 'For that reason,' he said, 'it is proper for us to hurry back to the mountain, like fishes to the sea, for if we linger here we might forget our commitment to the monastic way of life.' The commander marvelled at the man's great wisdom and expressed this just and true view of him when he said, 'Truly, this man is the servant of God for no uneducated man could possess such great wisdom unless he were guided by divine love.'

86 (54) Later Balacius, who was the commander of Egypt under Nestorius, the prefect of Alexandria, and a most committed supporter of the Arian wickedness, was persecuting the Church of Christ so violently that in his madness he would have virgins and monks stripped and beaten in public. Antony then sent him a letter, the substance of which was this: 'I see God's anger coming upon you. Stop persecuting the Christians or this anger, which threatens you with imminent death, will take hold of you.' The accursed man read the letter and laughed; spitting on it he threw it to the ground. He hurled many insults at the letter-bearers and ordered them to take the following message back to Antony: 'Since you are so concerned about the monks, you too will feel the force of my discipline.' But he who uttered these threats was immediately punished: five days later divine vengeance curbed his unbridled mouth. For he went out as far as the first staging post outside Alexandria, called Chaereus, together with Nestorius, the prefect I mentioned earlier. They were riding on the most gentle horses of all those trained by Balacius (to whom they belonged). While the horses were playing with each other as usual,

the gentler one, which Nestorius was riding, suddenly bit Balacius and knocked him to the ground. Its mouth open wide, it ripped his thighs apart and gnawed them to pieces. Although he was carried back to the city without delay, he died three days later. And so everyone realized that Antony's threats which I mentioned earlier had swiftly been fulfilled and that the persecutor had come to a fitting end.

87 (55) Antony was amazingly unassuming when he advised others who came to him, urging them to forget secular honour and seek the happiness of a more remote life. If there were any who were oppressed by those more powerful than themselves and who were unable to obtain justice, he defended them so strenuously that he seemed to be suffering the injustice on their behalf. Many found the words spoken by this exceptional old man useful; many, who had abandoned great riches and high military rank, were eager to join him in his way of life. To sum up an infinite number of points in a brief phrase, Christ granted Egypt an excellent doctor. Whose sadness was not transformed into joy in Antony's presence? Whose anger was not turned to peace? Was there anyone whose grief in bereavement was not allayed at the sight of Antony? Was there anyone who did not cast off his dissatisfaction with the poverty oppressing him and immediately scorn the opulence of wealth and rejoice in his poverty? What monk who had lost his enthusiasm was not invigorated by Antony's encouragement? What young man, inflamed with desire, did not dedicate himself to chastity as a result of Antony's advice? What person, tormented by the devil, went away without a cure? Was there anyone, distracted by the enemy's thoughts, who did not have the mental disturbance clouding his perceptions dispelled and who did not go back home in a serene state of mind?

88 Antony was able to perceive each person's misfortune for he had been granted the gift of discerning spirits on account of his virtuous life. He could therefore apply a cure for each disease, according to what wounds he found. And so it happened that as a result of his teachings all the devil's traps were exposed. There were also many girls who were engaged to be married: when they saw him they turned away from the very marriage bed, so to speak, and sank into

the embrace of mother Church. What more need I say? People came to him in great numbers from all over the world and all the different nationalities rejoiced to see this man fighting so valiantly against the devil. No one complained that his visit to Antony had been wasted; in fact they all found the efforts they had spent pleasurable and delightful. They received ample compensation for the tiring nature of the journey, as the outcome proved. After his death, although they all suffered the wound of bereavement together, it was as if each of them grieved for him as for his own father.

89 (56) As to what the end of his life was like, it is right that I should tell you about it and that you should hear about it, as you wish to, for this was also something concerning him which everyone else can imitate. He came as usual to visit the brothers who were living at the Outer Mountain. While he was there he learned from divine providence of his own death. He then began to speak in the following words, 'My dear sons, listen to your father's last thoughts; for I do not think that we will see you again in this life. Nature's laws compel me now to be released from this life after a century, which I have exceeded by five years.' This speech of his filled the hearts of his listeners with sorrow and his sad words provoked sighs and tears. They all embraced him as if he were now withdrawing from the world, but Antony spoke to them with great joy as if he were leaving foreign lands and was about to set out for his own country. He said that they should not allow idleness to creep into their way of life and they must guard their souls from sordid thoughts, behaving as if they were going to die each day, as he had said before. They should emulate the saints in all things and not go anywhere near the Melitian schismatics. 'For you are aware,' he said, 'of their long-standing perversity; neither should you join in communion with the Arians because their impiety is now obvious to everyone.' To these things he added that no Christian, seeing the secular powers fighting in support of the Arian and Melitian wickedness, should be frightened into departing from the truth of Christ; the heretics' defence was that of mere mortals and this deceptive illusion could not last for long. 'And so,' he said, 'true faith in Christ and the religious traditions of the fathers must be protected; this is what you have learned from

your reading of the Scriptures and what I have often reminded you of.'

90 (57) When he had finished speaking, the brothers forcibly detained him for they were very keen to gain the honour of their father's glorious end. But he protested against this for many reasons which he indicated even by his silence, but particularly because of that tradition which was taken for granted among the Egyptians. For it is customary for Egyptians to wrap in linen cloths the bodies of those they think worthy, and especially of the blessed martyrs, and to accord them the usual funeral rites; however, they do not bury them in the earth but lay them on beds at home and preserve them. Age-old custom, though pointless, has made it a tradition for this honour to be accorded to the dead. Regarding this matter Antony had often asked the bishops to put the people right by means of an ecclesiastical decree, and he himself addressed lay men and women quite sternly, saying that this was neither permissible nor pleasing to God. Did not the tombs of the patriarchs and prophets which have lasted until our day convince them of this? He told them that they should consider also the example of the Lord's body: it was placed in a tomb which was closed with a rock until the third day, the day of resurrection.[144] By these means he demonstrated that this Egyptian practice with regard to the dead was wrong, even in the case of the bodies of holy men. He would argue, 'Whose body is greater or more holy than the Lord's? Yet we know that it was buried in the ground according to other nations' customs.' His reasonable argument freed many from this deep-seated error, with the result that they buried their corpses in the earth and gave thanks to the Lord that they had been well taught.

91 And so, fearing, that the monks might fall into the same error and treat his body according to this particular custom, Antony hurriedly said goodbye to those who had gathered there and returned to his dwelling, the friend of his virtue.

(58) A few months later when his ageing limbs began to be troubled by some discomfort, he summoned two brothers whom some fifteen years earlier he had established a short distance away and who had begun to look after him now that he was old. He said to them, 'My

dear sons, I am going the way of the fathers, to use the words of Scripture,[145] for the Lord is now summoning me and I long to see heaven. But I warn you who are closest to me not to waste in one moment all the hard work you have put in over a long period. You must think that it is only today that you have started on your life of religious endeavour and allow the strength of your commitment to grow as if it had just begun. You are aware of the many different means the demons have of deceiving you; you have seen that their attacks are savage but that their strength has been rendered powerless. Draw inspiration from Jesus and set your faith in His name firmly in your minds: then all the demons will be put to flight by the sure faith. Remember also my words of advice and the instability of the human condition; re-examine this fluctuating life each day and then the heavenly prize will be awarded to you without delay. Avoid, too, the schismatics' and heretics' poisons and seek to imitate me in hating them because they are the enemies of Christ. You yourselves know that I have never held a conciliatory conversation with them on account of their perverted will and the war they persistently wage against Christ. Instead you should be concerned to keep the Lord's commandments so that after your death the saints may receive you into the eternal tabernacles[146] like well-known friends. Think on these things, be inspired by these things, repeat these things. And if you have any love for me, if you remember your father, if you wish to demonstrate an attitude of loving obedience, let no one carry my remains to Egypt, for I do not want my body to be preserved[147] for empty honours nor do I want those rites of the practice I have censured to be carried out for me. It is for this reason in particular that I have come back here. You must cover your father's humble body with earth and bury it. Carry out also this order given to you by this old man who is yours: let no one apart from your dear selves know the place of my tomb. I trust in the Lord that this humble body will rise uncorrupt at the appointed time of resurrection.[148] Let my clothes be divided in the following way: please give to Athanasius this sheepskin and the worn cloak[149] on which I am lying, because he gave it to me when it was new. Let bishop Serapion receive the other sheepskin. You must have my hair shirt. Farewell, you who are closest to me.

For Antony is departing: no longer will he be with you in the present life.'

92 (59) He had finished speaking and when his disciples had kissed him, he stretched his feet out a little and looked upon death with joy. They could tell by his cheerful expression that the holy angels who had come down to carry away his soul were present. When he saw the angels, he looked upon them as friends and breathing out his spirit he went to join the fathers, in accordance with the practice recorded in the Scriptures. His disciples carried out his orders: they wrapped his body (as he had told them to) and covered it with earth. And no one apart from them knows to this day where he is buried. The legatee[150] of the blessed Antony who had been deemed worthy of receiving the worn cloak and the sheepskin according to Antony's orders, embraces Antony in Antony's gifts: this garment causes him to remember with joy the paragon of holiness as if a large inheritance had made him wealthy.

93 (60) This was how Antony's life ended,[151] these were his principal virtues. Although, as I said before, I ought to have given a shorter account of them, yet these will enable you to understand how this man of God progressed from childhood to old age and how he always trampled on any doubts and never made any concessions to weariness or to his great age. Instead he maintained his commitment steadfastly: he did not change his clothes or wash his feet, nor did he request more delicate food. On account of his goodness, he retained his sharp eyesight and all his teeth (although they appeared somewhat worn down because of his old age), as well as his ability to walk, indeed the strength of his whole body, contrary to the laws of nature. In fact, his body looked healthier than those glistening bodies which are pampered by baths and luxurious living.

(61) To whom then, my brother, can we attribute the fact that his fame and love have spread throughout all the provinces, he who won fame not through the dazzling discourse of books that have been circulated far and wide nor by means of the arguments of worldly wisdom nor because of his family's nobility nor the accumulation of great wealth? To whom if not to Christ whose gift this is? Foreseeing Antony's devotion to His divine majesty He revealed this man who

was almost hidden in another world, set in the midst of such vast areas of solitude. He revealed him to Africa, Spain, Gaul, Italy, Illyria, even to Rome itself, the first city, as He had promised in the beginning. For this occurred as a result of the Creator's kindness, He who always raises His servants to nobility, even against their will, so that they might learn that virtue is possible and not beyond the bounds of human nature and so that all the best people might thus be impelled by the fruit of his labour to imitate his blessed life.

94 (62) Read this book very carefully to the brothers so that, when they learn about the faithful life of these outstanding monks, they may know that our Saviour Jesus Christ glorifies those who glorify Him and grants the nobility of fame to those who serve Him and who long not only for the kingdom of heaven but also wish to lead a life of withdrawal in remote mountain places. They do this so that they themselves might win praise for their virtues and so that others may be spurred on by their examples. But if it should prove necessary, read this also to the pagans so that they may in this way recognize not only that our Lord Jesus Christ is God, the Son of God, but also that to those who worship Him diligently and who believe in Him faithfully He grants the power to trample upon and cast out the demons whom they consider to be gods, but who are really deceivers of men and devisers of all corruption.

Evagrius' epilogue to his translation

And so we beg those sensible people who wish to read this piece of writing to look benevolently if we have been unable to convey the force of the Greek text in translating it into Latin: if this is the case, then it is contrary to our intention. We were unwilling to do this translation not because we bore any ill will but because we were well aware that the Greek text, when translated into Latin, might lose its power. Yet we thought it preferable for the Greek text to be subjected to this rather than that those who would read the Greek text in some form of translation should be cheated of a profit which could make them divine. May the almighty God who cooperated with this great man to produce such things cooperate also with us to imitate him, even in part, so that his name may shine clearly among all the people through the teacher and encourager and redeemer and our Saviour Lord Jesus with the Holy Spirit, to whom is splendour and everlasting power for ever and ever.

Life of Paul of Thebes by Jerome

There is disagreement over the exact date of Jerome's birth: was he born as early as 331 or perhaps as late as 347? Whatever the truth, it would seem that his Life of Paul of Thebes, *probably written at Antioch in 337[1] after he had deserted the desert of Chalcis and was once again staying with Evagrius, was to be his first published work: the only earlier writings we have from Jerome's pen are a few letters. He may have been inspired to write it when he saw the success of Evagrius' translation of the* Life of Antony. *It differs from the* Life of Antony, *however, in that it deals only with Paul's youth and extreme old age, and acts as a sort of preface to the* Life of Antony. *Jerome's intention, he tells us in his prologue, is to prove that Antony was not in fact the first person to choose a life of extreme asceticism in the desert. He does this by showing us the ninety-year-old Antony[2] coming to the realization that there is someone in the desert who is better than him. Moved by this, he decides to visit Paul even though he has no idea where he lives. He sets out and is guided by strange creatures, a satyr and then a centaur, until he finds the cave where Paul, now 113 years old, had been living for over ninety years! The meeting between the two hermits is both touching and gently amusing. They discuss Paul's death, which he knows is imminent, and compete with each other in humility. Paul tactfully sends Antony back to his cell to fetch a cloak so that Antony will not witness his death. Antony returns to find Paul's corpse still kneeling in prayer. He is at a loss as to how to bury him since he has no spade, but is miraculously helped by two friendly lions who come to dig the grave. He wraps Paul's body in the cloak which Athanasius had given him, in accordance with Paul's instructions.[3]*

On completion of this work Jerome sent it first to an old man, Paul of Concordia, a learned ascetic whom he had known while living in the region of Aquileia. He accompanied it by a letter[4] in which he says that he has worked hard to make the Life of Paul *readable and if his addressee finds it so, he will send him some more of his writings. Paul of Concordia was not the only one to read it: by the time Jerome set out to write the* Life of Hilarion, *he could speak of the public reaction to the* Life of Paul, *which had not been altogether favourable. Some had clearly criticized his account on the grounds that since Paul lived a life of such utter remoteness, there was no proof that he had actually existed. Jerome, however, had no doubts about Paul's existence. Whatever the truth – and the fact that Jerome tells us little of what Paul did during the long years of complete solitude perhaps increases the story's plausibility – Jerome's decision to focus on the meeting of Antony and Paul was a master stroke for it meant that the* Life of Paul *became associated with the* Life of Antony *and was deemed of interest as providing further information about Antony: Paul of Thebes could survive, as it were, by clinging on to Antony. This is not to say that Jerome's short account of Paul's long life is not very readable in its own right. If it is limited in the amount it tells us about Paul, it does tell us much about Jerome, his ideals and interests. We find in this work many of the characteristics of his later writings: his obsession with sex, his inability to write without literary allusions even when he is aiming at a simple style, his admiration for a life of withdrawal and extreme asceticism even though he now realizes, after attempting it for several years in the desert of Chalcis, that he himself is not suited for such a life.*

Prologue

1 It has often been a matter of discussion among many people as to which monk was the first to inhabit the desert. Some, going back further into the past, have ascribed the beginning to the blessed Elijah and to John; of these, Elijah seems to us to have been more than a monk, while John seems to have started to prophesy before he was born. Others, whose opinion is commonly accepted, claim that Antony was the first to undertake this way of life, which is partly true, for it is not so much that he came before all the others but rather that he inspired everyone with a commitment to this way of life. Amathas and Macarius,[1] Antony's disciples (of whom the former buried his master's body), affirm to this day that a certain Paul of Thebes was the originator of the practice, though not of the name, of the solitary life, and this is the view I also take. Some people make these and other claims as the whim takes them. They claim, for example, that there was a man living in an underground cave, with hair down to his feet, and they invent many unbelievable things which it is a waste of time to recount. Since their opinion is a bare-faced lie, it seems unnecessary to refute it. Seeing, then, that an account of Antony has been recorded in both Greek and Latin,[2] I have decided to write a few things about the beginning and end of Paul's life, more because these things have been neglected than because of any talent on my part. As to how he lived during the middle years of his life and what attacks of Satan he endured, no one knows anything for certain.

Life of Paul of Thebes

2 During the persecutions under Decius and Valerian, when Cornelius at Rome and Cyprian at Carthage shed their blood in blessed martyrdom, a violent storm ravaged many churches in Egypt and the Thebaid. At that time Christians longed to be killed by the sword for the name of Christ. But the cunning enemy was more keen to murder their souls than their bodies, and so he arranged for them to be put to death by slow torture. And as Cyprian himself, whom he put to death, said, 'Those who wished to die were not permitted to be killed.'³ So that the enemy's cruelty might be better known, we shall include two examples to ensure they are not forgotten.

3 When one martyr, remaining steadfast in the faith, refused to give in amidst the racks and the red-hot metal plates, the order was given for him to be smeared with honey and placed beneath the blazing sun, with his hands tied behind his back, so that he who had earlier survived the burning metal plates might succumb to mosquito bites. Another martyr, in the flower of his youth, was ordered to be taken off to a most delightful garden. There, amid the white lilies and red roses, beside which a gently murmuring stream meandered, while the wind plucked lightly at the leaves of the trees producing a soft whisper, he was made to lie down on a thick feather bed. He was left there, tied down by soft garlands to prevent him escaping. When everyone had gone away, a beautiful prostitute came up to him and began to stroke his neck with gentle caresses, and (what is improper even to relate) to touch his private parts with her hands: when his body was roused to lust as a result, this shameful conqueress lay down on top of him. The soldier of Christ did not know what to do or where to turn: he who had not yielded to tortures was being overcome by pleasure. At last, by divine inspiration, he bit off his tongue and spat it out in her face⁴ as she kissed him; and so the sense of lust was overcome by the sharp pain that replaced it.

4 While these things were happening, in the Lower Thebaid Paul was left a wealthy heir at the age of about sixteen, after his sister's marriage and the death of both his parents. He was highly educated

in both Greek and Egyptian letters, with a compassionate disposition and a profound love of God. As the storm of persecution rumbled on, he withdrew to a more distant and isolated spot. But to what does the accursed greed for gold[5] not drive the hearts of men? His sister's husband conceived a desire to betray the person he ought to have concealed; neither his wife's tears (as is usually the case), nor family ties, nor God who watches everything from on high, could dissuade him from this crime. He was on the spot, he was insistent, he practised cruelty as though it were kindness.[6]

5 As soon as this very wise young man realized what was going on, he fled to the mountainous regions of the desert to await an end to the persecution, making a virtue of necessity. He would move on a bit further into the desert, then stop for a while: repeating this pattern, he at last came to a rocky mountain at the foot of which was a small cave, its entrance blocked by a stone. Removing this (for it is human nature to want to discover what is hidden), he began to explore more eagerly: inside he found a large chamber, open to the sky above and covered by the spreading branches of an old palm tree. This indicated that there was a spring of clearest water, whose stream gushed forth and was immediately absorbed through a small crack in the ground which had produced it. There were, moreover, throughout the hollow mountain, a number of rooms in which were to be seen rusty stamps and hammers, used to stamp coins. According to Egyptian records this place had been a secret factory for minting money at the time when Antony was having an affair with Cleopatra.

6 Paul fell in love with this dwelling as if it had been offered to him by God, and spent the rest of his life there in prayer and solitude. The palm tree provided him with food and clothing. In case anyone should think this impossible, I call Jesus and his holy angels to witness that in the part of the desert close to Syria and the Saracens, I myself have seen monks (and I know that they still exist there), one of whom was enclosed for thirty years, living on barley bread and muddy water, while another survived in an old well (which the Syrians call a 'gubba' in their local dialect), living on five dried figs a day. These things will appear incredible only to those who do not believe that everything is possible for those who believe.[7]

7 But to return to the point where I digressed: when Paul had now been leading his heavenly life on earth for one hundred and thirteen years, while the ninety-year-old Antony was living in another part of the desert, it occurred to Antony (as he himself used to relate) that there was no monk in the wilderness more perfect than himself. But during the night while he was asleep it was revealed to him that there was someone else further into the desert interior who was far better than him and whom he ought to go and visit. As soon as dawn broke, the venerable old man, using a stick to support his weak limbs, conceived a wish to go, although he did not know where. It was now scorching midday and the sun was blazing down from on high, and yet he was not dissuaded from the journey he had set out on, for he said to himself, 'I believe that my God will show me my fellow servant as he has promised.' He had said no more than this, when he caught sight of a creature that was half man and half horse, to which the poets have given the name Hippocentaur. At the sight of it, he protected himself by making the life-giving sign on his own forehead and said, 'Hey you, where does the servant of God live?' The creature gave some kind of barbaric grunt, grinding out the words through his bristling lips rather than pronouncing them. By means of this rough speech he indicated a desire for friendly communication. Stretching out his right hand he indicated the route that Antony was seeking. Then crossing the open plain at a gallop, he vanished from the eyes of the astonished man. Now whether the devil had contrived these things so as to terrify Antony or whether, as often happens, the desert which abounds in monstrous creatures had produced this beast too, we are not sure.

8 Antony was amazed. Reflecting on what he had seen he went on his way. It was not long before he saw in the rocky valley a man of no great height, with a hooked nose, his forehead sprouting sharp horns, the lower part of whose body ended in goats' feet. At the sight of him, Antony, like a good soldier, seized the shield of faith and the breastplate of hope, but this animal brought him the fruits of the date palm to eat on his journey, as pledges of peace. When he realized this Antony stopped and on asking who he was, he received this answer from him: 'I am a mortal creature, one of the inhabitants of the desert

whom the pagans, deluded by various errors, worship, calling them fauns, satyrs and evil spirits. I am acting as envoy for my tribe. We ask you to pray for us to the Lord we share, for we know He came once for the salvation of the world, and His sound has gone out over the whole earth.'[8] As the creature said this, tears streamed down the aged traveller's face, tears which, in his great happiness, he shed as an indication of his feelings, for he rejoiced in Christ's glory and in the destruction of Satan. He was amazed to be able to understand the creature's speech and striking the ground with his staff he said, 'Woe to you, Alexandria, for worshipping monsters instead of God. Woe to you, you whore of a city, to which demons from all over the world have flocked in great numbers. What have you to say now? The wild beasts speak of Christ while you worship monsters instead of God.' He had hardly finished speaking when this frisky animal ran away as if borne on wings. In case anyone has scruples about believing this, it was proved to be true by what took place while Constantius was emperor, witnessed by the whole world. For a man of this kind was brought to Alexandria alive, providing the people with a marvellous spectacle. Later, when it was a lifeless corpse, salt was sprinkled on it to prevent the summer heat causing it to putrefy, and it was carried to Antioch for the emperor to see it.

9 But to proceed with my proposed account, Antony continued on his journey, seeing nothing but the tracks of wild animals and the immense vastness of the desert. He did not know what to do or which way to go. Already another day had passed and there was only one thing left: to remain confident that he would not be abandoned by Christ. He spent the whole second night in prayer and in the faint light of dawn he saw a she-wolf near by, panting with thirst and moving stealthily along to the foot of a mountain. He followed it with his eyes and when the wild beast disappeared into a cave he went up close and tried to look inside. His curiosity achieved nothing for the darkness prevented him seeing anything. But as Scripture says, *Perfect love casts out fear,*[9] and so, walking carefully and holding his breath, this cunning explorer entered the cave. Going in a bit further, he kept stopping to listen for a sound. At last, through the terrifying darkness of the night which made it impossible to see anything, he

discerned a light in the distance. As he quickened his pace in his eagerness, he bumped his foot against a stone, making a noise. When the blessed Paul heard this noise he closed and bolted a door that had been open. Then Antony fell down in front of this door and continued to beg to be allowed in until it was the sixth hour of the day or even later, saying, 'You know who I am, where I come from and why I have come. I know that I do not deserve to see you but I will not go away unless I do. Why do you, who welcome animals, drive a person away? I have sought you and I have found you: I knock that it may be opened to me.[10] If I do not get what I want, I shall die here in front of your door – and I trust you will bury my body when I am dead.'

He stood there thinking of these things, and remained transfixed.[11] In response the hero spoke a few words thus:[12] 'No one makes a request like this as a threat; no one attempts treachery with tears. Are you surprised if I do not welcome you, since you come here with the intention of dying?' Then Paul smiled and unbolted the door. When it was open, they embraced each other, and greeting each other by name, they joined in giving thanks to the Lord.

10 After the holy kiss, Paul sat down and began to speak to Antony as follows: 'Look at the person you sought with such effort: ugly grey hair covers his limbs which are rotting with old age. Look upon a man who will soon be dust. But because love endures all things,[13] tell me, I beg you, how the human race is getting on. Are new buildings rising up in the old cities? What government rules the world? Are there still some people alive who are in the grip of the demons' error?' While they were talking they noticed a raven land on the branch of a tree: it then flew down gently and placed a whole loaf of bread in front of them as they watched in amazement. When it had flown away Paul said, 'Look, the Lord who is truly loving and truly merciful has sent us our supper. For the last sixty years I have always received half a loaf,[14] but in honour of your arrival Christ has doubled His soldiers' rations.'

11 When they had given thanks to the Lord, they both sat down at the edge of a spring as clear as glass. Here a dispute arose as to which of them should break the bread and they continued to argue until the

day had almost turned to evening. Paul argued that it was the custom for the guest to do so, while Antony countered with the rights of age. At last it was decided that they should hold the bread at each end, and then if each one pulled towards himself, he would keep the bit left in his hands. Then they bent over the spring and drank a little of the water, and offering to God a sacrifice of praise, they passed the night in prayer. As soon as daylight returned to earth, the blessed Paul spoke thus to Antony, 'It is a long time, dear brother, since I learnt that you were living in these parts; it is a long time since God promised that you would be my fellow servant. But now, as the time of my death is close at hand when I will be released to be with Christ as I have always longed to do,[15] there remains for me a crown of righteousness now that I have run the course.[16] You have been sent by the Lord to cover my poor body with earth, or rather, to return earth to earth.'

12 When Antony heard this, he wept and groaned, and begged Paul not to leave him but to take him as his companion on that journey. But Paul said, 'You ought not to seek your own benefit but that of others.[17] It might be to your advantage to lay down the burden of the flesh and to follow the Lamb, but it is also beneficial for the other brothers to be instructed by your example. And so I beg you to go back, unless it is too much trouble, and bring me the cloak which bishop Athanasius gave you and wrap it around my poor body.' The blessed Paul asked this not because he was particularly bothered whether his corpse was naked or clothed as it decomposed (had he not for a long time been dressed in woven palm leaves?) but so that by going away Antony might be spared the grief caused by Paul's death. Antony was astonished that Paul had heard about Athanasius and his cloak. It was as if he saw Christ in Paul and so he worshipped God in his heart, but he dared make no further answer. Weeping in silence, he kissed Paul's eyes and hands and returned to the monastery that was later captured by the Saracens. His steps could not keep up with his will, but although his body was emaciated as a result of fasting and broken by old age, yet his will overcame his age.

13 Exhausted and breathless he at last arrived home, his journey over. Two of his disciples, who had started looking after him now that he

was getting old, ran to meet him, saying, 'Where have you been all this time, father?' He replied, 'Alas for me, sinner that I am. It is dishonest of me to call myself a monk. I have seen Elijah, I have seen John in the desert and now I have seen Paul in paradise.' And so, with lips tightly closed and beating his breast with his hands, he fetched the cloak from his little cell. When his disciples begged him to explain what this was all about, he said to them, '*There is a time for silence and a time for speech.*'[18]

14 Then Antony went out and returned the way he had come without taking even a small amount of food, for he longed for Paul, desiring to see him and to contemplate him with his eyes and with his whole heart. He feared the very thing that had in fact happened, namely that in his absence Paul would have given up the spirit he owed to Christ. When the next day dawned and there was still a three-hour journey left, he saw Paul among the hosts of angels, among the choirs of prophets and apostles, shining with a dazzling whiteness and ascending on high. Immediately Antony fell to the ground and threw sand over his head. Weeping and wailing he said, 'Why do you send me away, Paul? Why are you going away without saying goodbye? Are you leaving so soon, when I have only just got to know you?'

15 The blessed Antony later reported that he had run the rest of the way with such speed that he had flown like a bird. There was good reason to hurry for when he entered the cave he saw the lifeless corpse, in a kneeling position, its head erect and its hands stretched out towards heaven. At first he thought that Paul was still alive and so he knelt down beside him to pray, but when he heard no sighs from the praying man, as he usually did, he fell upon him in a tearful embrace, realizing that even as a corpse the holy man, by means of his reverent posture, was praying to God for whom all things live.

16 Antony therefore wrapped Paul's body up and brought it outside, singing hymns and psalms according to Christian tradition, but he was upset that he did not have a spade with which to dig the earth. His thoughts were in turmoil as he considered a number of alternatives, saying to himself, 'If I go back to the monastery, it is a four-day journey. If I stay here, I can do nothing more. Therefore let me die beside your warrior, Christ, as is fitting. Let me collapse and breathe

forth my last breath.' As he was pondering these things, behold, two lions came running from the inner desert, their manes flowing over their necks. At first Antony was terrified at the sight of them but when he focused his mind on God he was able to stand still without fear as if what he saw was a pair of doves. They came straight towards the corpse of the blessed old man and stopped there; wagging their tails in devotion they lay down at his feet, roaring loudly as if to show that in their own way they were lamenting as best they could. They then began to dig the ground near by with their paws: vying with each other to remove the sand, they dug out a space large enough for one man. They then went straight up to Antony, their necks bent and their ears laid back, and licked his hands and feet as if demanding a reward for their hard work. He realized that they were asking him for a blessing. Immediately he burst out in praise of Christ because dumb animals, too, were able to understand that there was a God, and said, 'O Lord, without whose assent no leaf flutters down from the tree and not a single sparrow falls to the ground, grant them what you know to be best.' Making a sign to them with his hand, he ordered them to depart. As soon as they had gone away, he bent his aged shoulders beneath the burden of the holy corpse. Laying it in the grave he piled the earth on top of it and made a burial mound according to custom. But when the next day dawned, in case this affectionate heir should possess none of the goods of the intestate man, he took the tunic that Paul had woven for himself out of palm leaves like a wicker basket. He then returned to the monastery and gave the disciples a detailed account of all that had happened, and on the feast days of Easter and Pentecost he always wore Paul's tunic.

17 At the end of this little work I would like to ask those who own so much land that they do not know it all, those who cover their homes in marble, those who thread the wealth of whole estates on to one string, 'What did this old man ever lack, naked as he was? You drink from jewelled cups but he was satisfied with the cupped hands that nature had given him. You weave gold into your tunics but he did not even have the shabbiest garment belonging to your slave. But then, paradise lies open to him, poor as he was, while hell will welcome you in your golden clothes. He was clothed with Christ

despite his nakedness: you who are dressed in silks have lost the garment of Christ. Paul who lies covered in the vilest dust will rise again in glory: heavy stone tombs press down upon you, you who will burn together with your wealth. Have a care, I ask you, for yourselves, have a care at least for the riches you love. Why do you wrap your dead in cloths of gold? Why does your ostentation not cease amidst the grief and tears? Or are the corpses of the rich unable to rot except in clothes of silk?'

18 I beg you, whoever you are who reads this, to remember the sinner Jerome: should the Lord grant him his wish, he would far rather choose Paul's tunic, together with his rewards, than the purple robes of kings, together with their punishments.

Life of Hilarion by Jerome

Jerome was not put off by the hostile reception he felt had greeted the publication of his Life of Paul. In 391, when he was settled at Bethlehem after the difficult years at Rome spent as Pope Damasus' secretary and the spiritual adviser of a group of aristocratic women, Jerome returned to the biographical genre. His Life of Hilarion was to be the longest biography he wrote. Jerome was apparently motivated by a desire to record Hilarion's outstanding deeds, to supplement the encomium of the Palestinian monk already written by Epiphanius[1] of Salamis in Cyprus who had known Hilarion personally. Now that Jerome was living at Bethlehem in Palestine he had no doubt heard much about Hilarion whose body had been brought back to his monastery near Gaza after his death in Cyprus[2] in 371. It has also been suggested that the Life of Hilarion reflects Jerome's own experiences,[3] and it may be that Jerome found Hilarion an attractive figure because of the similarities he saw in the ideals they held and the problems they faced.

The Life of Hilarion gives an account of Hilarion's life from his birth near Gaza in Palestine to his death in Cyprus, following him in his travels around the Mediterranean area. Hilarion models himself on Antony – and dresses in a tunic given to him by Antony[4] – but settles near his native village. Like Antony he is attacked by demons during his twenty-two years of solitude; like Antony he becomes famous against his will and is forced to perform miracles, particularly miracles of healing when the sick seek him out. These miracles are described in chapters 13–23. Chapters 24–30 tell of the growth in the number of monasteries springing up around him, to the point where Hilarion finds he must get away from it all and go in search of solitude once more. He sets off for Egypt, where, on the anniversary of Antony's death, he visits the Inner Mountain (30–31). But even in the vast deserts of Egypt he cannot find solitude, for his reputation continues to attract determined visitors.

From Egypt he travels by camel to Libya (34) and then by ship to Sicily (35–6) in search of peace and quiet. Unfortunately for him, he cannot stop performing miracles and so a crowd soon gathers there, too. Crossing to the coast of Dalmatia, Hilarion remains hidden for a few days on a country estate, but when he finds that a serpent is eating up the human and animal population of the area he has to intervene and cremate the monster on a pyre (39). This is immediately followed by a miracle involving a tidal wave (40) and the reputation Hilarion gains as a result forces him to move on to Cyprus where he spends his last years.

In its fullness and many of its details the Life of Hilarion is more similar to Athanasius' Life of Antony than either the Life of Paul or the Life of Malchus: like Antony, Hilarion gives away his property when he is orphaned as a teenager, struggles with demons, moves on in search of solitude and bequeaths his few belongings to his closest disciple. It differs, however, from all three in the way it focuses on the miracles performed by Hilarion. One might even say that it is in fact the first example of a saint's life in which the miracles provide the narrative material, and it was along similar lines that so many later hagiographies, including the Life of Martin and the Life of Benedict, were to run.

Prologue

1 As I set out to write the life of the blessed Hilarion, I call upon the Holy Spirit who dwelt in him, that he who bestowed virtues on that man might grant to me the speech to describe them, so that his deeds might be equalled by my words. For as Sallust says, the achievements of successful men are rated according to the talents with which they are praised by those authors who are able to praise them.[1] When Alexander the Great of Macedon (whom Daniel refers to as the ram or leopard or goat of goats),[2] reached Achilles' tomb, he said, 'Happy are you, young man, for you will have the benefit of a great spokesman of your achievement,'[3] referring of course to Homer. But I have to describe the life of a man so outstanding that if Homer were alive, he would envy me my subject or prove unequal to it. For although the holy Epiphanius, bishop of Salamis in Cyprus, who spent a great deal of time with Hilarion, composed a eulogy of him in a short letter which many people have read, yet it is one thing to praise a dead man using the conventions of the genre, another to give an account of the dead man's personal virtues. That is why, in taking up the work begun by Epiphanius I do him a service rather than any harm and I disregard what the critics say of it, for those who earlier found fault with my life of Paul will now perhaps also find fault with my life of Hilarion. If they criticize Paul for his solitude, they will criticize Hilarion for his sociability, believing that because Paul always remained out of sight he did not exist and because Hilarion was seen by many he should be regarded as of no importance. Their ancestors, the Pharisees, did exactly the same in the past: they did not approve of John's fasting in the desert, nor of the Lord and Saviour eating and drinking among the crowds. But I shall

put my hand to my intended task and pass by the dogs of Scylla with my ears blocked.

Life of Hilarion

2 Hilarion was born in the village of Thabatha[4] which is situated about five miles south of Gaza, a city in Palestine. Since his parents were given to idol worship, he was, so to speak, a rose flowering among thorns. They sent him to Alexandria where he was entrusted to a teacher of grammar and where he gave evidence of great talent and character, so far as his age allowed. In a short time, he endeared himself to all and developed into a practised speaker, and what was even more impressive than this was the fact that because of his faith in the Lord Jesus he took no pleasure in the madness of the circus or in the blood of the arena or in the excesses of the theatre: instead, all his desire lay in the communion of the Church.

3 When he came to hear of the famous name of Antony which was talked about by all the people of Egypt, he was fired with a desire to see him and so he set off for the desert. As soon as he saw him, he changed the garment he had been wearing and remained with Antony for about two months, studying the routine of his life and the austerity of his behaviour.[5] Hilarion was amazed by how frequently he prayed, how humble he was in welcoming the brothers, how severe he was in rebuke, how keen to encourage! No weakness ever caused him to break his rule of continence or give up his coarse diet. Later Hilarion could no longer put up with the crowds of people who came running to Antony on account of all kinds of illnesses or demonic attacks. Considering it unreasonable to have to endure in the desert the crowds of the cities and that he must rather begin as Antony had begun – for Antony, like a hero, was winning victories while he himself had not yet started on his military career – he returned to his home accompanied by a few monks. As his parents were now dead, he shared out their property between his brothers and the poor, keeping nothing at all for himself for he feared the example, or punishment, of Ananias and Sapphira, as narrated in the Acts of the Apostles.[6] He particularly

remembered the words of the Lord, who said, *Any one who fails to renounce everything that he has cannot be my disciple.*[7] At the time he was fifteen years old. And so, naked but armed with Christ, he went into the desert which lies to the left if you are travelling along the coast towards Egypt, seven miles from Majuma, the port of Gaza.[8] Although these were places full of bloodthirsty brigands and his neighbours and friends warned him of the risks involved, he despised death so as to escape death.

4 Everyone would have been amazed at his courage, they would have been amazed at his youth, were it not for the fact that in his heart there burned a flame and sparks of faith shone in his eyes. His cheeks were smooth, his body delicate and thin and unable to bear any hardship: it could be hurt by the slightest cold or heat. And so, dressed only in sackcloth and an overgarment of skins which the blessed Antony had given him as he set out, together with a rough peasant's cloak, he found pleasure in the vast and terrible desert between the sea and the marshland, eating only fifteen dried figs a day after sunset. As the area was notorious for brigands, he never used to stay in the same place. What was the devil to do? Where should he turn? He who had previously boasted, saying, *I will climb up to heaven and place my throne above the stars of the sky and I will make myself like the most High,*[9] saw himself conquered and trodden underfoot by a boy whose age would not yet allow him to sin.

5 So the devil tickled his senses and, as is his wont, kindled the flames of desire in Hilarion's adolescent body. The young disciple of Christ was forced to think about things which he knew nothing about and to watch things of which he had no experience filing past in his thoughts. Angry with himself he beat his chest with his fists as if he could drive out the thoughts by beating with his hands, saying, 'I will stop your kicking, you ass. I will feed you not on wheat but on chaff. I will make you weak with hunger and thirst; I will weigh you down with a heavy load. Through heat and cold I will strive to ensure that you think of food rather than of sexual gratification.' And so he would sustain his weakened existence by feeding it every three or four days with the juice of herbs and a few dried figs, praying frequently and singing psalms, and digging the soil with his hoe, so that the pain of

fasting might be increased by the pain of work. At the same time he would weave baskets out of reeds, imitating the rigorous existence of the Egyptian monks and the words of the Apostle, who said, *He who does not work will not eat.*[10] This way of life caused him to grow very thin: his body became so emaciated that it hardly clung to the bones.

6 One night he started to hear babies crying, sheep bleating, cattle lowing, women weeping, as well as lions roaring and the din of an army, in short, many different terrifying sounds. He was driven back by terror at this noise rather than by anything he could see. He realized that the demons were mocking him and so he fell down on his knees and made the sign of Christ's cross on his forehead. Armed in this way he fought more bravely as he lay there, but he half-wanted to see what he was terrified to hear and so he carefully looked around him in every direction. All of a sudden, in the moonlight, he saw a chariot with neighing horses rushing over him, but when he called upon Jesus, the earth immediately opened wide and the whole procession was swallowed up. Then he said, *He has thrown the horse and his rider into the sea,*[11] and *Some trust in chariots and some in horses, but we will be glorified in the name of our God.*[12]

7 Numerous were the temptations put before him and night and day the demons attacked him in every way: if I were to relate them all, I would exceed the limits of this book. Often naked women would appear to him as he lay resting, often the most splendid banquets would appear to him when he was hungry! Sometimes a howling wolf and a snarling fox leapt over him as he prayed, and when he sang the psalms a gladiatorial show appeared before him: one gladiator, mortally wounded, seemed to collapse at his feet and ask for burial!

8 At one time he was praying, his eyes fixed on the ground, and as often happens with human nature, his mind wandered from his prayer and he began to think about something else. Then a rider jumped on to his back, kicking Hilarion's sides and whipping his neck. 'Hey you,' he said, 'why are you falling asleep?' and cackling over him, he asked Hilarion whether he was growing tired and wanted some barley to eat.

9 From his sixteenth to his twentieth year he sheltered from the rain

and sun in the little hut he had woven together out of reed and sedge. Afterwards he built a small cell which remains to this day, five feet high, in other words, less than his own height but slightly wider than his body demanded, so that you might have taken it to be his tomb rather than his home.

10 He cut his hair once a year on Easter Day and right up to his death he would sleep on the bare earth or on a mat of rushes. He never washed the sackcloth once he had put it on, saying that it was unnecessary to expect cleanliness in a hair shirt. He never changed his tunic unless the previous one had been torn to shreds. He also knew the Holy Scriptures by heart and after his prayers and psalms he would recite the Scriptures as if God were there with him. It would take too long to give a detailed account of the successive stages of his ascent, so I will summarize them briefly, at the same time presenting his life to the reader's eyes, and then I shall return to the sequence of the narrative.

11 From the time he was twenty-one until he was twenty-seven, for three years he ate half a pint of lentils soaked in cold water and for the other three years he ate dry bread with salt and water. Then from the time he was twenty-seven until he was thirty, he lived on wild herbs and the uncooked roots of certain shrubs. From the time he was thirty-one until he was thirty-five his food consisted of six ounces of barley bread and lightly cooked vegetables without any oil. But when he sensed that his eyes were clouding over and that his whole body had contracted impetigo and some kind of rough skin disease, he added oil to the food I mentioned, and until the sixty-third year of his life he continued at this level of abstinence, tasting neither fruit nor beans nor anything else. Then when he realized that he was physically worn out and thought that death was close at hand, from the time he was sixty-four until his eightieth year he abstained from bread. He was fired by an incredible spiritual ardour, so that at the time of life when others are usually leading a more relaxed existence, it was as if he was entering the Lord's service as a novice. He would make himself a little soup out of flour and chopped vegetables, so that together the food and drink weighed no more than five ounces. Such was his dietary routine and never did he break his fast before

sunset, not even on holy days or when he was seriously ill. But now it is time to return to the proper sequence of events.

12 While he was still living in his little hut, at the age of eighteen, robbers came to find him in the night, either because they believed he had something which they could steal or because they felt offended that a boy, living on his own, was not afraid of their attacks. So from evening until sunrise they ran back and forth between the sea and the marshy ground but were unable to find the place where he was resting anywhere. Then when they discovered the boy in broad daylight, they said jokingly, 'What would you do, if robbers were to come to you?' To this he answered, 'A naked man does not fear robbers.' Then they said, 'But you might be killed!' 'I might,' he said, 'I might, and that is why I am not afraid of robbers, for I am ready to die.' Admiring his firmness and his faith, they then confessed how they had wandered about in the night and how their eyes had been blinded, promising that from now on they would lead reformed lives.

13 He had already spent twenty-two years in solitude and was known to everyone solely by his reputation, and was talked about throughout the cities of Palestine, when a woman from Eleutheropolis was the first to dare to intrude upon Hilarion, seeing that her husband despised her for being barren (for in fifteen years of marriage she had produced no child). To his great surprise she immediately threw herself at his feet. 'Forgive my boldness,' she said. 'Forgive the necessity that impels me. Why do you avert your eyes? Why do you try to ignore my requests? Do not look upon me as a woman but as a wretched creature. This sex gave birth to the Saviour. *Those who are well have no need of a doctor, but those who are ill.*'[13] At last Hilarion stood still and looked upon a woman for the first time for a long while. He asked her why she had come and why she was crying. When she told him, he raised his eyes to heaven and commanded her to have faith. As she departed, he followed her in tears and one year later he saw her with a son.

14 This marked the beginning of the miracles which became famous on account of another greater miracle. Aristaenete, the wife of Elpidius who was later made Praetorian Prefect, a woman well known among her own people and even more renowned among Christians,

was returning with her husband and three children from a visit to the blessed Antony. She stopped for a while at Gaza on account of her children's illness, for the three of them caught a semi-tertian fever there, either as a result of the noisome air or, as later became clear, to glorify Hilarion, the servant of God. The doctors despaired of them all and their mother was running back and forth between the bodies of her three children as if they were already dead. She lay sobbing, not knowing which of them to mourn first. When she heard that there was a monk living in the desert near by, she forgot the formalities expected of a grand lady – she could only think of the fact that she was a mother – and set out accompanied by her young maids and eunuchs: her husband was only with difficulty able to persuade her to make her journey seated on an ass. When she reached Hilarion, she said, 'I pray you, in the name of Jesus, our most merciful God; I implore you by His cross and His blood to give me back my three sons. May the name of our Lord and Saviour be glorified in the city of the Gentiles! May His servant enter Gaza and may the idol Marnas[14] fall to the ground.' When Hilarion refused, saying that he would never leave his cell and that he was not in the habit of going even into the village, let alone into the city, she threw herself on the ground, shouting over and over again, 'Hilarion, Christ's servant, give me back my children. May those whom Antony kept safe in Egypt be saved by you in Syria.' Everyone there was weeping and Hilarion himself wept as he refused her request. What more is there to say? The woman did not go away until he had promised that he would enter Gaza after dark. When he arrived there he made the sign of the cross on each child's bed and on their burning limbs, calling on the name of Jesus. What miraculous power! Sweat broke out on each of the boys as if from three fountains of water. In that same hour they took food and recognized their distraught mother, and thanking God, they kissed the holy man's hands. When this incident became known the news of it spread far and wide, people came flocking to him eagerly from Syria and Egypt, and as a result many came to believe in Christ and adopted the monastic way of life. For at that time there were as yet no monasteries in Palestine nor had anyone in Syria previously known a monk before St Hilarion. He was the founder and teacher of this way of life and this discipline in that province. The Lord Jesus had the elderly Antony in Egypt and in Palestine he had the youthful Hilarion.

15 Facidia was a small village near Rhinocorura,[15] a city of Egypt. A woman who had been blind for ten years was brought from this village to the blessed Hilarion and presented to him by the brothers (for there were now many monks with him). When she told him that she had spent all her money on doctors, he answered, 'If you had given to the poor what you have wasted on doctors, Jesus, the true doctor, would have cured you.' But when she cried out and begged for mercy, he spat on her eyes and at once the same miracle of healing occurred as when the Saviour did this.[16]

16 A charioteer from Gaza was struck in his chariot by a demon and was so completely paralysed that he was unable to move his hand or turn his neck. So he was brought to Hilarion on a bed, able only to move his tongue to entreat help. He was told that he could not be healed until he believed in Jesus and promised to give up his previous profession. He believed, he promised, he was healed, and the healing of his soul caused him more joy than that of his body.

17 There was also a young man of great strength called Marsitas, who came from the Jerusalem area. He was so proud of his own strength that he carried fifteen bushels of corn for a long time and over a long distance and considered it his highest achievement that he could beat the asses at carrying heavy loads. This man, possessed by a particularly wicked demon, did not leave chains or leg-irons or the bolts of doors intact; he had bitten off many people's noses and ears; he had broken some people's feet, other people's legs. Everyone was so terrified of him that he was dragged to the monastery like the most ferocious bull, loaded down with chains and ropes on all sides. When the brothers saw him they were very frightened (for he was extraordinarily large) and went to tell their father about him. Hilarion, seated as he was, ordered them to bring the man to him and to untie him. When he had been released, Hilarion said to him, 'Bow your head and come here.' The man trembled and bent his neck, not daring to look Hilarion in the face. All his fierceness had vanished and he now began to lick the feet of Hilarion as he sat there. When the demon which

possessed the young man had been cursed and tormented, on the seventh day it departed.

18 But I must also relate how Orion, a very wealthy man of the first rank from Aila, a city on the shores of the Red Sea, who was possessed by a legion of demons, was brought to Hilarion. His hands, neck, back and feet were weighted down with iron, and his wild eyes gave evidence of his ferocity and madness. As the holy man walked along with the brothers, giving an interpretation of some passage of Scripture, Orion broke free from the grasp of those who held him. Taking hold of Hilarion from behind he lifted him high in the air. Everyone started to scream for they were afraid he might break those limbs which had become so thin as a result of fasting. But the holy man smiled at them and said, 'Quiet! Let go of this wrestler of mine.' And then reaching back over his shoulders, he touched Orion's head, took hold of his hair and pulled him round in front of him. Next, holding both the man's hands tight, he trod on both his feet, muttering at the same time, 'Here is torture for you, you crowd of demons, here is torture for you.' When Orion screamed as his head touched the ground, his neck bent back, Hilarion said, 'O Lord Jesus, release this poor man, release this captive. As you have the power to overcome one, so you can overcome many.' I shall now tell you something very strange: from the mouth of this one man different voices were heard, sounding like the confused babble of a crowd. In this way Orion was cured and not long afterwards he came to the monastery with his wife and children, bringing numerous gifts as thanks. But the saint said to him, 'Have you not read what happened to Giezi[17] and to Simon?[18] Giezi accepted payment with the intention of selling the grace of the Holy Spirit, while Simon offered payment with the intention of buying it.' When Orion, in tears, said, 'Take them and give them to the poor,' Hilarion answered, 'You are better placed to distribute your own things for you walk through the cities and you know the poor. Why should I, who have abandoned what was mine, be keen to get hold of what belongs to someone else? Many people use the poor as a pretext for their greed; but compassion knows no cunning. No one spends his money better than the person who keeps nothing for himself.' Then he said to the unhappy man lying in the dust, 'Do not

be sad, my son. What I do for my own good, I do also for yours. For if I were to accept these things, I would offend God and the legion of demons would return to you.'

19 Who could pass over in silence what happened to a man from Majuma, the port of Gaza? While he was quarrying building stone on the sea-shore not far from Hilarion's monastery, he became totally paralysed. His workmates carried him to the saint and he was immediately cured and was able to return to his work. I ought to explain that the shore stretching from Palestine to Egypt, which is by nature soft, becomes rough because the sand hardens into rock and the gravel gradually solidifies, losing the feel of gravel though not the appearance.

20 There was also the case of Italicus, a Christian citizen of the same town, who kept horses to race in the Circus against those of one of the two magistrates of Gaza, a man who worshipped the idol Marnas. This custom has in fact continued in the Roman towns since the time of Romulus: in commemoration of the successful rape of the Sabine women, the charioteers race the seven laps round the circuit in honour of Consus, being the god of counsel.[19] Victory consists in exhausting the rival's horses. Since Italicus' rival had a magician who would use demonic spells to slow Italicus' horses down and make his own horses run faster on the track, Italicus went to the blessed Hilarion and begged him, not so much to harm his rival but rather to protect Italicus himself. The venerable old man considered it foolish to waste prayer on trivialities of this kind, so he smiled and said, 'Why do you not rather give the money you would get from the sale of the horses to the poor for the salvation of your soul?' The man answered that he was a public official and he did this not so much from choice but from compulsion: a Christian could not use magic arts but should seek help instead from a servant of Christ, especially against the people of Gaza who were enemies of God and who would revile the Church of Christ more than himself.[20] At the request of the brothers who were present, Hilarion ordered that the earthenware cup from which he usually drank should be filled with water and given to the man. Italicus took it and sprinkled the stable, the horses and their charioteers, as well as the chariot and the bars of the starting stalls. The people were terribly excited about what would happen, for the rival had

laughed at what Italicus had done and told everyone about it, while Italicus' supporters were jubilant, confident of victory. And so, when the starting signal is given, Italicus' horses fly forth while the other horses stand still, unable to move. The wheels grow hot beneath the chariot of Italicus' horses while the others can hardly see their backs as they fly past. The noise from the crowd becomes deafening – in fact even the pagans were shouting, 'Marnas has been beaten by Christ!' Then Italicus' furious opponents demanded that Hilarion, as the Christian magician, should be handed over for punishment. And so their decisive victory, at that race and at many later ones, was the cause of many believing in Christ.

21 A young man from the same port of Gaza was dying of love for a virgin of God who lived next door. Frequent touching, jokes, nods, whistles, and other things of this kind which usually lead to the loss of virginity, had brought him no success so he went all the way to Memphis:[21] he intended to confess his lovesick state and return to the virgin armed with magic devices. After a year spent learning from the priests of Aesculapius, not how to cure souls but how to destroy them, he came back confident of the violation he had already anticipated in his imagination. Beneath the threshold of the girl's house he buried some magic spells and strange figures engraved on sheets of bronze from Cyprus. At once the virgin started to rave, and casting off the veil from her head, she tore her hair, gnashed her teeth and called out the young man's name. The power of her love had turned to madness. So she was taken by her parents to Hilarion's monastery and handed over to the old man. At once the demon began to scream and shout out, 'I was the victim of violence! I was abducted against my will! How expertly I used to delude the people of Memphis with my dreams! What tortures, what torments I suffer! You force me to depart but I am tied up, imprisoned beneath the threshold. I cannot depart unless the young man who is holding me lets me go.' Then the old man said, 'Your strength must indeed be great, if you are held down by a string and a metal plate! Tell me, how did you dare to enter a girl dedicated to God?' 'I wanted to protect her virginity.' 'You wanted to protect it, you who betray chastity? Why did you not rather enter the one who sent you?' 'Why should I enter someone

who was possessed by my colleague, the demon of passion?' The saint refused to give the order to look for the young man or the magic charms until he had exorcized the virgin for he did not want it to look as if the demon had departed once it was released from the spells or that he himself had taken the demon's words seriously. For he firmly declared that demons are deceitful and cunning at pretence. Instead, once he had cured the virgin he scolded her, asking why she had behaved in such a way as to allow the demon to enter her.

22 It was not only through Palestine and the neighbouring cities of Egypt and Syria that Hilarion's fame spread, but also throughout the distant provinces. For Constantius, one of the emperor's assistants, whose red hair and pale skin made it obvious which province he came from (for his people, who are powerful even though they do not extend over a wide area, live between the Saxons and the Alemanni, in an area known to historians as Germany and now known as France), had for a long time – in fact from his infancy – been possessed by a demon which at night drove him to scream, to groan and gnash his teeth. He secretly applied to the emperor for a travel permit, openly telling him his reasons. Having also been given a letter for the governor of Palestine, he travelled to Gaza with great honour and a large retinue. When he asked the local authorities where Hilarion lived, the people of Gaza were much afraid: thinking that he had been sent by the emperor, they led him to the monastery, so that they might prove their respect for such a distinguished person and in the hope that if any of the wrongs they had done Hilarion in the past had offended him, their offence might be erased by their present dutifulness. At the time the old man was walking along the soft sands, humming to himself some passage or other from the psalms. Seeing a great crowd coming towards him, he stopped. Responding to all their greetings, he blessed them with a movement of his hand. One hour later he asked the others to go away but the visitor to stay, along with his servants and the officials accompanying him, for he understood from the man's eyes and his face the reason why he had come. On being questioned by the servant of God the man at once stood on tiptoe, so that his feet hardly touched the ground; roaring loudly he answered in the Syriac language in which he had been questioned. Coming

from the mouth of a barbarian who knew only French and Latin you would have heard words of perfect Syriac: neither the accent nor the breathing nor any idiom of the speech of Palestine was missing. Then the demon confessed by what means it had entered into the man. And so that the man's interpreters, who knew only Greek and Latin, might understand, Hilarion also questioned it in Greek. When the demon gave the same answer using the same words, giving as his excuse the many occasions on which magic spells had been laid upon him and the power of magic devices, Hilarion said, 'I do not care how you entered but I order you to depart in the name of our Lord Jesus Christ.' As soon as the man had been cured, with the naïvety typical of a peasant he offered Hilarion ten pounds of gold but he was given barley bread by Hilarion and was told that those who live on this kind of bread consider gold to be worth no more than mud.

23 It is not enough to mention only humans: every day brute animals that had gone wild were also brought to him. One of these was a Bactrian camel of enormous size which had already trampled many people to death. Restrained by very thick ropes, it was brought to Hilarion by thirty or more men making a great noise. Its eyes were bloodshot, it foamed at the mouth, its rolling tongue was swollen, and above every other source of terror there resounded its loud roar. The old man ordered it to be untied. At once those who had brought the animal and those who were with the old man all ran away, without exception. Hilarion went up to it by himself and said in Syriac, 'You do not frighten me, devil, with your huge body. You are exactly the same in a fox as in a camel.' While he was speaking he stood with outstretched hand. The beast came up to him, raging wildly and looking as if it was going to eat him, but immediately it knelt down, bending its head right to the ground to the amazement of all those present, suddenly displaying as much gentleness as it had previously shown ferocity. But the old man explained to them that in order to harm people the devil also enters into animals; he is inflamed with such great hatred of men that he is very keen to destroy not only them, but also their possessions. As an example of this he gave the fact that before the devil was allowed to tempt the blessed Job, he destroyed all Job's property. Hilarion said that no one ought to be

disturbed by the fact that at the Lord's command, two thousand pigs were destroyed by demons,[22] since those who had seen them would otherwise have been unable to believe that such a great number of demons had departed from one man if a large number of pigs had not at the same time fallen headlong to their deaths, proving that they were driven by many demons.

24 I would run out of time if I were to relate all the miracles Hilarion performed. For the Lord raised him to such great glory that even blessed Antony, hearing of his way of life, wrote to him and received his letters gladly. And if ever exhausted visitors came to Antony from the regions of Syria, he would say to them, 'Why did you want to put yourselves to the trouble of such a long journey when you have my son Hilarion near you?' As a result, then, of Hilarion's example, there sprang up countless monasteries throughout the whole of Palestine and all the monks flocked to him. When he noticed this, he praised the Lord's grace and encouraged each of them in their spiritual progress, telling them that the attractions of this world pass away, and that the true life is that which is earned by means of sufferings in the present life.

25 Wishing, however, to set them an example both of humility and of service, he used to make a tour of the monks' cells on certain appointed days before the grape harvest. When the brothers learned of this, they would all come together to meet him, and accompanied by this distinguished leader of theirs they would go from one monastery to another, carrying their own provisions because sometimes up to two thousand men were gathered together. But as time passed, each estate was glad to offer food to the neighbouring monks in order to welcome the holy men. An indication of Hilarion's determination not to neglect any brother, however humble, however poor, is provided by the following episode. On his way to the desert of Cades to visit one of his disciples, he arrived at Elusa together with a great number of monks. It happened to be the day on which the whole population of that town had gathered in the temple of Venus for the annual celebrations. (They worshipped her on account of Lucifer, to whose cult the Saracen people are devoted. But in fact the town itself is to a large extent semi-barbarous on account of its situation.) When

they heard that the holy man Hilarion was passing through (for he had often cured many Saracens possessed by demons), crowds of them went out to meet him together with their wives and children. They bowed their heads and shouted, '*Barech*,' a Syriac word meaning 'bless'. Hilarion received them in a friendly and humble manner, and entreated them to worship God rather than stones. At the same time he wept profusely, looking up to heaven and promising that if they believed in Christ, he would come and visit them often. How wonderful is the Lord's grace! They would not allow him to depart until he had marked out the foundations of the future church and until their priest, garlanded[23] as he was, had been marked by the sign of Christ.

26 Another year, when he was about to set off to visit the monasteries, he was making a list of those with whom he would stay and those whom he should visit in passing. The monks were aware that one of the brothers was rather stingy and they wished to cure him of this fault of his, so they asked Hilarion to go and stay with him. Hilarion said, 'Why do you wish to cause yourselves hardship and your brother annoyance?' When the stingy brother heard this, he blushed with shame, and with everyone's support, he managed, not without difficulty, to persuade the unwilling Hilarion to put his cell, too, on the list of stopping places. When they came to him ten days later, guards had been posted in the vineyard through which the monks were to pass to frighten away anyone who came close, by throwing stones and lumps of earth or by whirling their slings. So they all set off in the morning without eating any grapes, while the old man smiled and pretended not to know what had happened.

27 They were then welcomed by another monk whose name was Sabas (for it is right that we should mention the name of the generous monk, but not the name of the mean one). As it was Sunday, he invited them all into the vineyard so that before dinner-time they should relieve the exhaustion caused by the journey by eating some grapes. But the holy man said, 'Cursed is he who seeks the nourishment of the body before that of the spirit. Let us pray, let us sing psalms, let us perform our duty to the Lord and then we will hasten to the vineyard.' When the divine service was over, Hilarion, standing on higher ground, blessed the vineyard and sent his flock out to feed.

Those eating numbered no fewer than three thousand but although the vineyard had been estimated to contain one hundred flagons before they touched it, twenty days later it produced three hundred. Moreover, the stingy brother gathered a much smaller harvest than usual and even what he did obtain turned to vinegar. However, his distress came too late. The old man had previously predicted this to many brothers. He particularly detested those monks whose lack of faith made them hoard things for future use and who were concerned with wealth or clothing or any of those things which pass away with this world.

28 Finally, because Hilarion found that one of the brothers who lived about five miles away from him was excessively careful and anxious in tending his little garden and had saved a little money, he had driven him from his sight. The brother wanted to be reconciled with the old man and so he came often to the brothers, especially to Hesychius, of whom Hilarion was very fond. One day, then, he brought with him a basket of green peas, just as they were in their pods. Hesychius placed the basket on the table in the evening, but the old man cried out, saying that he could not bear the smell, and asked where it came from. When Hesychius answered that a brother had brought the monks the first fruits of his little garden, Hilarion said, 'Do you not notice this foul smell and the stink of greed in these peas? Throw them to the cattle, throw them to the brute animals, and see whether they will eat them.' When Hesychius put them in the manger as he had been told, the cattle were terrified and mooed more loudly than usual; they broke the ropes tethering them and stampeded off in all directions. For the old man had a spiritual gift which enabled him, from the smell of bodies or clothes or other things anyone had touched, to recognize which demon or vice was holding that person in its grip.

29 In the sixty-third year of his life, when he observed how large the monastery had grown and how many monks were living with him, as well as the crowds of people who brought to him those suffering from many different illnesses and possessed by unclean spirits, with the result that the whole desert around him was filled with all kinds of people, he would weep every day, remembering his former way of life with a feeling of unbelievable nostalgia. When the brothers

asked him why he was feeling so dejected, he said, 'I have returned once more to the world and received my reward in this life. Look how the people of Palestine and the neighbouring province consider me to be of some importance, and under the pretext of a monastery for the direction of the brothers, I possess worthless stuff.' But he was kept there by the brothers, especially by Hesychius who was devoted to the old man, venerating and loving him in an extraordinary way. When he had lived for two years in this state of dejection, that woman Aristaenete (whom I mentioned earlier – the wife of the Prefect at that time, though without any of the Prefect's ostentation) came to Hilarion, intending to go on to visit Antony, too. Hilarion, in tears, said to her, 'I would come too, if only I were not held prisoner in this monastery and if there were any point in going. But today it is two days since the whole world was bereaved of such a father.' She believed what he said and decided not to continue her journey. A few days later a messenger arrived bringing news of Antony's death.

30 Let others marvel at the miracles he performed; let them marvel at his incredible abstinence, his knowledge and his humility. Nothing in him astounds me so much as his ability to despise acclaim and honour. Bishops and priests, flocks of clerics and monks used to throng to him, as did large numbers of Christian women (a great temptation), as well as crowds of common people from every direction, from cities and from the countryside. Even powerful men and high officials came to receive bread and oil blessed by him. But Hilarion thought of nothing except solitude, so much so that one day he decided to go away. Having got hold of an ass (for he was so emaciated by fasting that he could hardly walk), he tried to set off quickly on his journey. However, when word got round it was as if some disaster had occurred and all business had been shut down: more than ten thousand people of various ages, both men and women, gathered to stop him leaving. But Hilarion was unmoved by their entreaties and striking the sand with his stick, he said, 'I will not make our Lord a liar. I cannot see the churches overturned, the altars of Christ trampled underfoot, the blood of my sons.' Everyone there understood that some secret had been revealed to him which he did not want to make known, but they still kept a watch on him to prevent him setting off. He therefore

resolved – and he called them all in a loud voice to witness – that he would not accept any food or drink until they let him go. After seven days of fasting he was at last released. Saying farewell to large numbers of people, he arrived at Betilium accompanied by a huge crowd. There he persuaded the crowds to return, choosing forty of the hermits who had supplies for the journey and who could travel while fasting. On the fifth day he reached Pelusium[24] and after he had visited the brothers in the neighbouring desert and those who lived in a place called Lychnios, he continued for a further three days until he arrived at the fort of Theubanum to visit Dracontius, bishop and confessor, who was living in exile there. Dracontius derived unbelievable consolation from the presence of such a distinguished man. Three days later after a difficult journey Hilarion reached Babylon to visit the bishop Philo, who was also a confessor. (For the Emperor Constantius, a supporter of the Arian heresy, had deported both of them to that area.) Departing from there after three days Hilarion came to the town of Aphroditon where he met the deacon Baisanes (who, because of the scarcity of water in the desert, used to hire out camels to take those who were on their way to visit Antony). There Hilarion revealed to the brothers that the anniversary of Antony's death was at hand and that he ought, in Antony's honour, to mark it by keeping watch for a night in the place where Antony had died. And so after travelling for three days through the vast and terrifying desert, they came at last to a very high mountain and found there two monks, Isaac and Pelusianus, Isaac having been Antony's interpreter.

31 Since the opportunity presents itself and we have reached this point, it seems right to give a brief description of the place where the great Antony lived. There is a tall and rocky mountain, about a mile in circumference, that produces water at its foot, some of which is absorbed by the sand while some flows down to the lower area, gradually forming a stream. Above this stream grow innumerable palm trees which make the place very pleasant and comfortable. Here you might have seen the old man Hilarion rushing from one place to another with the blessed Antony's disciples. 'Here,' they said, 'he used to sing psalms; here he used to pray. Here he would work and here he would rest when he was tired. He planted these vines and

bushes himself. This little garden he made with his own hands. He worked very hard to construct this pond to irrigate his garden. This is the hoe he used for many years to dig the ground.' Hilarion lay on Antony's bed and kissed it as if it were still warm. In area Antony's cell was just large enough for a sleeping man to stretch out in. Moreover, when they climbed to the top of the mountain, going with great difficulty along a spiral path, they were shown two cells of the same size in which Antony used to stay when he wished to escape the crowds of visitors and the company of his disciples. These cells were in fact hewn into the living rock, with only the doors added. Afterwards they came to a little garden: 'You see this orchard,' said Isaac, 'planted with fruit trees and green vegetables. About three years ago it was devastated by a herd of wild asses. Antony commanded one of the asses, the leader of the herd, to stand still while he beat its sides with his stick. "Why are you eating what you did not sow?" he demanded. From then on the animals never touched the fruit trees or the vegetables, only the water which they often used to come and drink.'[25] Then the old man Hilarion asked them to show him the site of Antony's tomb. As they led him away on his own, it is not known whether they showed it to him or not. They say that the reason why it was kept secret in accordance with Antony's order was to prevent Pergamius, the wealthiest man in those parts, from moving the saint's body to his estate and building a martyr's shrine for it.[26]

32 Then Hilarion returned to Aphroditon and lived in the neighbour-ing desert, retaining only two brothers with him. He practised such a degree of abstinence and silence that according to him only then did he really begin to serve Christ. The skies had not opened for three years, causing those regions to become parched: people said that even the elements were mourning the death of Antony. The inhabitants of that place also got to hear of Hilarion's reputation: men and women, pale-faced and with bodies emaciated with hunger, earnestly entreated this servant of Christ, as the blessed Antony's successor, to bring rain. When he saw them he was terribly upset. Raising his eyes to heaven and lifting both hands on high, he instantly obtained what they desired. However, as soon as it had been watered by the rains, that parched and sandy region unexpectedly produced such an enormous number

of serpents and poisonous animals that if the many people who were bitten had not rushed to Hilarion they would have died immediately. Once all the farmers and shepherds had applied to their wounds the oil blessed by Hilarion, they recovered completely.

33 Seeing that there, too, he was accorded extraordinary honour, he went to Alexandria, intending from there to cross the desert to the more remote Oasis.[27] And because he had never stayed in the cities since he had begun to be a hermit, he stayed with some monks whom he knew well in Bruchium, outside Alexandria. They welcomed the old man with great joy, but as night drew near they suddenly heard his disciples saddling the ass and Hilarion preparing to depart. So they threw themselves at his feet and begged him not to do this: prostrated before the threshold they protested that they would sooner die than lose such an important guest. He answered them, 'I am in a hurry to leave because I do not want to cause you any trouble. You will no doubt learn from later events that my sudden departure was not without good cause.' The next day people from Gaza and the Prefect's lictors entered the monastery (for they knew that Hilarion had arrived there the previous day). When they were unable to find him they said to each other, 'Surely what we heard must be true? He is a magician and has knowledge of the future.' For after Hilarion's departure from Palestine and the destruction of his monastery, when Julian had succeeded as emperor, the city of Gaza had sent a petition to the emperor asking that both Hilarion and Hesychius be put to death: consequently a decree had gone out throughout the world that the two of them were wanted.

34 Departing, then, from Bruchium Hilarion crossed the pathless desert and entered the Oasis where he spent about a year. But because his fame had reached this far, too, so that now he could no longer find a hiding place anywhere in the east, where many people knew of him both by hearsay and in person, he thought of sailing to some remote islands, so that he whom the land had made famous might at any rate be concealed by the sea. At about this time Hadrian, a disciple of his, arrived from Palestine with the news that Julian had been killed and that the new emperor, Jovian,[28] was a Christian: Hilarion ought to return to the remains of his monastery. When Hilarion heard this,

he rejected the idea. Instead he hired a camel, crossed the great desert and reached the city of Paretonium, a city on the coast of Libya. There the unfortunate Hadrian, wishing to return to Palestine because he did not want to lose the renown which had hitherto been associated with his master's name, reproached him strongly. At last, after secretly packing up the things the brothers had sent Hilarion, Hadrian set off without Hilarion's knowledge. In this connection, as there is no other opportunity to tell it, I would only mention this (so as to inspire fear in those who fail to respect their masters): shortly afterwards this man caught leprosy and rotted away.

35 The old man, accompanied by a man from Gaza, boarded a ship bound for Sicily. He intended to pay the fare by selling a codex of the Gospels which he had written in his youth with his own hand. More or less half-way across the Adriatic, the son of the ship's master was seized by a demon. He began to cry out, saying, 'Hilarion, servant of God, why do you not allow us to be safe on the sea? Leave me be until I reach land, for I do not want to be cast out here and fall headlong into the deep.' To which Hilarion replied, 'Stay, if my God lets you stay. But if he casts you out, why should you blame me, I who am a sinful man and a beggar?' He said this so that the sailors and the traders who were on the ship should not betray him when they reached land. Shortly afterwards the boy was exorcized when the father and the others present promised that they would not tell anyone Hilarion's name.

36 As they approached Pachynus, a promontory in Sicily, Hilarion offered the ship's master his copy of the Gospels to pay for his passage and that of the man from Gaza. But he did not want to accept it, especially when he saw that they possessed nothing apart from that codex and the clothes they were wearing, and in the end he swore that he would not take it. But the old man, passionately confident in the consciousness of his poverty, was all the happier for not having any worldly possessions and because he was considered a beggar by the inhabitants of that area.

37 Calculating, then, that traders coming from the east might reveal his identity, he fled inland, some twenty miles from the sea; and there, at a deserted farm, he would tie up bundles of wood each day and

place them on his disciple's back. He sold them in the neighbouring village and bought a little bread as sustenance for them both and for those who happened to visit them. But in accordance with the words of the Bible, *A city set on a hill cannot be hidden*,[29] it happened that when a certain guard who was possessed by a demon was in Saint Peter's Basilica[30] in Rome, the unclean spirit within him cried out, 'A few days ago Hilarion, the servant of Christ, arrived in Sicily but no one has recognized him and he thinks that he can remain hidden. I shall go and betray him.' The man immediately boarded a ship in the harbour together with his young servants and sailed to Pachynus. The demon led the way and as soon as the man fell to the ground in front of the old man's hut, he was immediately cured. This marked the beginning of Hilarion's miracles in Sicily and as a result huge crowds of the sick but also of devout people were drawn to him; so much so that one of the most high-ranking men, suffering from dropsy, was cured on the very day that he came to Hilarion. When the man later offered Hilarion numerous gifts, he heard the words used by the Saviour to his disciples, *You have freely received, freely give*.[31]

38 While these things were happening in Sicily, Hilarion's disciple Hesychius was looking all over the world for the old man, combing the coastal areas and penetrating into the deserts. He was confident of one thing only, namely that wherever Hilarion might be, he would not be able to remain hidden for long. Three years had now passed when at Methone he heard from a certain Jew who sold cheap trinkets to the people that a Christian prophet had appeared in Sicily, performing so many miracles and signs that he was thought to be one of the holy men of old. Hesychius questioned him about his clothes, his gait and his language and particularly about his age, but he was unable to find out anything, for his informant asserted that he only knew of the man by hearsay. Hesychius then set sail on the Adriatic and reached Pachynus after a prosperous voyage. He asked for news of the old man in a little village on the curved shore and as everyone gave him the same answer, he learned where Hilarion was and what he was doing. They were particularly amazed by the fact that after such impressive signs and miracles Hilarion had not accepted even a crumb of bread from anyone in that area. To cut a long story short,

the holy man Hesychius threw himself down at his master's feet and watered his feet with tears. Finally Hilarion raised him up and after two or three days of conversation, Hesychius was told by the man from Gaza that the old man was no longer able to live in those regions but wished to move to some barbarian peoples where his name and reputation would be unknown.

39 And so Hesychius took him to Epidaurus,[32] a town in Dalmatia, where he stayed for a few days on a nearby country estate, but even there he was unable to remain hidden. For an extraordinarily large serpent (of the kind called a '*boa*' in the local language, because they are so large that they often swallow whole cattle),[33] was devastating the whole province far and wide, devouring not only cattle and flocks but also farmers and shepherds which it drew to itself with its powerful breath. Hilarion gave orders that a pyre should be built for it and after sending up a prayer to Christ, he called the serpent forth and commanded it to climb the pile of wood. He then set fire to the pyre. Then, while all the people watched, he burned the huge beast to ashes. After this he was deeply troubled as to what he should do and where he should turn and so he planned another escape; and ranging over distant countries in his thoughts, he grieved that although his tongue was silent about himself, his miracles would not keep quiet.

40 At that time, as a result of an earthquake that shook the whole world after the death of Julian, the seas burst their bounds. Ships were dumped on steep mountainsides and hung there, as if God was threatening a second flood or as if everything was reverting to ancient chaos. When the people of Epidaurus saw this, namely the churning waters and the huge masses of swirling waters dashing on to the shores, they feared that their town would be completely overwhelmed (as they had already seen happen elsewhere). They therefore went to see the old man, and placed him on the shore as if they were preparing for battle. As soon as he made the sign of the cross three times in the sand and held his hands up against the sea, amazing as it is to relate, the sea that had swelled up to an enormous height stopped in front of him; seething for a long time and apparently furious at this obstruction, it gradually subsided. To this day the people of Epidaurus and the neighbouring region talk of this and mothers tell their children

about it so that the memory might be handed down to posterity. That which was said to the apostles, *If you have faith, you will say to this mountain, move into the sea, and it will happen*,[34] can be fulfilled literally, if anyone has such faith as the Lord ordered the apostles to have. For what difference does it make whether the mountain moves down into the sea or the huge mountains of the waves that are fluid elsewhere suddenly grow solid and turn to rock in front of the old man's feet?

41 The whole city was astounded and news of this extraordinary miracle spread as far as Salona. When the old man learned of this, he stole away by night in a little boat; after two days he found a cargo ship and went on to reach Cyprus. Between Malea and Cythera the pirates who had abandoned their fleet (propelled not by sails but by oars) on the shore, attacked them in two large vessels. As the waves beat them on all sides, all the oarsmen who were on the ship were terrified: they wept and rushed about and prepared the poles. As if it were not sufficient for one person to report it, they all crowded round to give the old man the news that pirates were coming. Hilarion looked at the pirates in the distance, smiled, and turning to the disciples, said, 'You of little faith, why are you afraid?[35] I suppose these are more numerous than Pharaoh's army? And yet they were all drowned by the will of God.' Even as he spoke the enemy ships were drawing very close, their prows foaming, now only a stone's throw away. So Hilarion went and stood in the prow of the ship, and holding his hand up to them as they approached, he said, 'No need to come any further.' It is hard to believe but at once the ships withdrew and though the oars impelled them in the opposite direction, their attack moved back. The pirates, still unwilling to retreat, were amazed. Using all their physical strength they tried to reach the ship but were driven back to the shore much faster than they had come.

42 I shall leave out the rest in case I should seem to be filling the volume with miracles. I will only say this, that as he sailed through the Cyclades before a favourable wind, Hilarion heard on every side the voices of unclean spirits shouting from the cities and villages and running down to the shore. After entering Paphos, the city in Cyprus made famous by the poets' songs, which has on several occasions been destroyed by earthquakes and whose ruins alone now provide evidence

of what it once was, he lived in obscurity two miles outside the city, relieved that he could live in peace for a few days. However, before twenty days had passed, all those throughout the whole island who were possessed by unclean spirits began to cry out that Hilarion, the servant of Christ, had arrived and that they must hurry to him. This was what Salamis, Curium, Lapetha[36] and the other cities proclaimed, while many declared that they knew Hilarion and that he was truly the servant of God but that they did not know where he was. Within thirty days or not much more, two hundred people, men as well as women, came flocking to him. When he saw them he was upset that they would not leave him in peace, and keen to get his own back in some way, he lashed them so forcefully with his prayers that some of them were cured immediately, others after two or three days and certainly all of them within one week.

43 He stayed there, then, for two years, always planning how he might escape. During this time he sent Hesychius to Palestine to convey his greetings to the brothers and to visit the ashes of his monastery, telling him to return in the spring. Hilarion wanted to sail to Egypt once more, to that area called Bucolia,[37] because there were no Christians there but only a barbarian and savage tribe, but when Hesychius returned he persuaded Hilarion instead to climb to a more remote area on the island of Cyprus itself. After a long search Hesychius found a place twelve miles from the sea and led Hilarion into the remote and harsh mountains to a place which could hardly be reached even on hands and knees. On entering, Hilarion saw before him a remote and terrifying place. For although it was surrounded on all sides by trees and there was also water flowing down from the brow of the hill, a most delightful garden and many fruit trees (the fruit of which he never picked for his food), yet there were also near-by the ruins of a very ancient temple from which the sound of an enormous number of demons (as he himself related and his disciples still testify) could be heard night and day. You might have imagined that there was an army there! It pleased Hilarion greatly that he would have his adversaries near by, and so he remained there for five years.[38] He was comforted by the fact that Hesychius often came to visit him during this time, at what was now the final period of his life, because

no one – or only the occasional person – was able – or dared – to climb up to see him, owing to the fact that the place was in such a difficult and rugged location and on account of the large number of ghosts there (as rumour had it). But one day as he was leaving his garden Hilarion saw a man who was totally paralysed lying in front of his door. He asked Hesychius who this man was and how he had been carried there. The man replied that he was the agent of the estate to which the garden where they were belonged. Hilarion wept and held out his hand to the man lying there. 'In the name of our Lord Jesus Christ,' he said, 'I say to you, get up and walk.' The speed of the miracle was astounding: the words were still on the speaker's lips when the man's limbs had grown strong enough for him to get up and stand. As soon as people heard about this, the needs of many other people overcame even the problems of the place's situation and the fact that there was no path up to it, while all those in the surrounding villages were concerned with nothing so much as keeping watch to prevent Hilarion somehow slipping away. For a rumour concerning him had spread, to the effect that he was unable to stay in the same place for long. He did this not from a lack of stability or some kind of childish restlessness but because he wanted to avoid public acclaim and importunate requests. For he always longed for silence and a life in obscurity.

44 In the eightieth year of his life, then, while Hesychius was absent, Hilarion wrote him a short letter in his own hand, as a kind of will, leaving all his wealth to him (that is, his copy of the Gospels and the sackcloth tunic, hood and cloak), for his servant had died a few days earlier. Then there came from Paphos many devout men to visit the sick man, particularly because they had heard that he had stated that he was now about to pass to the Lord and that he would be freed from the shackles of the body. There came also a holy woman called Constantia whose daughter and son-in-law Hilarion had saved from death by anointing them with oil. Hilarion made them all swear that they would not preserve his body after his death even for a minute, but that they should immediately cover him with earth in the little garden there, dressed just as he was in his haircloth tunic and hood, with his rough cloak.

45 By now there was but little heat in his breast and there seemed nothing left in him of a living man apart from his mind, and yet he spoke with his eyes wide open, 'Depart, my soul, depart. What are you afraid of? Why do you hesitate? You have served Christ for nearly seventy years and do you now fear death?' With these words he breathed his last. He was buried in the ground at once, so that the news of his burial reached the city before news of his death.

46 As soon as the holy man Hesychius heard of this, he travelled to Cyprus. Pretending that he wanted to live in Hilarion's little garden (for he did not want the inhabitants to be suspicious and keep watch over him), he managed after about ten months, at great risk to his life, to steal Hilarion's body. Bringing it to Majuma, he buried it in the old monastery, after whole troops of monks and townspeople had accompanied the funeral procession. Hilarion's tunic, hood and cloak were undamaged while his whole body remained perfect, as if he were still alive, giving off such a fragrance that you would think it had been anointed with perfumed oils.[39]

47 I feel it would be wrong, right at the end of this book, not to mention the devotion of that most holy woman, Constantia. On receiving the news that Hilarion's dear body was now in Palestine, she died there and then, proving even by her death the genuine affection she had for the servant of God. For she had been in the habit of spending the nights awake at his tomb and conversing with him as if he were really there to help her in her prayers. To this very day you will find extraordinary rivalry between the people of Palestine and those of Cyprus, the former arguing that they possess Hilarion's spirit, the latter his body. And yet in both places great miracles occur each day, though more so in the garden on Cyprus, perhaps because he loved that place more.

Life of Malchus by Jerome

The Life of Malchus *was written during Jerome's early years at Bethlehem: as Evagrius is mentioned as bishop of Antioch in the preface to the work, it cannot have been composed before 389. It is likely that it was written shortly before the* Life of Hilarion. *The preface presents a characteristically belligerent Jerome, still determined to fight for the cause of Christian asceticism and the superiority of the life of chastity. It was not long after writing the* Life of Malchus *that Jerome became deeply embroiled in controversy over this issue when he challenged the views on virginity and marriage held by Jovinian: it was a controversy which was to lead him to write his most famous work of polemic and abuse, the work* Against Jovinian.[1] *But already in the* Life of Malchus *his overwhelming attachment to the concept of chastity is evident. The work, though couched in terms of a colourful and exciting account of one individual's experiences in the desert, is less of a biography than an essay on the ideal of chastity.[2] Neither can it really be termed hagiography: the account is given by Malchus himself in the first person, no mention is made of any cult surrounding him, and the only incident which might be regarded as miraculous is the episode where the lion kills Malchus' master and fellow slave but does not seek to harm Malchus or his female companion in their flight from slavery.*

The preface also informs us that Jerome was, at the time of writing, planning a major work, a history of the Christian Church with a clearly polemical bias. He hoped to describe the beginnings of the Church and its growth through times of persecution and martyrdom, but also how it had declined in virtue as it increased in wealth and power. Presumably he was here thinking of the way the Church had developed in the course of the fourth century, becoming open to charges of laxity and compromise with the secular world: compromise of this kind was what drove so many into the arms of asceticism at this time.

The Life of Malchus, *like the* Life of Hilarion, *is full of interesting and vivid details, with occasional references to public figures adding authenticity to the account. Malchus' story of his adventures provides us with incidental information about monastic life in Syria in the early fourth century, about travel conditions in the area, and about the customs of the nomad population. Jerome's prime concern may have been to produce a work of propaganda for the life of chastity, but in doing so he has produced a short masterpiece of the narrative art.*

1 Those who intend to fight a naval battle first turn the rudder in the calm waters of the harbour, pull at the oars and prepare the grappling irons and hooks. They accustom the soldiers, ranged along the decks, to keep their balance even when their feet slip and the footing is precarious, so that when it comes to the real battle they will not fear what they have learned in the mock battle. In the same way I who have long been silent (for he who finds my speech painful has forced me to remain quiet), desire first to practise on a minor work and to rub away, so to speak, any rust from my tongue, so that I might become capable of undertaking a more extensive account. For if the Lord should grant me life and if my critics should stop persecuting me now that I am a fugitive and a prisoner, I have decided to write an account of the Church of Christ from the coming of the Saviour down to our time, in other words, from the apostles down to the dregs of our own period, showing by what means and through what agents the Church was born, and how it grew up under the persecutions and was crowned by the martyrs, and how, under the Christian emperors, it became more powerful and wealthy but less rich in virtues. But I shall deal with these matters elsewhere; for the moment, let us deal with the matter in hand.

2 Maronia is a tiny village about thirty miles east of the city of Antioch in Syria. While I was living in Syria as a young man, this village, after having a number of landlords or owners, came into the possession of my close friend bishop Evagrius[1] whom I mention at this point to show where I got my information from. There lived in that village an old man called Malchus, a name which means 'king'. He was a Syrian by birth and language, a true native of that place. There was

also an old woman living with him as his companion, so decrepit that she seemed close to death. Both of them were so devout and wore away the threshold of the church so assiduously that you might have taken them to be Zacharias and Elisabeth from the Gospel,[2] except that John was not with them. When, out of curiosity, I asked the neighbours about them – what was it that bound them together, was it marriage, family ties or the bond of the spirit? – they all with one accord answered that they were holy people, pleasing to God, and they told me some extraordinary things about them. Drawn by my desire to find out more, I went up to the man and inquired of him with great interest whether these things were true. This is what he told me:

3 'My son,' he said, 'I was a tenant farmer on a small piece of land at Nisibis,[3] and my parents' only child. When they put pressure on me to marry because I was the only scion of their stock and their sole heir, I replied that I would rather be a monk. How my father threatened me and with what wheedling words my mother tried to make me betray my chastity, you may judge from this fact alone, that I ran away from my home and my parents. As I could not go east because of the proximity of Persia and the Roman military presence, I turned my steps westwards, taking with me some few provisions which might just keep me from destitution. What more is there to say? At last I came to the desert of Chalcis which lies between Immae and Beroea,[4] a little to the south. There I found some monks and I attached myself to them as their disciple, earning my living by manual work and restraining the lustfulness of my flesh by fasting.

'After many years I conceived a desire to return to my country and to console my mother in her widowhood while she still lived (for I had already heard that my father had died). I then planned to sell my small property and to donate part of the proceeds to the poor, to use another part to establish a monastery and the rest (why do I blush to confess my lack of faith?) I intended to keep for my own expenses. My abbot began to protest that it was the temptation of the devil and that under the pretext of a virtuous intention were concealed the secret attacks of the old enemy: in other words, the dog was returning to its vomit.[5] "Many monks," he said, "are deceived in this way for the devil never shows himself openly." He set before me several examples from the Scriptures, including the one where in the beginning the devil tricked Adam and Eve through the hope of divinity. When the abbot failed to persuade me, he fell on his knees and begged me not to desert them, not to destroy myself and not to look back once I had my hand on the plough.[6] Unfortunately for me, I won a most miserable victory over my mentor, for I believed that he was more concerned for his own comfort than for my welfare. He escorted me from the monastery as if he were accompanying a funeral procession and at the last moment he spoke these words of farewell, "I see, my son, that you are marked by Satan's branding-iron: I do not ask your reasons and I accept no excuses. The sheep that leaves the sheep-fold immediately exposes itself to the wolf's jaws."

4 'As one travels from Beroea to Edessa,[7] the public highway is bordered by desert across which Saracens constantly wander, leading a nomadic existence. Fear of these people causes travellers in those regions to group together in large parties so that they might protect each other from the danger threatening them. There were in my party about seventy travellers: men, women, old people and young, as well as small children. Suddenly the Ishmaelites, riding on horses and camels, swooped on us. They wore their hair long, bound by a fillet, their bodies half naked, wearing cloaks and broad boots. From their shoulders hung quivers and they carried their bows unstrung and brandished long spears. They had come not for battle but for booty. We were captured, divided up and dragged off in different directions. Meanwhile, I, the heir to property, regretted too late my decision to return home: lots were drawn and I was taken into slavery together with one of the young women, both of us to serve one master. We were led, or rather, carried high on camels, and fearing that we might fall off at any moment we hung suspended rather than sat as we crossed the vast desert. Half-cooked meat was our food and camels' milk our drink.

5 'At last, after crossing a great river, we reached the interior of the desert. There we bowed our heads when ordered to pay homage to the mistress and her children, as is the custom of that tribe. Here, as if I were a prisoner, I learned to walk around in different clothes, in

other words, naked. For the heat of that climate was so oppressive that it did not allow one to cover anything other than one's private parts. I was assigned the task of looking after the sheep as they grazed, and in comparison with my other misfortunes I found this occupation a comfort for I rarely saw my masters and my fellow slaves. I felt that I was rather like the holy Jacob and I reminded myself of Moses, both of whom had once been shepherds in the wilderness. I lived on fresh cheese and milk; I prayed without ceasing and sang the psalms I had learned in the monastery. I enjoyed my captivity and gave thanks to God for his judgement because I had discovered in the desert the monk whom I had been about to lose in my own country.

6 But nothing is ever safe when the devil is around! How manifold and unspeakable are his wiles! For his malice found me out even in my hiding place. My master, seeing his flock grow and detecting in me no hint of dishonesty (for I knew that the Apostle had commanded us to serve our masters as faithfully as one serves God)[8] wished to reward me so as to make me more faithful to him. So he offered me my fellow slave, the woman who had once been captured with me, as a wife. When I refused her, saying that I was a Christian and was not allowed to marry a woman whose husband was still alive (for her husband had been captured with us but had been carried off by a different master), my owner became implacable in his fury. He drew his sword and was on the point of attacking me. Had I not at once anticipated him by taking the woman in my arms, he would have shed my blood on the spot.

'Now night had fallen, all too soon for me; it seemed even darker than usual. I led my new wife into a derelict cave, with sorrow as our bridesmaid, for we both detested each other but would not admit it. At that moment I really felt the pain of my captivity. I threw myself on the ground and began to lament the monastic state which I was losing, saying, "Is it for this that I have been preserved, wretch that I am? Have my sins brought me to the point where I, a virgin with greying hair, should become a husband? What was the point of renouncing my parents, my country, my family property for the Lord, if I now do the very thing which I rejected them in order to avoid doing? Or perhaps I am suffering all this because I was homesick.

What are we to do, my soul? Are we to perish or win the victory? Shall we await the hand of the Lord or stab ourselves with our own sword? Turn your sword upon yourself, for your death, my soul, must be feared more than that of the body. Chastity preserved has its own martyrdom, too. Let this witness of Christ lie unburied in the desert: I shall be both martyr and my own persecutor." With these words I drew my sword which gleamed in the darkness and turned its point towards myself. "Farewell, unhappy woman," I said. "Take me as a martyr rather than in marriage." Then she threw herself at my feet, saying, "I beg you in the name of Jesus Christ, I implore you by the crisis of this moment, do not shed your blood for I will be blamed for it. Or if you are determined to die, turn the sword on me first. It would be better for us to be united in this way. Even if my husband were to come back to me, I should preserve the chastity which captivity has taught me. I would rather die than lose it. Why should you die to avoid marrying me? I would die if you wished to be united with me. So take me as a partner in chastity and cherish the bond of the spirit rather than that of the body. Let our masters believe you to be a married man, let Christ know you as a brother. We shall easily convince them that we are married when they see us loving each other in this way." I admit I was astounded. Admiring the woman's virtue, I loved her more than a wife. But never did I see her body naked, never did I touch her flesh, for I was afraid to lose in peacetime what I had preserved in time of conflict. Many days passed in this form of marriage.[9] Our union made us dearer to our masters and there was no suspicion that we might escape: sometimes I was away for a whole month in the wilderness as a trusted shepherd of the flock.

7 'After a long time, as I was sitting alone in the wilderness with nothing to see apart from earth and sky, I began to turn things over in my mind and to remember amongst other things the companionship of the monks, and in particular the face of the abbot who had taught me, who had held and lost me. Absorbed in these thoughts, I watched a huge number of ants swarming along a narrow path. You could see that their loads were larger than their bodies. Some were dragging grass seeds in the forceps of their jaws; others were piling up soil from

pits and blocking off the flow of water with dams of earth. Some, mindful of the coming of winter, were chopping off the seeds which were brought in, to prevent the sodden earth turning their granaries into grass; others, in solemn lamentation, were bearing out the bodies of the dead. And what is more amazing, in this enormous procession not one of the ants going out got in the way of those going in; it was rather the case that if they saw one which had collapsed beneath the bundles and burdens, they helped it by putting their shoulders to the load. What more need I say? That day provided me with a wonderful spectacle which reminded me of Solomon when he directs us to the shrewdness of the ants and rouses our sluggish minds by means of this example.[10] I began to tire of captivity, to miss the monastic cells and to long to imitate those ants which work together for the common good, and where all things belong to everyone since each owns nothing of his own.

8 'As I went back to bed the woman came to meet me: my expression could not conceal my sadness of heart. She asked why I was so downcast. I told her the reasons. I encouraged her to escape. She did not refuse. I demanded silence; she gave me her promise. Continuing our conversation in whispers, we wavered between hope and fear. In my flock I had two unusually large goats which I slaughtered. I then made their skins into bags; their meat I prepared as food for the journey. As soon as evening came, when our masters thought we were lying asleep by ourselves, we set out on our journey, carrying the bags and the bits of meat. On reaching the river ten miles away, we inflated the bags of skin. Climbing on to them we entrusted ourselves to the water and paddled slowly across with our feet, so that as the river carried us downstream and set us on the opposite bank a long way from the place where we had entered the water, our pursuers might lose our trail. But meanwhile the meat had become sodden and some of it had fallen out, so that it promised scarcely three days' worth of food. We drank until we could drink no more, preparing ourselves for the thirst to come. We ran, constantly looking behind us and tending to move on at night rather than during the day, both on account of the danger of attacks from the Saracens who roamed that area far and wide, and on account of the excessive heat of the

sun. I shudder even as I recall it, poor creature that I am, and even though I know that I am safe, my whole body still trembles.

9 'After three days, we saw indistinctly in the distance two people on camels approaching at great speed. At once my mind feared the worst and began to think that our master was planning to put us to death: the sun seemed to turn dark. We realized that we had been betrayed by our tracks across the sand: in our terror we noticed a cave on our right leading deep down beneath the ground. And so, although we were afraid of poisonous animals (for vipers, basilisks and scorpions as well as other creatures of this kind tend to seek the shade, wishing to escape the burning sun), we entered the cave, but immediately took shelter in a pit on our left, just inside the entrance, not going any further in case we should run into death while trying to escape death. We reasoned to ourselves that if the Lord helps those in trouble, we would be safe here; if he rejects sinners, this would provide us with a tomb. What do you imagine was our state of mind, what terror do you think we felt when, in front of the cave, at no distance at all, there stood our master and one of our fellow slaves: they had now reached our hiding place by following our tracks. How much worse is death anticipated than death actually inflicted! Again my tongue stammers with distress and fear as if our master were calling us, and I hardly dare utter a word. He sent the slave to drag us out of the cave while he held the camels; drawing his sword, he waited for us to come out. Meanwhile the servant had come about three or four paces in and we could see his back from our hiding place (for such is the nature of eyesight that when someone comes into the dark out of the sunlight he can see nothing). Then his voice echoed through the cave: 'Come out, you villains, come out to die. What are you waiting for? Why do you delay? Come out, the master is calling and waiting patiently.' He was still speaking when suddenly, through the darkness, we saw a lioness attack the man; when she had strangled him, she dragged his bloody body inside. Dear Jesus, what terror was ours at that moment, what joy! Unbeknown to our master we watched as our enemy died. When our master noticed that the slave was taking a long time, he suspected that the two of us were resisting the one man. Unable to control his anger, he came into the cave gripping his

sword, and with furious shouts he rebuked the slave for taking such a long time, but before he reached our hiding place he was seized by the wild beast. Who would ever believe that before our very eyes a beast would fight to protect us? But although one cause of fear had been removed, we were presented with the prospect of a similar death for ourselves, unless it was better to endure a lion's ferocity than a man's anger. Shuddering inwardly, not even daring to move, we awaited the outcome, with only the consciousness of our chastity like a wall to protect us in the midst of these horrendous dangers. The lioness, wary of a trap and sensing that she had been seen, soon[11] picked up her cub in her teeth and carried it out, leaving the lodging to us. However, we were not confident enough to rush out immediately but waited a long time, and while planning our escape, we kept imagining that we would meet the lioness again.

10 'When that day had passed and our terror had abated, we went out at evening and saw the camels (known as dromedaries on account of their exceptional speed) chewing the cud. We mounted them and refreshed by new provisions, we at last arrived at the Roman fort after ten days spent crossing the desert. Brought before the tribune, we set forth a detailed account of events. Then we were sent across to Sabinianus,[12] the ruler of Mesopotamia, where we received a price for the camels. As that abbot of mine had by now fallen asleep in the Lord, I returned to that place and joined the monks once more, entrusting my wife to the virgins, for I loved her as a sister although I did not entrust myself to her as if she were my sister.'

The elderly Malchus told me this when I was a young man. I have related it to you, now that I myself am an old man. To the chaste I have unfolded a story of chastity: I exhort those of you who are virgins to preserve your chastity. Tell this story to later generations so that they may know that amid swords, amid wild beasts and desert regions, chastity is never taken captive, and that a person who is dedicated to Christ can die but cannot be defeated.

Life of Martin of Tours
by Sulpicius Severus

Sulpicius Severus wrote his Life of Martin *not long before Martin's death near Tours on 11 November 397. The fact that it was written while Martin was still alive accounts for the lack of description of his death,*[1] *that part of a saint's life which usually formed the climax of the hagiography, as in the cases of Antony, Paul of Thebes, Hilarion and Benedict. In every other way, the* Life of Martin *is a classic hagiography, documenting the whole life of the saint but concentrating on his spiritual achievements, the qualities which drew others to him and the manifestations of God's power working through him. Of course, the* Life of Martin *is an early instance of the genre, following in the footsteps of Athanasius'* Life of Antony *and Jerome's three biographies, but was itself destined to become one of the principal models for later hagiographers.*[2] *Nor did it have to wait long for its influence to spread: in Sulpicius' Dialogues, written in about 400, one of the main characters, Postumianus, claims that the* Life of Martin *has already been read in Rome, Carthage and Egypt.*[3]

It would seem that Sulpicius had first heard about Martin from his friend Paulinus with whom he had studied at Bordeaux. Martin had cured Paulinus of an eye complaint[4] *and when Paulinus mentioned Martin enthusiastically, Sulpicius was inspired to go and visit the great man himself,*[5] *during 393 or 394. Martin apparently urged Sulpicius to follow the example of Paulinus and cut himself loose from the ties of wealth and career. By 395 Sulpicius had indeed taken the decision to give up his legal career to become a servant of God. He sold his property and gave the money to the poor, keeping only one estate, that known as Primuliacum, which probably lay between Toulouse and Narbonne. Here he was to spend the rest of his life, leading a quasi-monastic existence, surrounded and visited by fellow Christians, rich and poor alike. Like his friend Paulinus, who had settled at Nola, Sulpicius spent much of his time in literary activities, promoting Martin's reputation as Paulinus was doing for St Felix. To what extent Sulpicius' life after his conversion imitated that of the monks at Martin's monastery is unclear. We know little about his life after about 404 but it seems probable that he lived until the 420s.[6] Sulpicius' literary output consists of the* Life of Martin, *three letters, the* Dialogues *and the* Chronicles, *a sacred history from creation down to Sulpicius' own time.*

Sulpicius' primary aim, as expressed in the preface to his biography of Martin, was to write an account of this most saintly man so that the example of Martin might awaken the enthusiasm of others for the ascetic life. He also hopes that his reward for this will be everlasting life. In stating these two purposes Sulpicius is consciously turning the aims of his classical predecessors – and Sallust in particular – on their head. Sallust, in his account of the conspiracy of Catiline, had spoken of the human desire to achieve everlasting fame: acknowledging this desire in himself he decided to seek fame not in political life, but by writing history. Sulpicius, too, acknowledges this human desire but criticizes Sallust for believing that fame is either anything worth having or that it can indeed be everlasting if it depends on human memory. The only worthwhile goal, according to Sulpicius, is everlasting life, the reward God grants for a life well spent.

Although Sulpicius does not mention Sallust by name, he clearly has him in mind. This concern to confront the aims of classical historiography[7] may indicate that Sulpicius intended his work to be read not only by Christians but also by those whose devotion to classical culture might stand in the way of commitment to Christianity.

Another underlying aim of the Life of Martin *may have been to explain Sulpicius' conversion to those who found it hard to understand why he should have given up his wealth and career. However, it would seem that the work failed to win all its readers over: in the* Letters *and* Dialogues *Sulpicius continues to defend Martin – and therefore his own way of life – in the face of a certain amount of scepticism.*

Sulpicius' portrayal of the man who, in his eyes, combined perfectly the roles of monk and bishop, can be divided according to the following sections: after the dedicatory letter, addressed to Sulpicius' friend Desiderius, and the preface, chapters 2–10 provide an account of Martin's life until he was made bishop of Tours and moved to a cell at Marmoutier; chapters 11–24 record his miracles as bishop, miracles associated not only with healing but with his work as missionary – of a rather thuggish type[8] – among the pagans of Gaul. The final three chapters (25–7) tell of Sulpicius' own meeting with Martin and his experience of the great man's humility, kindness and impressive intellect and eloquence.

Dedicatory letter:
Severus, to Desiderius, his dearest brother

I had in fact decided, dear brother who shares one soul with me, to conceal the little book I wrote about the life of the holy Martin within its covers and to keep it imprisoned inside the walls of this house, for being of a very diffident nature, I wanted to avoid people's criticisms. I feared that my unpolished style might offend my readers – as I am sure will happen – and I should be deemed deserving of general censure for having had the temerity to appropriate a subject better left to more competent writers. But I was unable to deny you when you asked me for it again and again, for what would I not do for love of you even if it meant a loss of self-respect on my part? However, in bringing this book out for you, I am confident that you will keep your promise and not hand it over to anyone. And yet I am afraid you may serve as an exit door for it and once it has got out it cannot be called back.[1] But if that happens and you see some people reading it, you must ask the readers kindly to attach more weight to the subject matter than to the words and if by chance some infelicity of language should strike their ears, to bear it patiently, because the kingdom of God is not founded on eloquence but on faith. They must remember that salvation was preached to the world not by orators (although the Lord could of course have done this too if it had been useful), but by fishermen. And so, from the moment I set myself to write because I considered it wrong to keep the virtues of such a great man concealed, I decided not to be embarrassed by any solecisms. I have never acquired any great learning in these matters and if I have perhaps dipped into these studies in a small way, I have forgotten everything I learnt due to lack of practice over a long period. But one way of avoiding the necessity of making such a difficult defence would be to suppress the name of the author when the book is published, if you think this is a good idea. In that case you must erase the title on the front so that the page may be dumb, announcing only its subject matter (and that is enough), not its author. Farewell, my venerable brother in Christ, you who are the hero of all good and holy people.

Preface

I.1 Many mortals, vainly devoted to study and worldly acclaim, have then sought to immortalize their reputation, or so they believed, by using their pen to give an account of the lives of famous men.[2] (2) But although this did not bring them everlasting fame the hopes they had conceived did however bear some small fruit because they prolonged their memory, although in vain, and by presenting the examples of great men they stimulated in their readers a considerable desire to emulate these people. However, these concerns were irrelevant for that blessed and eternal life. (3) For what use to them was the acclaim – which will vanish with this world – accorded to their writings? Or what benefit did posterity gain from reading about Hector's battles or about Socrates' philosophy? It would be foolish to imitate these men – indeed it would be madness not to combat them most energetically, seeing that as they estimate human life by present actions alone, they have entrusted their hopes of immortality to fables and their souls to tombs. (4) Indeed they believed that they should seek perpetuity for themselves only with regard to human memory although it is man's duty to seek everlasting life rather than everlasting renown, and not by writing or fighting or playing the philosopher, but by living in a pious, saintly and religious manner. (5) But this human error, handed down through literature, has become so prevalent that it has clearly found many who wish to emulate this vain philosophy or this foolish heroism. (6) For these reasons I think it would be useful if I were to write a detailed record of the life of this most saintly man as an example to others in the future. It would serve to rouse the enthusiasm of its readers for the true wisdom, for heavenly military service and for divine heroism. In doing so we will also be pursuing our own advantage in such a way that we may expect not empty renown from our fellow men but an everlasting reward from God. For even if we ourselves have not lived in such a way as to be an example to others, we have at least made an effort to prevent a man who deserves to be imitated from remaining unknown. (7) I shall therefore undertake to write the life of St Martin, showing what he did both before he became bishop and while he was bishop, although it was impossible for me to get access to everything about him. Consequently those things of which he alone was aware cannot be known because he did not seek praise from men but wished to conceal all his virtues, as far as it lay in his control. (8) And yet, even among those facts which are known to us, we have omitted many because we believed it was sufficient for the salient points alone to be noted. We also had to consider the readers for we did not wish an excessive accumulation of facts to cause them to lose interest. (9) I therefore beg those who are to read this to believe what I say and not to think that I have written anything except what has been learned on good authority and proved to be true. If this were not the case I would have preferred silence to falsehood.

Life of Martin

II.1 Martin, then, was born in Sabaria,[3] a town in Pannonia, but he was brought up in Italy, at Pavia. His parents were not of the lowest rank as far as worldly status goes, but they were pagans. (2) His father was first a soldier and later a military tribune. Martin himself, as a young man, followed him into the army and fought in the élite cavalry regiment under the emperor Constantius and then under the Caesar Julian.[4] He did not do so willingly, however, because from just about his earliest years the holy childhood of this remarkable boy preferred to aspire to God's service. (3) For when he was ten years old, he took refuge in the church against his parents' wishes and demanded to be made a catechumen,[5] (4) and it was not long before he was completely converted, in an extraordinary way, to the work of God. At the age of twelve, he longed for the desert, and he would have satisfied this desire if he had not been prevented by the weakness of his young age. Yet his mind was always intent either on the monastic cells or on the church and already in childhood he was planning what he later carried out with devotion. (5) But when the rulers gave out an edict to the effect that the sons of veterans were to be enrolled in the army, his father, who was hostile to his holy actions, betrayed him: at the age of fifteen Martin was arrested, put in chains and bound by military oaths. He was content with the company of only one slave – and in fact they exchanged roles so that the master served the slave to such an extent that it was usually Martin who pulled his slave's boots off and cleaned them, and when they took their meals together it was more often Martin who served at table. (6) He was in the army for about three years before his baptism but he remained free from the vices in which men of this kind usually become entangled. (7) He showed great kindness to his fellow soldiers, extraordinary love, superhuman patience and humility. It is unnecessary to praise his frugality which he practised in such a way that already at that time he might have been taken to be a monk rather than a soldier. These qualities of his bound all his fellow soldiers so closely to him that they adored him with extraordinary affection. (8) Although he had not yet been born again in Christ, in performing good works he behaved like a candidate for baptism: he supported those in trouble, he brought help to the wretched, he fed the poor, he clothed the naked and kept nothing of his military salary for himself apart from what he needed for food each day. Already at that time he was not deaf to the gospel for he took no thought for the morrow.[6]

III.1 One day, then, in the middle of a winter more bitterly cold than usual (so much so that many perished as a result of the severity of the icy weather), when Martin had nothing with him apart from his weapons and a simple military cloak, he came across a naked beggar at the gate of the city of Amiens. The man begged the people who were passing to have pity on him but they all walked past him. Then Martin, who was filled with God's grace, understood that this man had been reserved for him, since the others were not showing him any mercy. (2) But what was he to do? He had nothing apart from the cloak he was wearing, for he had already used up the rest of his things for a similar purpose. So he seized the sword which he wore at his side, divided the cloak in two, gave half to the beggar and then put the remaining piece on again. Some of the bystanders began to laugh because he looked odd with his chopped-up cloak, but many who were more sensible sighed deeply because they had not done the same despite the fact that, because they had more than Martin, they could have clothed the beggar without themselves being reduced to nakedness. (3) The following night, therefore, when Martin had fallen asleep, he saw Christ clothed in the part of his cloak which he had used to cover the beggar. He was told to look very carefully at the Lord and to recognize the clothing which he had given. Then he heard Jesus saying in a clear voice to the host of angels standing all around, 'Martin who is still a catechumen covered me with this cloak.' (4) Undoubtedly, when the Lord declared that He Himself was clothed in the person of this beggar, He was recalling His own words (for He had once said, 'As often as you do this to one of the least, you have done it to me.')[7] And He deigned to reveal Himself in the clothing which the beggar had received in order to confirm His witness to such a good deed. (5) This most blessed man was not puffed up with human pride by this vision. Instead he acknowledged God's goodness in his deed and now that he was eighteen years old, he was impatient to be baptized. However, he did not immediately give up his military career for he was persuaded by the entreaties of his tribune with whom he had a close relationship. In fact the tribune promised that once the period of his tribuneship was over, he himself would withdraw from the world. (6) As Martin was kept waiting for this for about two years, after his baptism he continued as a soldier though only in name.

IV.1 Then the barbarians invaded Gaul and the Caesar Julian[8] assembled his army at the city of the Vangiones[9] and set about paying the soldiers a bonus. They were called out one by one, as was the custom, until it was Martin's turn. (2) Then he judged that the time was right to request his discharge, for he thought it would be dishonest to accept a bonus payment if he did not intend to serve as a soldier. So he said to the Caesar, (3) 'Up till now I have fought for you; allow me now to fight for God. Let someone who intends to fight accept your bonus. I am a soldier of Christ, I am not allowed to fight.'(4) The tyrant was furious at these words and claimed that Martin was refusing to do his duty as a soldier not out of religious conviction but out of fear of the battle that was to take place the next day. (5) But Martin was not intimidated. In fact, he stood all the more firm when terror tactics were used against him. 'If,' he replied, 'you ascribe this to cowardice rather than to faith, tomorrow I shall stand unarmed before the front lines. With neither shield nor helmet but with the sign of the cross to protect me, in the name of the Lord Jesus I will push my way into the enemy's formations without being harmed.' (6) The order was therefore given for him to be taken back and thrown into prison so that he would keep his promise to be thrust unarmed at the barbarians.(7) Next day the enemy sent envoys to sue for peace, surrendering themselves and all their belongings. Who then could doubt that this victory was really due to the blessed man to whom it was granted not to be sent unarmed into battle? (8) Although the good Lord could have kept his soldier safe amidst the swords and weapons of the enemy, he none the less removed the necessity for battle so that the holy man's gaze would not be outraged even by the deaths of others. (9) For it was right that Christ should offer his soldier no other victory than one where no one died and where the enemy was driven to surrender without bloodshed.

V.1 After leaving the army, Martin went to visit the saintly Hilary,[10] bishop of Poitiers, whose faith in theological matters had been tested and was well known at that time, and spent some time with him. (2) This same Hilary attempted to tie Martin more closely to himself and to bind him to the service of God by making him a deacon, but Martin refused time and time again, pleading that he was unworthy. So Hilary, a man of penetrating intellect, understood that the only way in which Martin could be tied down was if Hilary were to confer on him a position which might seem to involve a degree of humiliation. So he suggested that he should be an exorcist.[11] Martin did not refuse to be ordained to this position for he did not want it to look as if he was rejecting it as not sufficiently prestigious. (3) Shortly afterwards he was admonished in his sleep to visit, out of a spirit of loving concern, his native land[12] and his parents who were still in the clutches of paganism. So with St Hilary's consent he set off, after being made to promise, by means of numerous entreaties and tears, that he would return. It was with sadness, so they say, that he set off on this long journey, testifying to the brothers that he would have to endure many tribulations. Later events proved this to be correct. (4) First of all, while crossing the Alps he lost his way and fell among brigands. When one of these raised his axe and prepared to strike Martin on the head, another restrained his arm as he was about to strike. However, they tied Martin's hands behind his back and handed him over to one of the brigands to be guarded and stripped of his belongings. When this brigand led him to a more remote spot and began to question him as to who he was, Martin replied that he was a Christian. (5) The brigand asked whether he was frightened. Then Martin declared with firm conviction that he had never felt so safe because he knew that the Lord's mercy was closest at hand when one was in danger; instead, Martin felt sorry for him because, being a brigand, he was unworthy of Christ's mercy. (6) Martin undertook to set forth the gospel and preached the word of God to the brigand. To cut a long story short: the brigand was converted to the faith and accompanied Martin to set him on the right road, begging him to pray to the Lord on his behalf. This same man was later seen leading a religious life, and in fact the story I have just related is said to have been heard from him.

VI.1 Continuing on his way, Martin had passed Milan when the devil, taking on human form, came up to him and asked where he was going. Receiving Martin's reply, to the effect that he was going where the Lord called him, he said to Martin (2), 'Wherever you go and whatever you attempt, the devil will oppose you.' Then Martin answered in the words of the prophet: '*The Lord is my helper; I will not fear what a man can do to me.*'[13] At once the enemy disappeared from his sight. (3) And so he carried out his intention to set his mother free from the error of paganism while Martin's father continued in wickedness. However, Martin saved many by his example. (4) By then the Arian heresy had spread throughout the world and especially in Illyricum. Since Martin was almost the only one to fight most strenuously against the heretical beliefs of the priests and because many tortures were inflicted on him (for he was publicly beaten and finally driven to leave the city) he returned to Italy. When he learnt that the church in Gaul had also been thrown into confusion by the departure of St Hilary who had been driven into exile[14] by the power of the heretics, Martin established a monastic cell for himself in Milan. There too Auxentius,[15] the chief instigator and leader of the Arians, persecuted him relentlessly: he inflicted many injuries on Martin and expelled him from the city. (5) Judging it necessary to yield to circumstances, Martin withdrew to an island called Gallinara,[16] accompanied by a priest, a man of great virtues. Here he lived for a time on the roots of grasses. During that period he ate some hellebore, a plant said to be poisonous. (6) But when he felt the power of the poison attacking him and death close at hand, he managed by his prayers to repel the danger threatening him and immediately all the pain left him. (7) Not long afterwards, when he learnt that the emperor had now repented and had granted St Hilary permission to return from exile,[17] Martin set out for Rome to try and meet Hilary there.

VII.1 As Hilary had already passed through, Martin followed in his footsteps to Poitiers where he was most warmly welcomed by Hilary. Martin then erected a monastic cell for himself not far from the town.[18] At that time a certain catechumen attached himself to him, wishing to learn how to live according to the teachings of such a holy man. A few days later this man fell sick, suffering from violent attacks of fever. (2) It happened that Martin had just gone away: after an absence of three days he returned to find a lifeless body. Death had come so suddenly that the man had departed this mortal life without being baptized. The grieving brothers were performing their sorrowful duties around the body laid out in their midst when Martin came running up, weeping and wailing. (3) But then, as his whole mind became filled with the Holy Spirit, he told the others to leave the little room where the body lay. He locked the door and threw himself down upon the lifeless limbs of the dead brother. And when Martin had lain in prayer for a while and felt that the power of the Lord was present through the spirit, he raised himself a little and stared into the dead man's face, fearlessly awaiting the outcome of his prayers and the Lord's mercy. Two hours had scarcely passed when he saw the dead man slowly move each limb and open his eyes, blinking to regain his sight. (4) Then he turned with a great cry to the Lord, filling the tiny cell with shouts of thanksgiving. On hearing this those who had been standing outside immediately rushed in. It was an extraordinary sight: they saw the man whom they had left as dead now alive. (5) And so, restored to life, he immediately underwent baptism. He lived for many years afterwards and was the first to provide evidence and testimony to Martin's spiritual powers. (6) He used to relate how when he left the body he was taken to the court of the Judge and that he heard the grim sentence that he was to be condemned to the dark places and to the hordes of common people. Then two angels pointed out to the Judge that this was the man for whom Martin was praying and so the order was given for him to be taken back by the two angels, handed over to Martin and restored to his former life. (7) It was from that moment that the name of the blessed man first shone forth so that he who was already considered by everyone to be a holy man, was now also considered truly worthy of the apostles.

VIII. 1 Not long afterwards, while Martin was passing through the estate of Lupicinus, a man who was held in high esteem in the eyes of this world, he was greeted by cries of grief from a crowd of mourners. (2) He went up to them in concern and inquired what this wailing was about: they explained to him that a young slave belonging to the household had hanged himself. When he learned of this, he entered the little room in which the corpse was lying, and shutting out all the people, he lay down on the body and prayed for a short while. (3) Soon the face showed signs of life and the dead boy, his eyelids still heavy, raised himself up towards Martin's face. Slowly and with great effort he managed to get up, and taking hold of the blessed man's hand he stood up and then walked with him to the entrance of the house while the whole crowd looked on.

IX. 1 At about this time, Martin was considered as a candidate for the bishopric of Tours. But since he could not easily be torn from his cell, a certain Rusticius, one of the citizens, pretending that his wife was ill, threw himself at Martin's feet, thus managing to make him come out. (2) Then, when crowds of citizens had been arranged along the route, Martin was escorted as far as the city more or less under guard. What was extraordinary was that an incredible number of people not only from that town but also from neighbouring towns gathered to cast their votes. (3) They all shared one will, one wish, one opinion: Martin was the most worthy to become bishop and fortunate was the church which had such a bishop! A few, however, including some of the bishops who had been summoned to install the prelate, wickedly rejected him, saying that he was despicable: a person with such a scruffy appearance, dirty clothes and unkempt hair was unworthy of the episcopate. (4) But those who had a more sensible attitude found such foolishness ridiculous: while wishing to find fault with him, these bishops were actually proclaiming him to be an outstanding person! In fact they were unable to do anything other than what the people were planning in accordance with the Lord's will. However, among the bishops present, someone called Defensor is said particularly to have opposed Martin. In this connection it was noticed that he was afterwards severely reprimanded by a reading from the prophets. (5) For it happened that the reader whose turn it was to read on that day had been prevented by the crowds from arriving and the men in charge were anxiously awaiting the man who was missing, when one of the bystanders took the psalter and seized upon the first verse he came to. (6) This was the psalm verse: *Out of the mouths of babes and sucklings you have perfected praise because of your enemies, so that you might destroy the enemy and the defender.*[19] When he read this, the cries of the people rose up and the opposition party was thrown into confusion. (7) They believed that it had been by God's will that this particular psalm had been read so that Defensor might hear this testimony to his deeds, he who out of the mouths of babes and sucklings had been at the same time revealed as the enemy and destroyed now that the Lord's praise had been perfected in Martin.

X.1 It is not in our power to give a full account of his behaviour and his greatness after he had succeeded to the episcopate. In fact, with the utmost constancy he continued the same as before. (2) There was the same humility of heart, the same poverty of clothing. Full of authority and grace, he fulfilled the high office of bishop without abandoning his monastic commitment and virtue.[20] (3) For a time, therefore, he used a little cell adjoining the church; then when he could no longer bear the disturbance caused by those who flocked to see him, he built himself a cell some two miles outside the city.[21] (4) This place was so remote and secluded that it was equal to the solitude of the desert. For on one side it was bounded by the sheer rock of a high mountain, while on the level side, it was enclosed by a gentle bend in the river Loire. It could be approached by only one path and that a very narrow one. Martin lived in a small cell made of wood and (5) a number of the brothers lived in a similar manner, but most of them had made shelters for themselves by hollowing out the rock of the mountain which overlooked the place. There were about eighty disciples who had chosen to lead a life in accordance with their blessed master's example. (6) No one there possessed anything of his own, everything was shared.[22] They were not allowed to buy or sell anything (as is the practice with most monks). No craft was practised there, apart from that of the scribes; the young were set to this task while the older ones spent their time in prayer. (7) It was rare for anyone to leave his own cell except when they gathered at the place of prayer. They all received their food together after the period of fasting. No one drank any wine unless illness forced him to do so. (8) Most of them were dressed in camel-skin garments: they considered the wearing of any softer material to be reprehensible. This is all the more remarkable since many of them were said to be noblemen who had been brought up in a very different way but had voluntarily adopted this life of humility and endurance. Later we saw several of them become bishops. (9) For what city or church did not long to have a priest from Martin's monastery?

XI.1 Let me now deal with the rest of the miracles which he performed during his episcopacy. There was a place, not far from the town and next to the monastery, which people wrongly considered to be sacred, on the grounds that martyrs had been buried there. (2) In fact there was also an altar there thought to have been set up by previous bishops. But Martin was not quick to believe things which were doubtful and so he kept asking the older priests and clerics to reveal to him the martyr's name and the date of his passion. He said he was troubled by one major misgiving, namely the problem that ancestral tradition had handed down no information that was coherent and indisputable. (3) For some time Martin refrained from going to this place. Since he was uncertain, he did not disparage the cult but neither did he give his authority to the people in case the superstition should flourish. But one day he went there, taking with him a few of the brothers. (4) Then, standing on the tomb itself, he prayed to the Lord to reveal who was buried there and what his special merit was. Then he turned to the left and saw an ugly and ferocious-looking shade standing near by. He ordered him to tell them his name and his special merit. He gave his name and confessed his crime: he had been a robber, executed for his crimes and mistakenly venerated by the people. He said that he had nothing in common with the martyrs since they were remembered for their glory, while he was remembered for his punishment. (5) What was extraordinary was that those present heard his voice as he spoke but could not see him. Then Martin revealed what he had seen and ordered them to remove from the place the altar that had stood there. In this way he set the people free from the error of that superstition.

XII. 1 It happened during the following period that while he was on a journey he came across the corpse of a pagan which was being carried out for burial in accordance with superstitious funeral rites. Seeing in the distance a crowd of people coming towards him, he stopped for a while, not knowing what it was. For he was about five hundred paces away so it was difficult to make out what he was seeing. (2) However, because he could see a group of peasants and the linen cloths laid over the corpse fluttering in the wind, he thought that they were performing pagan sacrificial rites, for it was the custom for the peasants of Gaul, in their pitiable delusion, to carry demonic representations, covered with a white veil, over their fields. (3) And so Martin raised his hand and made the sign of the cross against those who were coming towards him. He ordered the crowd to stop and to set down what they were carrying. And now you would have seen an amazing thing. These miserable people first became rigid like rocks; (4) then, when they made a great effort to move forward, they found that they were unable to move any further and went spinning round in a ridiculous whirling movement until they were overcome with dizziness and set down the burden of the corpse. They looked round at each other in amazement, wondering in silence what had happened. (5) But when the holy man understood that these people had gathered for a funeral, not for a religious ceremony, he raised his hand once more and granted them the power to depart and to carry the corpse. He therefore forced them to stop when he wanted and allowed them to depart when he wanted.

XIII.1 Again, when he had destroyed a very ancient temple in a certain village and had undertaken to chop down a pine tree standing beside the shrine, the priest of that temple, together with a whole crowd of pagans, began to put up resistance. (2) And although these people had at the Lord's command done nothing while the temple was being knocked down, they refused to allow the tree to be cut down. Martin was at pains to make it clear to them that there was nothing sacred about a tree stump; they should rather follow God, whose servant he was; in fact, they ought to chop down that tree because it was consecrated to a demon. (3) Then one of them, who was bolder than the rest, said, 'If you have any faith in your God whom you claim to worship, we will cut down this tree ourselves and you must catch it as it falls. If your Lord is with you, as you claim, you will escape injury.' (4) Then Martin promised that he would do so for his confidence in the Lord made him fearless. At this point the whole crowd of pagans agreed to these terms, and they readily assented to the loss of their tree, as long as it managed to crush the enemy of their rites as it fell. (5) And so, when that Pine tree began to lean to one side so that there was no doubt as to which way it would fall when it was cut down, Martin was tied up and placed, as the peasants wished, in the spot where everyone was convinced the tree would fall. (6) They then began to chop at the pine with great joy and excitement. A crowd of amazed onlookers stood at a distance. And now the pine was gradually starting to sway to and fro and, on the point of falling, it threatened its own destruction. (7) Standing some way away the monks grew pale: terrified by the danger which was now close at hand, they had lost all hope and confidence and were now only awaiting Martin's death. (8) But he trusted in the Lord and waited without fear. The pine gave a crashing noise as it fell and Martin raised his hand to meet it as it was falling, as it came crashing down on top of him, and he made the sign of salvation to block the tree's path. As a result the tree fell in a different place (you would have thought it had been pushed back by some kind of whirlwind) so that it came close to crushing the country folk who had been standing in a safe place. (9) Then shouts rose to the skies for the pagans were shocked by the miracle, while the monks wept for joy and the name of Christ was proclaimed by all of them together. It was generally agreed that on that day salvation came to that region. For there was hardly anyone in that huge crowd of pagans who did not ask for the laying-on of hands and who did not believe in the Lord Jesus, abandoning the error of impiety. It is true that before Martin came there were only a very few, or rather, there was hardly anyone in those regions who had received the name of Christ, but by means of his miracles and his example the name of Christ grew so strong that there was no longer any place in that area which was not full of churches or monasteries filled with people. For in those places where he had destroyed the pagan shrines, he immediately built either churches or monasteries.

XIV. 1 At about the same time Martin performed a miracle of no less value by means of a similar kind of deed. In one village he had set fire to a most ancient and famous shrine and the balls of flame were being carried by the driving wind on to the nearest, or rather, adjoining house. (2) As soon as Martin noticed this, he quickly ran and climbed up on to the roof of the house, throwing himself in the path of the flames as they came towards him. Then an extraordinary thing occurred: you would have seen the fire turned back against the force of the wind, so that there appeared to be a sort of conflict between the elements fighting each other. And so, as a result of Martin's special power, the fire only had an effect in the place where it was ordered to do so. (3) In another village, called Leprosus, Martin wanted to knock down a temple which had been richly ornamented by the pagan superstition, but he was so strongly resisted by a crowd of pagans that he was driven back, not without injury. (4) Consequently he withdrew to the neighbouring area, where he spent three days fasting and praying, clothed in sackcloth and ashes. He prayed to the Lord for divine power to destroy that temple since human hands could not demolish it. (5) Then suddenly two angels, armed with spears and shields, appeared to him like heavenly soldiers, saying that they were sent by the Lord to disperse the crowds of peasants and to bring assistance to Martin to prevent anyone resisting him while the temple was being demolished. The angels told him to go back and finish off faithfully the task that he had begun. (6) So he went back to the village and as the pagan crowds looked on in silence he completely demolished the temple belonging to the false religion and reduced all the altars and statues to dust. (7) Seeing this, the villagers realized that the divine will had rendered them speechless and panic-stricken to stop them resisting the bishop, and as a result almost all of them converted to the Lord Jesus: they shouted out in public, confessing that they should worship Martin's God and neglect the idols that were unable to help them.

XV.1 I shall also relate what happened in a village of the Aedui. While Martin was destroying another temple, a furious crowd of pagan villagers attacked him. When one of them who was braver than the others drew his sword and aimed a blow at him, Martin threw back his cloak and offered his bare neck to the man who was on the point of hitting him. (2) The pagan did not hesitate to strike but when he raised his right arm higher, he fell backwards. Overwhelmed by fear of the divine, he begged for mercy. (3) That story is not unlike the following one: when someone wanted to stab Martin with a knife while he was destroying some idols, the weapon was knocked from the man's hands as he struck the blow, and disappeared. More often, however, when the country people tried to prevent him destroying their shrines, he would restrain the minds of these pagans by means of his holy teaching in such a way that when the light of truth was revealed to them, they would destroy their own temples themselves.

XVI.1 He also possessed such a powerful gift of healing that there was hardly a sick person who came to him who was not restored to health on the spot. (2) At Trier[23] there was a girl in the grip of such a terrible paralysis that for a long time now she had been unable to use her body for the normal human functions: she was nearly dead in every part of her body, her pulse was almost non-existent and her breathing faint. (3) Her grieving relatives were at her bedside, waiting only for her death, when suddenly the news came that Martin had arrived in that city. As soon as the girl's father learned of this, he ran breathlessly to ask for help for his daughter. (4) By chance Martin had already entered the church. There, in full view of the congregation and the many other bishops present, the old man embraced Martin's knees, lamenting loudly and said, 'My daughter is dying from a terrible wasting disease and, what is more cruel even than death, only her breathing proves that she is still alive – in her flesh she is already prematurely dead. I ask you to come to her and bless her, for I am confident that through you she must be restored to health.' (5) Martin was filled with confusion at these words and stood there horrified; he tried to avoid what was asked of him by saying that this was not part of his special power, that the old man was mistaken in his judgement and that he himself was not worthy to be used by the Lord to reveal a sign of His power. The father, in tears, persisted all the more determinedly, begging Martin to come and see the dying girl. (6) Finally, Martin was prevailed upon to go by the bishops standing round him and so he went along to the girl's house. A huge crowd was waiting outside the doors to see what the servant of God would do. (7) First of all he lay down on the ground and prayed – this being his usual weapon in such circumstances. Then he examined the sick girl and asked for some oil. When he had blessed her, he poured the power of this holy liquid into the girl's mouth and immediately her voice was restored to her. (8) Then, little by little, as Martin touched each of her limbs, they began to come to life, until she got up and walked with steady steps as the people looked on.

XVII.1 At the same period, the slave of a man called Taetradius who was of proconsular rank, was possessed by a demon tormenting him to death with great pain. When Martin was asked to lay his hand on him, he ordered that the man should be brought to him. But it was utterly impossible for the evil spirit to be brought out from the cell where it was, so fiercely did it attack those who tried to enter with its rabid bites. (2) Then Taetradius threw himself at the blessed man's feet, begging him to come along to the house where the possessed man was being held. But Martin said that he was unable to enter a house that belonged to a pagan, an adherent of a false religion. (3) For at that time Taetradius was still entangled in the error of paganism. So he promised that if the demon was driven out of the boy, he would become a Christian. (4) Then Martin laid his hand on the boy and cast forth the unclean spirit from him. When he saw this, Taetradius believed in the Lord Jesus and was immediately made a catechumen; not long afterwards he was baptized and continued always to have an extraordinary affection for Martin as the person responsible for his salvation. (5) During this same period and in the same town, as Martin was entering a house belonging to the head of some family, he stopped on the very threshold, explaining that he could see a horrifying demon in the entrance hall to the house. When he ordered it to depart, the demon seized the owner's cook, who was in the inner part of the building. The wretched thing began to tear him with its teeth and to maul anyone it came across. The house was thrown into confusion, the household members panicked, and the people turned and ran. (6) Martin stood in the way of this raving creature and first ordered it to stop. But when it raged and showed its teeth and, with mouth wide open, threatened to bite him, Martin put his fingers in its mouth and said, 'If you have any power, eat these.' (7) But then, as if it had received white-hot metal in its jaws, it withdrew its teeth a long way, refusing to touch the holy man's fingers. Forced by these punishments and torments to flee from the body of the man who was possessed, it was not allowed to leave through his mouth but was expelled in a flow of diarrhoea, leaving behind it foul traces.

XVIII.1 Then, when a sudden rumour concerning barbarian movements and attacks had thrown the city into a panic, Martin gave the order that a man possessed of a demon should be brought before him. He commanded it to state publicly whether this news was true. (2) It then confessed that it was accompanied by ten demons who had spread the rumour throughout the population so that this fear, if nothing else, might drive Martin from that town; it admitted that the barbarians were not planning an attack at all. And so, as soon as the unclean spirit had confessed these things in the middle of the church, the city was freed from the fear and confusion rife at that time. (3) At Paris, as Martin was entering the city gate accompanied by huge crowds, to everyone's horror he kissed a leper with a piteous face and blessed him. At once the man was cleansed from all his misfortune, (4) and on the following day he came to church, his skin radiantly healthy, and gave thanks for the health he had recovered. One should not omit to mention the fact that bits of material pulled from Martin's cloak and hair shirt often had a powerful healing effect on those who were sick: (5) when tied to the fingers or applied to the neck of the patients, their illnesses were frequently dispelled.

XIX.1 When the daughter of Arborius, a man who had been Prefect and who was of a perfectly holy and faithful nature, was burning with a very serious quartan fever, her father placed on the girl's chest, while the fever was at its height, a letter from Martin which happened to have been delivered to him, and immediately the fever was dispelled. (2) This event had such an effect on Arborius that he immediately offered his daughter to God and dedicated her to perpetual virginity. He went to find Martin and presented his daughter to him as a living witness to his special powers, seeing that she had been cured by him even though he was not present. Arborius would not allow anyone other than Martin to put the virgin's robes on her and to consecrate her. (3) When Paulinus,[24] a man who was later to become a great example, began to suffer from a serious eye complaint and quite a thick grey film had spread across his pupil and now covered it, Martin touched his eye with a little brush. All the pain vanished and the eye was restored to the healthy state it had previously enjoyed. (4) Once Martin himself fell, rolling down from the upper room: as he fell over the uneven steps of the ladder he suffered multiple injuries. While he lay half dead in his cell in absolute agony, an angel appeared to him at night to wash his wounds and to anoint the bruises on his battered body with a healing ointment. The following day he was so much better that one might have thought he had never had any accident. (5) But it would take a long time to go through all the details: these stories – a few out of many – must suffice. Let it be enough that we have not removed the truth from the salient points and that we have avoided tiring the reader by relating too many.

XX.1 But let me include some lesser events among these great achievements. Our age has become so depraved and corrupted that it is almost exceptional for a priest to have the strength not to yield to flattery of the emperor. When a number of bishops from different parts of the world came together to visit the emperor Maximus,[25] a man of a fierce nature who was proud of his victory in the civil wars, the revolting sycophancy of all of them towards the emperor was noted, as was the fact that their priestly dignity had, as a result of their despicable weakness, stooped to the level of imperial clients: in Martin alone did the apostolic authority remain intact. (2) For even though he had to intercede with the king on behalf of a number of people, he demanded rather than begged, and although he was frequently invited, he refused to dine with Maximus, saying that he could not share the table of a person who had deprived one emperor of his sovereignty, another of his life.[26] (3) Finally Maximus protested that he had not taken up power voluntarily, but that he had used arms to defend the sovereign power imposed upon him by the soldiers[27] in accordance with the divine will: he did not think that God's will could be at odds with someone who had gained such a remarkable victory, and none of his enemies had been killed except in battle. Martin was at last convinced by his arguments or by his entreaties and attended the banquet, while the ruler was extraordinarily pleased to have achieved this. (4) The guests who were present, as if invited to celebrate some feast day, were illustrious men, the top-ranking people. There was the Prefect and consul Evodius, the most just man there has ever been, two counts invested with supreme power, the emperor's brother and his uncle. The priest who had come with Martin sat between these two, while Martin himself was seated on a chair beside the emperor. (5) About half-way through the banquet, according to custom an attendant brought a libation bowl to the emperor who told him that it should be given instead to the most holy bishop, for the emperor hoped and wished to receive the cup from the bishop's hand. (6) But when Martin had drunk from it, he passed the bowl to his priest, no doubt thinking that no one was worthier to drink immediately after himself and that it would not be in his power to put the emperor himself or those who were closest to the emperor before the priest. (7) The emperor and all those present were so amazed by what he had done that they actually approved of an act which humiliated them. And the news spread through the palace that Martin, at the emperor's banquet, had done something which none of the bishops had done at dinners hosted by lesser officials. (8) To this same Maximus Martin predicted long in advance that if he went to Italy where he planned to go to wage war against the emperor Valentinian, he ought to be aware that he would be victorious in the first onslaught but that he would die shortly afterwards. (9) That is indeed what we saw happen: when Maximus first arrived, Valentinian turned and fled, but about a year later, when he had regained his strength, he captured Maximus within the walls of Aquileia and killed him.

XXI.1 It is certain that angels often appeared to Martin, even going so far as to enter into conversation and talk with him. But as for the devil, Martin could see him so easily and so clearly that whether he retained his own form or turned himself into various evil shapes, Martin could recognize him, whatever his disguise. (2) But when the devil realized that he could not escape, he would frequently hurl abuse at Martin, because he was unable to deceive him by his wiles. One time he burst into Martin's cell with a loud roar, holding in his hand a bull's bloody horn. He showed his bloody hand, and glorying in the crime he had just committed, he said, 'Where is your power, Martin? I have just killed one of your friends.' (3) Then Martin called the brothers together and told them what the devil had revealed. He told them to go carefully round all the cells to find out who had suffered this fate. They reported that none of the monks was missing but that one peasant, hired to transport some wood, had gone into the forest. Martin therefore ordered some of them to go and meet him; (4) he was found not far from the monastery, already on the point of death. As he breathed his last, he revealed to the brothers the cause of his deadly wound: when his oxen were yoked together, as he was tightening the straps which had come undone, an ox shook his head free and drove his horns into the peasant's groin. A short while later he yielded up his life. It is for you to decide by what judgement of the Lord this power was granted to the devil. (5) What was amazing about Martin was that he foresaw long in advance not only what we mentioned earlier but many things of this kind whenever they happened, or he made them known to the brothers as soon as they were revealed to him.

XXII.1 The devil appeared to Martin in the most diverse forms in his attempts to trick the holy man by means of a thousand harmful devices. Sometimes he appeared transformed into the person of Jupiter, sometimes that of Mercury and often even of Venus and Minerva. Martin, always unafraid, protected himself against him by making the sign of the cross and with the help of prayer. (2) Often one could hear abuse hurled at him by the throng of demons using foul language, but Martin knew that all these things were deceptive and an illusion and was therefore unmoved by their taunts. (3) Some of the brothers also claimed that they had heard a demon accusing Martin in foul language of having received into the monastery after their conversion some brothers who had once lost the grace of baptism as a result of various sins, and the demon had set forth their individual sins. (4) Martin resisted the devil and answered firmly that the old faults had been purged away by a better way of life: by the Lord's mercy those who had ceased to sin would be absolved from their sins. When the devil retorted that forgiveness was not appropriate for guilty people and that no mercy could be obtained from the Lord for those who had once fallen into error, Martin is said to have then exclaimed in these words; (5) 'If you, you wretched creature, ceased to persecute people and repented of your deeds, particularly at this time when the Day of Judgement is close at hand, then I, who trust completely in the Lord Jesus Christ, would promise you mercy.' How saintly of Martin to anticipate the Lord's goodness! Although he was unable to offer a guarantee of it, he did show his feelings. (6) And since we have started to discuss the devil and his devices, it does not seem irrelevant – in fact, it seems to be at the heart of the matter – to mention what happened, for a good deal of Martin's special powers are revealed in this event and a story which has the status of a miracle should rightly be recorded as a warning, in case anything similar should occur in future.

XXIII.1 Clarus[28] was a young man of the highest nobility who later became a priest and now is blessed as a result of his fortunate death. After abandoning everything and going to join Martin, it was not long before he shone forth at the very summit of faith and all virtues. (2) It happened that after he had built a hut for himself not far from the bishop's monastery and while many of the brothers were living with him, a young man called Anatolius, professing to be a monk and making a show of every form of humility and innocence, came to him and for a time lived a communal life with the others. (3) Then, as time went on, he claimed that angels regularly conversed with him. As no one put any faith in what he said, he used certain signs to force a number of the brothers to believe him. Finally he went so far as to declare that messengers went back and forth between himself and God: he now wanted to be considered one of the prophets. (4) But there was no way that Clarus could be forced to believe even though Anatolius threatened him with God's anger and immediate punishment for not believing in a saint. (5) At last Anatolius is said to have burst forth with these words: 'Look! Tonight the Lord will give me a white tunic from heaven and dressed in this, I shall remain in your midst. The fact that I have been presented with a tunic from God will be a sign to you that I am the power of God.' (6) Then great indeed was the expectation of all when they heard this claim. At about midnight the whole monastery appeared to shake with a loud noise as of people stamping the ground. You would have seen the cell in which the young man was being kept light up with repeated flashes and you would have heard the sound of people rushing about inside, as well as a sort of murmur of numerous voices. (7) Then when all was silent Anatolius came out. He summoned one of the brothers called Sabatius and showed him the tunic he was wearing. (8) Sabatius was astonished and called the others. Clarus himself came running, and when a light had been brought they all carefully examined the garment. It was extremely soft, exceptionally white, dazzlingly bright and made of a material that could not be identified; but when inspected by curious eyes and fingers, it seemed to be an ordinary tunic. Clarus then told the brothers to begin praying that the Lord might reveal to them more clearly what it was. (9) So the rest of the night was spent in hymns and psalms. When daylight came, Clarus grasped Anatolius by the hand, intending to take him along to see Martin, for he was well aware that Martin could not be deceived by the devil's wiles. (10) Then the wretched man began to struggle and shout, saying that he was forbidden to show himself to Martin. When they forced him to go against his will, the tunic vanished in the hands of those who were dragging him along. (11) And so who can doubt that it was also Martin's special power that made it impossible for the devil to keep his deception secret or disguise it any longer once it was going to be brought before Martin's eyes?

XXIV.1 It was noticed that at about the same time there was a young man in Spain who became so carried away when he gained influence as a result of performing numerous miracles that he claimed to be Elijah. (2) Many people foolishly believed this and so he went further and said that he was Christ: so great was the deception he caused that a bishop by the name of Rufus worshipped him as God (which is why we saw this man later stripped of the episcopacy). (3) A large number of the brothers have reported to us that at the same period there was someone in the East who boasted that he was John, from which we can deduce that when pseudo-prophets of this kind appear, the coming of the Antichrist is imminent, for in these men he is already working the mystery of his iniquity. (4) I think I ought to mention what exceptional cunning the devil used to try and tempt Martin at that time. One day he appeared to Martin who was praying in his cell: he was preceded by a bright light with which he also surrounded himself in the hope of more easily tricking Martin by means of a feigned brightness. He wore a royal robe and was crowned with a diadem made of gold and jewels, wore gilded sandals, had a serene expression and a look of joy – no one could have looked less like the devil! (5) When Martin first saw him he was stunned and for a long time they both maintained a profound silence. Then the devil spoke first, 'Martin, recognize who you are looking at. I am Christ. Intending to come down to earth I wished to reveal myself first to you.' (6) When Martin remained silent and said nothing in reply to these words, the devil dared to repeat his bold claim. 'Martin, why do you hesitate? Believe, since you can see: I am Christ.' Then, as a result of the spirit's revelation, Martin understood that it was the devil, not the Lord, and so he said, 'The Lord Jesus did not foretell that He would come in splendid clothes and with a shining crown; I will not believe that Christ has come unless He wears the same garments and has the same appearance as at the time of His suffering, and unless He bears the marks of the cross.' At these words the devil immediately vanished like smoke. He filled the cell with such a strong smell that he left clear proof that he was the devil. In case anyone should happen to think this incident mere fiction, I actually learned of it, as I mentioned earlier, from the mouth of Martin himself.

XXV.1 After having heard about his faith, his life and his virtue for a long time, we were burning with a desire to meet him and so we gladly undertook a long journey to see him. At the same time, because I was already very keen to write his life, we partly questioned the man himself (in so far as it was possible for him to be questioned) and partly tried to find out from those who had been present or who knew of his deeds. (2) You cannot believe the humility and kindness with which he welcomed me at that time. He was very pleased, rejoicing in the Lord that we had considered him so important as to undertake a long journey to seek him out. (3) Wretched creature that I am – I hardly dare to admit it – when he was kind enough to invite me to share his holy meal, he himself brought the water to wash our hands. In the evening he washed our feet himself and we did not have the courage to resist or refuse: I was so overwhelmed by his authority that I would have thought it sinful not to allow him to do so. (4) All his conversation with us was concerned with the need to leave behind the seductions of this world and our secular burdens so that, free and untrammelled, we might follow the Lord Jesus. He insisted to us that the most outstanding model of our time was that famous man Paulinus, whom we mentioned earlier: he who gave up immense riches to follow Christ and was thus almost the only one in our time to have fulfilled the precepts of the Gospel. (5) It was him we must follow, insisted Martin, it was him we must imitate: the present age was fortunate in having an example of such great faith and virtue, since, according to the words of the Lord, the rich man who had many possessions, had by selling everything and giving to the poor made possible the impossible by means of his example.

(6) And then, how full of gravity and dignity were his words and his conversation! How sharp and how forceful he was, how readily and easily he solved Scriptural problems! (7) And because I know that many find it hard to believe this (for I have seen some who refused to believe even when I myself told them about it), I call Jesus and our shared hope to witness that I never heard from anyone's lips so much knowledge, so much wisdom, so much excellent and pure speech. (8) With regard to Martin's virtues this eulogy does not go very far, but it is amazing that not even this grace was lacking to an uneducated person.

XXVI.1 But now the book demands an end and I must conclude this account, not because I have exhausted all there is to say about Martin but because like those lazy poets who write carelessly at the end of their work, we are giving up, overwhelmed by the amount of material. (2) For even if a full account of his deeds might in some measure be given, no account, I truly believe, no account could ever provide a full description of his inner life, his daily behaviour and his soul which was always focused on heaven: I mean his perseverance and moderation in abstinence and in fasting, his ability to stay awake and pray, and the nights as well as days he spent in this way, the fact that he had no time spare from God's work to which he devoted himself, whether in activity or at leisure, while going without both food and sleep except in so far as the demands of nature forced him to partake of them. (3) In truth, I will admit that not if Homer himself, as they say,[29] emerged from the underworld could he give an accurate account of this: everything in Martin is so much greater than can be expressed in words. Never did any hour or moment pass when he was not absorbed in prayer or concentrating on reading, although he never allowed his mind to relax from prayer, even during his periods of reading or if he happened to be doing something else. (4) Without doubt, just as in the case of blacksmiths who strike their anvil during the break in their work as a kind of relaxation from their hard work, so Martin always prayed even while he seemed to be doing something else. (5) O truly blessed man, in whom there was no guile: no one did he judge, no one did he condemn, never did he return evil for evil. He bore all insults with such patience that, although he was the priest of the highest rank, he allowed himself to be hurt with impunity by the lowest of the clergy, nor did such behaviour lead him to remove them from their position or reject them from his love, as far as it depended on him.

XXVII.1 No one ever saw him angry, never worked up, never mournful, never laughing: he was always one and the same. Bearing an expression of joy that was in some way heavenly, he seemed above human nature. There was never anything on his lips except Christ, (2) never anything in his heart except devotion, peace and forgiveness. He often used to weep even for the sins of those who appeared to be his critics and who tore at him with their poisonous tongues and viperous jaws while he remained detached and calm. (3) In fact we knew some people who envied his virtue and his life and who hated in him what they did not see in themselves and what they were unable to imitate. And it was said (what a grievous and lamentable scandal!) that most of his critics, few in number though they were, were actually bishops. (4) It is certainly unnecessary to name them, although many of them bark at us, too. It will suffice that if any one of them should read this and recognize the truth, he should blush with shame, for if he grows angry, he will be admitting that he is the one who is meant, although we might have had others in mind. (5) But we cannot evade the fact that if there are people of this kind, they will hate us as well as a man like Martin. (6) I am certain that this little work will please all holy people. For the rest, should anyone read this without faith, he will be sinning. (7) Driven to write by faith in these things and by the love of Christ, I am confident that I have given a clear account of things and spoken the truth; and the reward prepared by God, as I hope, will await not whoever reads this but whoever believes it.

Life of Benedict by Gregory the Great

Life of Remedut by Gregory of Graf

The Life of Benedict *is unusual in that it was not written as a self-contained work but forms the second book of Gregory's* Dialogues, *a work in four books*[1] *which aims to do for the saints of Italy*[2] *what Palladius and others had done for the saints of Egypt, and what Sulpicius Severus had done for St Martin of Gaul some two centuries earlier. The* Dialogues *were written by Pope Gregory I in 593 or 594, apparently at the request of some of his friends, who had urged him to write something on the subject of the miracles performed by recent Christians in Italy to show that God had not abandoned His people, even though it must have sometimes seemed like it in that period of catastrophes of all kinds.*

Gregory, born in about 540, had been pope since 590. He grew up at the time of the invasions of the Goths and pursued a successful public career, as was expected of someone with his family credentials and excellent education, but renounced this way of life in order to live as an ascetic in Rome. However, it was not long before he was brought out of monastic retirement by the pope at the time: he ordained Gregory deacon and sent him on a mission to Constantinople to ask for military aid from the emperor. On his return some years later, Gregory withdrew to the monastery once more but continued to act as Pope Pelagius' secretary. When this pope died of the plague which was scourging Rome, Gregory was chosen as his successor, much against his will, for he hated to exchange the peace of the monastic life for the administrative burden of high office. Yet he proved himself to be a pope of great distinction at a time of crisis in Italy, and indeed was forced to take on the role of civil ruler to negotiate with the Lombards, who were now threatening to destroy Rome. Despite his official responsibilities he managed to write several major works,[3] *as well as leaving over eight hundred letters which are the prime source for our knowledge of Gregory's life.*

The Life of Benedict *differs from previous Christian biographies in that, in accordance with the subtitle of the* Dialogues, *it concentrates primarily on the miracles performed by St Benedict, at the expense of information about his teachings, his character or appearance. The dialogues of the title take place between Gregory and his deacon Peter: the miracle stories, of varying lengths, are interspersed with Peter's questions and Gregory's theological and scriptural reflections. The dialogue form had already been used in Greek and Latin literature by such writers as Plato, Cicero, Seneca and Tacitus, but took on a new lease of life in Christian literature when it was used for the defence of the faith against pagans, Jews or heretics,*[4] *for philosophical debate (as in the case of Augustine's early works written at Cassiciacum) and for more biographical – but still basically didactic – purposes, as in the case of the* Dialogues *of Sulpicius Severus and Palladius'* Dialogue on the Life of John Chrysostom *at the beginning of the fifth century. It is with this latter category that Gregory's* Dialogues *have most in common.*

Gregory's Dialogues *soon reached a wider audience than the friends for whom it was originally written. In the west we find that writers such as Adomnan, in his* Life of St Columba, *and Bede, in his* Life of Cuthbert *and* The Ecclesiastical History of the English People, *were clearly familiar with the work. It was one of the works translated into Old English under King Alfred the Great, along with Gregory's* Pastoral Rule. *In the east the work was translated in the eighth century into Greek by Pope Zacharias, which enabled it to become known in the Byzantine world. The text of the* Dialogues *continued to be copied throughout the Middle Ages: it sometimes appeared as a whole but often, because of the importance of Benedict for the history of monasticism, the second book was copied on its own or together with the text of the* Rule of Benedict. *The very miracle stories which seem to have caused many modern readers to dismiss the work as unworthy of Gregory were what made the* Life of Benedict *so popular among medieval readers as an inspiration to the Christian life.*

Prologue

There was a man whose life was worthy of veneration, Benedict by name and blessed by grace.[1] From his very childhood he possessed the wisdom of old age; his behaviour made him seem older than he was and he took no interest in sensual pleasures. While he still lived upon this earth, he despised as if it were dust the world and its splendour which he could have freely enjoyed for a time. Benedict came from a free-born family from the district of Nursia[2] and had been sent to Rome for a liberal education. But when he noticed that many students fell headlong into vice, he stepped back, as it were, just as he was about to enter the world, fearing that if any worldly knowledge should touch him, he, too, would then fall, body and soul, into the bottomless abyss. And so, after abandoning the study of literature and leaving his father's home and property, wishing to please God alone, he went in search of the habit of a holy way of life. He therefore withdrew, knowledgeably ignorant and wisely unlearned.

2 I do not know of all this man's deeds, but the few that I am going to describe I learned of from the account of four of his disciples, namely Constantine, an extremely respectable man who succeeded Benedict as the head of the monastery; Valentinian who was for many years in charge of the Lateran monastery; Simplicius, who was the third person to rule his community after him; and Honoratus who is still in charge now of the cell in which Benedict first lived.[3]

Life of Benedict

I.1 And so, after abandoning his literary studies he decided to make for the solitary places, accompanied only by his nurse who loved him dearly. When they came to the place which is called Effide, many people from the nobility detained them there out of love. While they were staying at the church of St Peter, this nurse of his asked the neighbouring women if she could borrow a sieve to sift the chaff. She then carelessly left it lying on a table, and it happened to fall off and broke in two pieces. As soon as Benedict's nurse came back and found it, she burst into tears on seeing that the utensil that had been lent to her was broken.

2 When Benedict, who was a devout and affectionate boy, saw his nurse crying, he felt sorry for her in her grief: he took away with him both halves of the broken sieve and began to pray, in tears. When he got up from his prayer, he saw beside him the utensil in one piece: no mark was to be found on it to show where it had been broken. Then he tenderly reassured his nurse and gave her back the mended sieve which he had taken away in pieces. Everyone in that place got to hear of this and it was regarded with such awe that the inhabitants hung the sieve up at the entrance to the church so that all their contemporaries as well as future generations might know from what point of perfection the young boy Benedict had started on the grace of that way of life. For many years it remained there where everyone could see it, hanging above the doors of the church even to this day at the time of the Lombard invasions.

3 But Benedict was keen to experience the evils of the world more than its praises, to be exhausted by working hard on God's behalf more than to be exalted by the acclaim of this life. So he secretly ran away from his nurse and withdrew to a remote place called Subiaco, about forty miles from the city of Rome, where there are springs of cool, clear water: all this water first collects in a broad lake and then flows down into a river.

4 As he fled to this place, a monk called Romanus met him on his way and asked him where he was going. When he learned of Benedict's

plan, Romanus kept it secret and offered his assistance. He gave to Benedict the habit of the holy way of life and served him as best he could. When the man of God arrived there he made his home in a very cramped cave and stayed there for three years, unknown to anyone except the monk Romanus.

5 This man Romanus lived close by in a monastery under the rule of Father Adeodatus. But out of devotion he would steal away from this abbot of his and regularly bring Benedict bread which he had surreptitiously been able to smuggle out from his own rations. There was no path from Romanus' cell to this cave because of a high cliff projecting above it, but Romanus used to tie the bread to a very long rope and let it down from this cliff. He had also hung a little bell on this rope so that at the sound of the bell the man of God would know that Romanus was bringing him bread and that he should come out and fetch it. But the old enemy looked maliciously on Romanus' kindness and on Benedict's meal. One day when he saw the bread being lowered, he threw a stone at the bell and broke it. In spite of this, Romanus still continued to look after Benedict by appropriate means.

6 But the almighty God wanted Romanus to rest from his exertions and Benedict's life to be revealed as an example to men, so that the light placed on the candlestick might shine brightly and give light to all those in his house.[4] There was a priest living some distance away who had prepared himself a meal for the Easter celebrations. The Lord graciously appeared to this man in a vision, saying, 'You are preparing delicious food for yourself while my servant is tormented by hunger over there.' The priest got up at once and went to the place on Easter Day itself, taking the food that he had prepared for himself. He went looking for the man of God over steep mountains and through deep valleys and in the caverns in the earth until he found him hiding in his cave.

7 When they had prayed and blessed the almighty Lord, they sat down together and had a delightful conversation about their life. Then the priest who had come said, 'Come on, let us eat, for today it is Easter.' The man of God replied, 'I know that it is Easter, because I have been granted the privilege of seeing you.' He was certainly

isolated from people, seeing that he was unaware that it was Easter Day! Then the venerable priest stated it once more, saying, 'Today really is the day of the Lord's resurrection, Easter Day. It is not right for you to fast. I have been sent for this very reason, so that together we might partake of the gifts of the almighty Lord.' And so they thanked God and shared the food, and when the meal was over and they had finished conversing, the priest returned to his church.

8 At about this time some shepherds also found Benedict concealed in his cave. When they saw him through the bramble bushes, clothed in animal skins, they thought he was some wild beast, but when they came to know God's servant, many of them were transformed and their bestial mentality changed into the grace of devoutness. As a result Benedict's name became known to all throughout the neighbouring areas and it happened that from that time onwards he began to be visited by large numbers of people who brought him food for his body and from his lips took back the food of life in their hearts.

II One day, while he was alone, the tempter came to him. A little bird, commonly known as a blackbird, began to flutter around his head, coming up close to his face in such an insistent manner that the holy man could have caught it in his hand if he had wanted to. Instead he made the sign of the cross and the bird flew away. However, when it had gone, it was followed by a feeling of carnal temptation stronger than any the holy man had ever experienced. For the evil spirit presented to his mind's eye a woman whom he had seen some time earlier, and the sight of her set the soul of God's servant on fire, making it burn so violently that his heart could hardly contain the flame of passion. Benedict almost decided to abandon the wilderness, overcome by sensual pleasure.

2 Suddenly he was touched by heavenly grace and came to himself once more. Seeing some dense bushes with nettles and brambles growing near by, he took off his clothes and threw himself naked into those sharp thorns and stinging nettles. Rolling around in them for a long time, he emerged with sores and scratches all over his body. These wounds to his skin allowed him to remove the mental wound from his body by turning the pleasure to pain. The external pain served as a beneficial punishment for he thereby managed to extinguish

the fire burning sinfully within him; and so by transforming the fire he gained a victory over sin.

3 From that time onwards, as he himself later told his disciples, he managed to control the temptation of sexual pleasure so completely that he never experienced it in the slightest. Afterwards, many people began to abandon the world and to hasten to learn from him, for now that he was free from the vice of sexual temptation, it was right that he should become a teacher of virtue. That is why Moses orders that Levites should enter service from the age of twenty-five but from their fiftieth year they should become guardians of the vessels.[5]

4 PETER: I now have some understanding of this text but I would still like you to explain it more fully.

GREGORY: It is obvious, Peter, that when one is young the temptation of the flesh is at its strongest, but from one's fiftieth year the body's heat begins to cool. The sacred vessels are the minds of the faithful: that is why it is necessary for the chosen ones, while they are still victims of temptation, to be subordinate, to serve and tire themselves out in works of obedience; but after the heat of temptation has receded and the mind attains the peace of age, they are the guardians of the vessels for they then are made the teachers of souls.

5 PETER: Yes, I agree with what you say. But now that you have revealed the secrets of this particular text, I beg you to continue with the account you started on of the life of this just man.

III GREGORY: As temptation receded then, the man of God produced a more abundant harvest of virtues, now that he had, as it were, pulled out the weeds from the cultivated soil. As word of his exemplary life spread, his name became increasingly famous.

2 Near by there stood a monastery where the abbot of the community had died. The whole community came to the venerable Benedict and begged him, with earnest entreaties, to become their abbot. For a long time he refused and put them off, predicting that his way of life would not suit the brothers, but at last he had to yield to their entreaties and gave his consent.

3 In that monastery[6] Benedict preserved the life according to a rule, allowing no one, by unlawful behaviour, to turn aside to right or left from the path of the monastic life, as they had done previously. As a

result the brothers of whom he was in charge became insanely angry and began to accuse each other for having asked this man to be their abbot, since their deviant behaviour clashed with his standard of rectitude. When they saw that under his leadership unlawful things were no longer lawful, they were aggrieved at having to abandon their habits, for they found it hard that their minds, which were set in their ways, should be forced to think new things (for the life of the virtuous is always a burden to the wicked). As a result they tried to devise a means of killing him.

4 Having decided upon a plan, they put poison into his wine. When the glass vessel containing that deadly drink was offered to their abbot as he reclined at table so that he might bless it in accordance with monastic custom, Benedict stretched out his hand and made the sign of the cross: the goblet broke as soon as this sign was made, even though it was not within his reach. It shattered as if he had thrown a stone at this vessel of death instead of making the sign of the cross. The man of God understood at once that it had contained a deadly drink because it could not bear the sign of life. He got up immediately and with a calm expression and without any agitation he called the brothers together and addressed them, saying, 'May God almighty have pity on you, my brothers. Why do you wish to do this to me? Did I not say to you at the beginning that your ways and mine were incompatible? Go and seek an abbot for yourselves who suits your ways, because after this you definitely cannot have me.'

5 Then he returned to the place of his beloved solitude and lived with himself, alone in the sight of Him who watches from on high.

PETER: I am not really clear what is meant by the phrase 'he lived with himself'.

GREGORY: The way of life of those monks who had united to conspire against him was so completely different from his own that if the holy man had wished to force them to remain under his rule for a long time and against their will, he might perhaps have exceeded his strength and lost his peace and turned his mind's eye away from the light of contemplation. Each day, exhausted by their refusal to be corrected, he would have neglected his own affairs and might perhaps have abandoned himself without finding them. For whenever we are taken outside ourselves by becoming excessively preoccupied, we remain ourselves but we are no longer with ourselves because we utterly fail to see ourselves as we wander all over the place.

6 Would we say that someone was with himself if he were to go away to a distant country where he spent part of the inheritance he had received and then had to hire himself out to one of the citizens, feeding the man's pigs and watching them munch acorns while he went hungry? When he then begins to think of the good things he has lost, it is about him that Scripture says, *Returning to himself, he said, How many workers there are in my father's house who have plenty of bread!*[7] If he were with himself, how could he return to himself?

7 I would therefore say that this venerable man lived with himself because he always kept watch over himself, always seeing himself in the Creator's eyes, constantly examining himself and not allowing his mind's eye to stray outside himself.

8 PETER: Then how about what is written concerning the apostle Peter when he had been led out of prison by the angel? *When he returned to himself, he said, Now I know for sure that the Lord sent his angel to snatch me from the hand of Herod and from every expectation of the Jewish people.*[8]

9 GREGORY: There are two ways, Peter, in which we are carried outside ourselves: either we fall beneath ourselves by some lapse of thought, or we are raised above ourselves by the grace of contemplation. So the man who fed the pigs fell beneath himself because his mind wandered and because of his filthiness, but he whom the angel released and whose mind was caught up into a state of ecstasy, was outside himself, certainly, but above himself. Both of them returned to themselves, the former when he came back to his senses from the error of his deed, the latter, when from the heights of contemplation he returned to his former, normal state of mind. And so the venerable Benedict lived with himself in solitude, in so far as he kept himself within the walls of his thought, but whenever the ardour of contemplation swept him up on high, he undoubtedly left himself beneath himself.

10 PETER: What you say is clear. But please answer this: was he right to abandon the brothers once he had taken charge of them?

GREGORY: In my opinion, Peter, bad men who have ganged up together ought to be endured with patience if there are some good men among them who can be helped. But when the fruit from good men is completely lacking, effort on behalf of the bad is sometimes wasted, especially if there exist sufficient opportunities for bringing better fruit to God. Who should the holy man have remained to protect, when he saw that they had all united to persecute him?

11 We should also mention what often happens in the mind of those who are perfect: when they see that their efforts are fruitless, they move elsewhere to find more fruitful work. This is the reason why that outstanding preacher[9] who longed to be released and to be with Christ, for whom to live was Christ and to die was profit,[10] who not only sought painful struggles for himself but also inspired others to endure similar things, after suffering persecution at Damascus, got hold of a basket and a rope so that he could escape and arranged for himself to be let down secretly.[11] Would we say that Paul feared death when he claims to be eager for it for the sake of Jesus' love?[12] No, but when he saw that his hard work was bearing less fruit there, he saved himself for more fruitful work elsewhere. God's fearless fighter refused to be imprisoned and went in search of battle in the open.

12 It was the same with the venerable Benedict: if you listen carefully, you will soon realize that in abandoning those who could not be taught and by remaining alive himself he was able to bring many others back to life from spiritual death.

PETER: Clear reason and the fitting evidence you have adduced prove that what you say is true. But I ask you to stop digressing and get back to your account of this great abbot's life.

13 GREGORY: As the holy man increased in virtues and miracles in this wilderness, he inspired many people to gather there to serve the almighty God – so many, in fact, that he built twelve monasteries there with the help of Jesus Christ, the almighty Lord. To each of these monasteries he assigned groups of twelve monks, as well as one abbot for each group. He did however keep a few monks with him, thinking that they would still benefit from his personal instruction.

14 At that time religious men from Roman noble families began to join him, too, and entrust their sons to him so that he might raise

them for the almighty Lord. Euthicius and the patrician Tertullus also handed over their offspring, Maurus and Placidus, on whom their hopes of good fortune rested. Of these two, Maurus[13] was slightly older, and as he was growing into a young man of fine character, he began to act as his master's assistant, while Placidus was still only child. IV In one of these monasteries that he had built all around that area was a monk who could not stand still to pray. As soon as the brothers had bent down to start praying, this man would go outside and engage in worldly and ephemeral activities, letting his thoughts wander. After being repeatedly told off by his abbot, he was taken to the man of God, who also rebuked him in strong terms for his foolishness. Returning to the monastery he could only just manage to hold fast to the admonition of the man of God for two days: on the third day he reverted to his usual practice and began to wander around when it was time for prayer.

2 The abbot of his monastery, whom Benedict had appointed, reported this to the servant of God who said, 'I will come and correct him myself.' So the man of God came to this monastery, and while the brothers were devoting themselves to prayer at the regular time, he saw that after the psalm-singing this monk who could not remain at prayer was being pulled outside by a little black boy[14] tugging at the fringe of his garment. Then Benedict whispered to the abbot of the monastery, who was called Pompeianus, and to Maurus, God's servant, 'Can you not see who is pulling this monk outside?' When they answered, 'No,' he said to them, 'Let us pray that you too might see whom this monk is following.' After praying for two days, the monk Maurus saw him, but Pompeianus, the abbot of the monastery, was unable to see him.

3 And so the next day, after the prayers were finished, the man of God went out of the chapel and found the monk standing outside. Benedict struck the man with his staff for being so spiritually blind and from that day on, the man no longer fell victim to the little black boy's persuasiveness. Instead, he was able to remain still during prayer: it was as if the old enemy had been beaten and no longer dared to try and control his thoughts.

V Among the monasteries that he had built in that area there were three at the top of mountain cliffs. It was very hard for the brothers always to go down to the lake when they had to fetch water, especially since the steep mountainside meant that those who climbed nervously down it were in great danger. So a delegation of brothers from these three monasteries came to Benedict, God's servant, and said, 'It is difficult for us to go all the way down to the lake each day for water. The monasteries must therefore be moved from this site.'

2 Benedict gave them kind reassurances and sent them away. That same night he climbed the rocky mountain together with the little boy called Placidus whom I mentioned earlier. There he spent a long time in prayer and when he had finished praying, he placed three stones there to mark the spot. Then he returned to his monastery, unnoticed by anyone.

3 The following day, when these same brothers came back to him about the water they needed, he said, 'Go and make a little hollow in the rock where you find three stones piled on top of each other. The almighty God can produce water even on the top of that mountain to spare you the trouble of such an awkward descent.' They went and found the moisture already seeping out of the rock that Benedict had mentioned. When they had made a hollow in it, it was immediately filled with water welling up in such abundance that it flows even to this day, pouring down from the mountain top right to the bottom.

VI On another occasion a certain Goth, poor in spirit,[15] came to adopt that way of life and Benedict, the man of the Lord, welcomed him most warmly. One day Benedict ordered that this man should be given a metal tool (known as a bush-hook because of its similarity to a hook), so that he could cut away the thorn bushes in an area where they planned to create a garden. The place which the Goth had undertaken to clear was situated on the very edge of the lake. When the Goth attacked the thick brambles energetically, the metal tool shot out from the handle and fell into the lake where the water was so deep that there was now no hope of retrieving the hook.

2 On losing the tool, the Goth ran trembling with fear to the monk Maurus and reported what he had lost and apologized for his carelessness. The monk Maurus took care immediately to inform Benedict, the servant of God. On hearing this, Benedict, the man of

the Lord, went to the spot, took the handle from the Goth's hand and plunged it into the lake: immediately the metal tool came up from the deep and fitted into the handle. Benedict gave the iron tool back to the Goth straight away, saying, 'Here you are. Get on with your work now. There is no need to be upset.'

VII One day when the venerable Benedict was keeping to his cell, Placidus, the boy I mentioned earlier who was one of the holy man's monks, went out to fetch water from the lake. Lowering the bucket he was holding into the water without due care, he overbalanced and fell in after it. The current immediately took hold of him and dragged him into the middle, almost an arrow's flight away from the bank. Although the man of God was inside his cell, he realized at once what had happened and quickly called Maurus, saying, 'Run, brother Maurus. That boy who went to fetch water has fallen into the lake and the current is already carrying him away.'

2 Then a remarkable thing happened which no one had experienced since the apostle Peter: after asking for a blessing and receiving it, Maurus, at the abbot's command, ran swiftly right to the place where the boy was being swept away by the current. Although he thought he was running on land he was actually moving over the surface of the water. He grabbed the boy by his hair and ran back, still at great speed. As soon as he reached the bank, he came to himself and, looking behind him, he realized that he had run over the water. He would never have dared to do this! He trembled with shock at what he had done.

3 Maurus went back to his abbot and told him what had happened. Benedict, that venerable man, tried to attribute this not to his own merits but to Maurus' obedience, but Maurus took the opposite view. He said that this had happened solely as a result of Benedict's order and that he himself had no part in a miracle he had performed without even knowing it. Then the boy who had been saved came forward to arbitrate in this friendly dispute in which both parties were vying for humility. He said, 'When I was pulled out of the water I saw the abbot's sheepskin cloak above my head and I watched him pull me from the waters.'

4 PETER: These are certainly very impressive things that you are

recounting: they will serve to edify many people. However, I find that the more I drink the miracles of this good man, the thirstier I become.

VIII GREGORY: The people of this area for miles around were now fervent in their love of the Lord God, Jesus Christ. Many abandoned the secular life and bent their spiritual neck beneath the light yoke[16] of the redeemer. But wicked men have a tendency to be jealous of others' virtue which they cannot be bothered to strive for themselves. And so it happened that a priest of the neighbouring church, Florentius by name (the grandfather of our subdeacon Florentius), was smitten by the malice of the old enemy and began to envy the holy man's devotion, to denigrate his way of life and, as far as he was able, to keep visitors away from Benedict.

2 When Florentius realized that he could not stop Benedict's progress and that the reputation of his way of life was growing and that many were continually being called to a better life as his reputation spread, the flames of jealousy burned all the more within him. For he longed for the praise which Benedict's way of life brought him but he was not willing to lead a life worthy of praise. Blinded by this dark jealousy, he went so far as to poison the bread he gave to the servant of the almighty God for a blessing. The man of God took it with thanks but the poison hidden in the bread was not hidden from him.

3 At mealtimes a raven used to come out of the nearby wood and take bread from Benedict's hand. This time, when it came as usual, the man of God threw down in front of the raven the bread that the priest had handed him, saying, 'In the name of the Lord Jesus Christ, take this bread and drop it somewhere where no one can find it.' Then the raven, opening its beak wide and spreading its wings, began to run around the bread, cawing, as if to indicate that it wanted to obey but was unable to carry out the order. Again and again the man of God told him to do it, saying, 'Pick it up, pick it up. Do not be afraid. Just drop it where it cannot be found.' After hesitating a long time, the raven took the bread in its beak, picked it up and flew away. Three hours later it came back, after having thrown the bread away, and received its usual ration from the hands of the man of God.

4 Then the venerable father, seeing that the priest burned with a desire to kill him, grieved for him more than for himself. But as this man Florentius could not kill his master's body, he was fired with a determination to destroy the souls of Benedict's disciples. And so, before their very eyes, he sent seven naked girls into the garden of the cell where Benedict was to be found: holding hands, these girls danced for a long time in front of the disciples so as to inflame their minds with degrading lust.

5 The saintly man saw this from his cell and feared greatly that those disciples who were still young would succumb. As he understood that this was all aimed at him alone, he let envy have its way. In all the places of prayer that he had built he appointed priors for the groups of brothers, and together with a few monks whom he took with him, he moved his place of residence.

6 But as soon as the man of God had, by his humility, managed to escape Florentius' hatred, the almighty God struck this man in a terrible manner. While the priest was standing on the terrace, rejoicing at the news of Benedict's departure, the terrace on which he was standing collapsed, crushing and killing Benedict's enemy while the rest of the house remained undamaged.

7 Maurus, the man of God's disciple, thought that this ought to be reported immediately to the venerable father Benedict who was still only ten miles away. He sent a message saying, 'Come back, for the priest who was persecuting you has been killed.' When Benedict the man of God heard this, he began to sob with grief, either because his enemy was dead or because his disciple was exulting over his enemy's death. And so he imposed a penance on this disciple because he had dared to rejoice when sending news of his enemy's death.

8 PETER: What you say is amazing – quite astonishing! For in the water pouring from the rock I see Moses,[17] in the iron which came back from the depths of the water I see Elisha,[18] in the walking on water I see Peter,[19] in the obedience of the raven I see Elijah,[20] and in the grief at the death of his enemy I see David.[21] In my estimation, Benedict was filled with the spirit of all just men.

9 GREGORY: Actually, Peter, Benedict the man of the Lord possessed

the spirit of only one person, of Him who has filled the hearts of all the elect by granting them the grace of the redemption. John said of Him, *He was the true light who illuminates every man coming into this world*,[22] and it is also written of Him, *Of his fullness we have all received*.[23] For the holy men of God might possess special powers from the Lord but they could not grant them to others. But He who grants the signs of special power to the humble is He who promised His enemies that he would give them the sign of Jonah:[24] He was willing to die in the presence of the proud and rise again in the presence of the humble with the result that the former saw in Him something to despise and the latter saw something they had to love and venerate. As a result of this mystery it happened that while the proud see the contempt of death, the humble on the other hand receive the glory of power over death.

10 PETER: Please tell me now where the saint moved to and whether he displayed any miraculous powers there.

GREGORY: When the saint moved, he changed his place but not his enemy. For after this the battles he endured were all the harder because he found himself fighting openly against the master of evil in person. The fortification known as Casinum[25] is situated on the side of a high mountain which holds Casinum in a broad pocket and then stretches its summit, as it were, towards the sky: the distance from the fortification to the summit is three miles. There was a very old shrine there where Apollo was worshipped by the foolish country folk in accordance with ancient pagan practice. Around the shrine a grove of trees had grown up, also consecrated to the demons, and here, even at this time, large numbers of pagans in their madness used to expend great effort on their sacrilegious sacrifices.

11 When the man of God arrived there he smashed the statue, overturned the altar and cut down the grove. In the temple of Apollo itself he built a shrine to St Martin[26] and where the altar of Apollo had stood he built a shrine to St John, and by preaching ceaselessly he called to the faith all those living in the vicinity.

12 But the old enemy could not endure this in silence and so he appeared before the eyes of the abbot, not secretly or in a dream but in a clear vision. With loud cries he complained that he was being

attacked: even the brothers could hear his words although they were utterly unable see his shape. As the venerable abbot reported to his disciples, this old enemy appeared to his bodily eyes in a most hideous shape, all on fire, looking as if he were launching a ferocious assault on Benedict, his mouth and eyes shooting flames. Everyone could hear what he was saying. First he called Benedict by name, and when the man of God made no reply, he immediately started to abuse him. When he shouted 'Benedict, Benedict,' and saw that Benedict would not answer, he then added, 'Cursed, not blessed!²⁷ What have you got to do with me? Why are you persecuting me?'

13 But now we must expect new attacks by the old enemy on the servant of God. The devil, wishing to wage war against Benedict, against his will provided him with opportunities for victory.

IX One day as the brothers were building rooms at this monastery, they found a stone lying in the middle which they decided to use for their building. When two or three of the monks found it impossible to move it, more of them came to help but the stone remained immovable, as if it were rooted to the ground. It was obvious, then, that the old enemy was sitting on it in person, seeing that the hands of such strong men were unable to move it. Faced with this difficulty, they sent a message to the man of God, asking him to come and drive the enemy away by means of prayer, so that they could lift the stone. Benedict came at once and when he had said a prayer and given a blessing, the stone was lifted so quickly that it was as if it had never been weighted down.

X Then the man of God decided that they should dig the soil at that spot. On digging down quite deep, the brothers discovered a bronze idol there. They threw it into the kitchen for the time being: at once fire appeared to shoot out and it seemed to all the monks that the whole kitchen building would burn down.

2 As they attempted desperately to put the fire out by throwing water on it, the man of the Lord arrived, alerted by all the noise. He realized that this fire existed in the eyes of the brothers but not in his own. He immediately bowed his head in prayer and restored the sight of those brothers whom he found to be deceived by the imaginary fire, so that they could perceive that the kitchen building was standing

intact, instead of seeing the flames which were an illusion created by the old enemy.

XI Another time, the brothers were working on a wall which needed to be made a little higher, as circumstances demanded. The man of God remained within the walls of his tiny cell, spending his time in prayer. The old enemy appeared to him, taunting him, and indicated that he was going to visit the brothers at their work. The man of God quickly sent a messenger to the brothers to warn them, saying, 'Be careful, brothers! An evil spirit is on its way to you at this moment.' The messenger had hardly finished speaking when the evil spirit knocked down the wall that was being built. As it collapsed it crushed a young monk, the son of a decurion. They were all very upset and deeply shocked, not by the collapse of the wall but because their brother had been crushed. In profound sorrow they hastened to report this to their venerable abbot Benedict.

2 Then the abbot gave orders for the injured boy to be brought to him. They could only carry him in a cloak because the stones from the collapsed wall had crushed not only his arms and legs but all his bones. The man of God told them to bring the boy into his cell and put him straight away on the psiathium (in other words, the rush mat) on which Benedict used to pray. He then told the brothers to go outside, closed the door and lay down to pray with even greater intensity than usual. Then something marvellous happened: in the very same hour he sent this boy, now recovered and as healthy as before, back to his work so that he could help the brothers to finish the wall, even though the old enemy had thought he could insult Benedict by causing this boy's death.

3 At this period the man of God began to have the power of the spirit of prophecy, to predict the future and to report to those who were present what was happening far away.

XII It was the custom at the monastery for the brothers not to eat or drink anything whenever they went on some errand outside the monastery and this rule was strictly observed. One day the brothers went out on an errand and were forced to stay out until rather late. They decided to stop off at the home of a devout woman; so they entered her home and had a meal there.

2 Returning to the monastery a bit later, they sought their father's blessing as usual. He immediately asked them, 'Where did you eat?', to which they answered, 'Nowhere.' 'Why are you lying like this?' he said. 'Did you not go into such and such a woman's hut? Did you not receive such and such food? Did you not have this many drinks?' When the venerable father gave them specific details of the woman's hospitality, the kinds of food and the number of drinks, they recalled everything they had done and fell trembling at his feet, confessing their guilt. He immediately forgave them, knowing that they would not in future do such things in his absence, now that they knew that he was present with them in spirit.

XIII The brother of his monk Valentinian, whom I mentioned earlier,[28] was a layman but a devout one. Every year he used to come from his home to the monastery without having eaten anything, so as to receive a prayer from the servant of God and to see his brother. One day, on his way to the monastery, he was joined by a fellow traveller who was carrying food to eat on the journey. As it was now getting rather late, this man said, 'Come on, brother, let us have some food, so that we do not get tired on the way.' The other man answered, 'Certainly not, brother. I will not do so because it is my custom always to come to see the venerable father Benedict without having eaten anything.' On receiving this answer, his fellow traveller was quiet for a while.

2 But later, when they had gone a little further on their journey, he again suggested that they should eat. However, the one who had decided to arrive without having eaten anything refused, and the one who had invited him to eat said nothing, agreeing to go a little further still without eating. They continued on their journey but then, as it was getting late, the walkers began to get tired. Along their route they came across a meadow and a spring – everything which gave the impression of offering delightful refreshment. Then the fellow traveller said, 'Look, here is water, here is a meadow. This is a lovely spot where we can be refreshed and rest a while. Then we will be able to finish our journey in good shape.' As these words pleased his ears and the place pleased his eyes, Valentinian's brother was persuaded by this third invitation: he consented and joined his companion in a meal.

3 In the evening he arrived at the monastery. When he was brought into the presence of the venerable father Benedict, he asked for a prayer for himself. But at once the saint reproached him for what he had done on the way, saying, 'What is the matter, brother? The malicious enemy who spoke to you in the person of your fellow traveller could not persuade you the first time, nor the second, but the third time he persuaded you and made you do what he wanted.' Then the man admitted his guilt, caused by his weakness. He threw himself down at Benedict's feet and began to weep for the wrong he had done, feeling all the more ashamed because he realized that he had done wrong in front of father Benedict's eyes, even though he was far away.

4 PETER: I see that the saint's heart contained the spirit of Elisha, since he was present to his disciple even when he was far away.[29]

GREGORY: You must be quiet for the moment, Peter, so that you can hear about even more wonderful things.

XIV At the time of the Goths, their king Totila heard that the holy man possessed the spirit of prophecy, and so he set off for Benedict's monastery.[30] He stopped at some distance from it and sent a message to Benedict to say that he was coming. Immediately an order came back from the monastery that he should come, but Totila, being of a devious mentality, tried to test whether the man of the Lord really possessed the spirit of prophecy. He gave his boots to one of his guards, who was called Riggo, and made him dress up in his royal robes. He then ordered him to go to the man of God as if he himself were the king. As Riggo's attendants, Totila sent three counts who were closer to him than any others, namely Vult, Ruderic and Blidin. They were to walk beside Riggo while the servant of God was watching so as to maintain the pretence that Riggo was king Totila. He also added other trappings of power as well as more guards so that both the trappings and the purple garments might make Benedict believe that this man was the king.

2 When Riggo, dressed in these splendid garments and accompanied by a large number of attendants, entered the monastery, the man of God was seated at some distance. He saw Riggo approaching and as soon as he was within earshot he called out, 'Take off what you are

wearing, my son, take it off. It does not belong to you.' At once Riggo fell to the ground, terrified at having dared to try to trick such a great man. All those who were coming to see the man of God with him were thrown to the ground in terror. Getting up again they dared not go any closer to him but returned to their king. Trembling with fear they told Totila how quickly they had been discovered.

XV Totila then went in person to see the man of God. Seeing him seated some distance away, Totila dared not approach him but threw himself to the ground. Two or three times the man of God said to him, 'Get up,' but Totila did not dare to get up from the ground and stand upright in front of him. So Benedict, the servant of the Lord Jesus Christ, was himself humble enough to approach the king, who was lying on the ground. He raised Totila up and then rebuked him for what he had done and in a few words foretold everything that would happen to him, saying, 'You do much wrong, you have done much wrong: now at last put a stop to your wicked behaviour. You will enter Rome, you will cross the sea, you will reign for nine years and in the tenth year you will die.'

2 On hearing this, the king was terribly frightened. He asked for a prayer and then departed and from that time onwards he behaved with less cruelty. Not long afterwards he reached Rome and went on to Sicily and in the tenth year of his reign, by the judgement of the almighty God, he lost his kingdom together with his life.[31]

3 Moreover, the bishop of the church at Canosa[32] used to come and visit this servant of the Lord, and the man of God loved him very much on account of his virtuous life. While the bishop was discussing with Benedict king Totila's entry into Rome and the destruction of that city,[33] he said, 'The king is going to destroy that city and render it uninhabitable.' But Benedict replied, 'Rome will not be destroyed by the pagans. Instead it will be devastated by storms, by lightning, whirlwinds and earthquakes, and as a result it will fade away.' The mysteries of his prophecy have become clearer to us than the light of day, for in this city we see walls crumbling, houses demolished, the churches destroyed by a whirlwind, and its buildings, weakened by great age, lying on the ground in spreading ruins.

4 However, his disciple Honoratus,[34] from whom I learnt this, states

that he did not himself hear it from Benedict but claims that the brothers told him that Benedict had said this.

XVI At about the same time a cleric at the church of Aquinum[35] was being tormented by a demon. The venerable Constantius, bishop of that church, had sent him to visit many martyrs' shrines to find a cure, but the holy martyrs of God refused to grant him the gift of health, for they wanted to reveal how great the grace in Benedict was. And so the cleric was taken to Benedict, the servant of the almighty God, who poured forth prayers to the Lord Jesus Christ and managed to drive out the old enemy there and then from the man who was possessed. When he had been cured, Benedict ordered him, 'Go, and from now on do not eat meat and never dare to advance to holy orders. The day you dare to violate a holy order, you will immediately find yourself in Satan's power once more.'

2 And so the cleric went away cured, and for a time he kept the man of God's commandments (for a recent punishment tends to fill the mind with terror). But after several years, when all his elders had departed this life and he saw that those who were younger than him were being promoted before him in holy orders, he ceased to respect the man of God's words as if the passing of time had caused them to be forgotten, and he was ordained. At once the devil who had left him seized him again and continued to torment him until he had driven out his soul.[36]

3 PETER: As I see it, this man Benedict penetrated even the secrets of divinity, for he understood that this cleric had been handed over to the devil so as to prevent him entering a holy order.

GREGORY: How could he not have known the secrets of divinity seeing that he kept the divinity's commandments? For it is written, *He who is united to the Lord is one spirit.*[37]

4 PETER: If he who keeps close to the Lord becomes one spirit with the Lord, why is it that the same outstanding preacher also said, *Who has known the mind of the Lord or who has been his counsellor?*[38] For it seems very odd not to know the mind of the person with whom one becomes one.

5. GREGORY: In so far as holy men are one with the Lord, they do know the mind of the Lord. For this same Apostle also said, *For what*

man knows a man's thoughts except the spirit of the man which is within him? Similarly no one comprehends the thoughts of God except the spirit of God.[39] So as to show that he knew the thoughts of God, he added, *But we have received not the spirit of this world but the spirit which is from God,*[40] and he also said, *What no eye has seen, nor ear heard, nor the heart of man conceived, what God has prepared for those who love Him, He has revealed to us through His spirit.*[41]

6 PETER: If then the thoughts of God were revealed to this Apostle through the spirit of God, how come he said, before the passage I quoted just now, *How deep are the riches and wisdom and knowledge of God! How incomprehensible are His judgements and how inscrutable His ways?*[42] But as I say this, another problem occurs to me. For the prophet David speaks to the Lord, saying, *With my lips I have declared all the judgements of your mouth,*[43] and since it is a greater achievement to declare one's knowledge than merely to possess it, why is it that Paul stated that the judgements of God are incomprehensible, but David claims not only to know all these things but even to have declared them with his lips?

7 GREGORY: I have just given a brief answer to both these points, when I said that holy men are aware of the Lord's thoughts in so far as they are with the Lord. All who follow the Lord with devotion are, by means of their devotion, with God, but as they are still oppressed by the weight of corruptible flesh they are not with God. They know the hidden judgements of God, therefore, in so far as they are joined to Him, but in so far as they are separated from Him, they do not know them. The fact that they do not yet penetrate His secrets fully shows that His judgements are incomprehensible; but because their minds are united to Him, by dwelling on the words of holy Scripture or on such secret revelations as they may receive, they understand them, and know these things and declare them. And so the judgements which God does not utter they do not know but those which God speaks forth they do know.

8 That is why the prophet David, after he had said, *With my lips I have declared all the judgements,* immediately added, *of your mouth,* as if he were really saying, 'I could have known and declared those judgements which I knew you had spoken. For those which you

yourself had not spoken, you undoubtedly conceal from our minds.' And so the prophet's view is in agreement with that of the Apostle because the judgements of God are incomprehensible, and yet, those which have been uttered from his mouth can be declared by human lips. For the things that are spoken by God can be known by men but those which are concealed cannot be known.

9 PETER: In dealing with my little query your reasoning has made the whole thing clear. But if there are any more miracles of this man left, please go on.

XVII GREGORY: A nobleman named Theopropus had been converted as a result of father Benedict's admonishments. He was trusted by Benedict and enjoyed familiarity with him on account of his virtuous life. One day when this man entered Benedict's tiny cell, he found him weeping bitterly. He waited quietly for a long time but when he realized that Benedict's tears would not cease and that the man of God was not weeping in prayer, as he normally did, but in grief, he asked what the reason was for his great unhappiness. The man of God immediately answered, 'This whole monastery that I built and everything that I made for the brothers has been handed over to the pagans according to a judgement of the almighty God. It is with difficulty that I have managed to obtain permission to remove the souls from this place.'

2 The prophecy which Theopropus heard at that time we see fulfilled, for we know that Benedict's monastery has been destroyed by the Lombards. During the night, while the brothers were asleep, the Lombards recently entered it and plundered everything.[44] However, they were unable to capture a single person, for almighty God carried out His promise to His faithful servant Benedict. He had promised that if Benedict handed the possessions over to the barbarians, He would protect the souls. In this matter, I see that Benedict was in the same position as Paul, who received the life of all his companions as a consolation when his ship lost all its cargo.[45]

XVIII On another occasion, our friend Exhilaratus whom you have known since his conversion, was sent by his master to bring to the man of God at his monastery two wooden vessels full of wine, commonly known as casks. He brought one, but hid the other one on his way. However, nothing that happened far away could escape the notice of the man of God, so he accepted the one flask with thanks, but as the boy was leaving he warned him, 'Be careful, my boy, not to drink from the hidden cask. Tip it up carefully and you will find what is inside.' Deeply embarrassed, the boy left the man of God. On his way back, wishing to test the truth of what he had been told, he tipped the cask up, and at once a snake slipped out of it. Seeing what he had found in the wine, this boy Exhilaratus was horrified at the wicked thing he had done.

XIX Not far from the monastery there was a village, where a large number of the inhabitants had been converted from the worship of idols to faith in God as a result of Benedict's admonishments. There were also some nuns there and Benedict, God's servant, took the trouble to send his brothers there regularly to give them spiritual encouragement. One day, he sent someone as usual but the monk whom he sent, after he had advised the nuns, was asked by them to accept a few handkerchiefs which he hid inside his tunic. As soon as he returned home, the man of God began to reproach him severely, saying, 'How has iniquity entered into your bosom?' The man was speechless with surprise because he had forgotten what he had done and could not understand why he was being chastised. So Benedict said to him, 'Was I not present when you received the handkerchiefs from the handmaidens of God and put them inside your tunic?' The monk immediately threw himself at Benedict's feet: he repented of his folly and pulled out the handkerchiefs hidden inside his tunic.

XX One day, the venerable abbot was taking bodily nourishment, and now that evening had come, one of his monks (the son of a high-ranking official) was holding the lamp for him at the table. The one in charge of the lamp was standing beside the man of God as he was eating, and he began to reflect in a spirit of pride, saying to himself, 'Who is this man, that I should have to stand beside him while he eats, and hold his lamp and work as his servant?' At once the man of God turned to him and began to reproach him severely, saying, 'Make the sign of the cross on your heart, brother! What is this that you are saying? Make the sign of the cross on your heart!' Benedict immediately called the brothers, told them to take the lamp from the monk's hands and ordered him to relinquish his task and to go that very moment and sit quietly by himself. When the brothers asked him what had been going on in this man's heart, Benedict gave them a detailed account of how the monk had become puffed up with the spirit of pride and how he had silently murmured in his thoughts against the man of God. It then became evident to everyone that nothing could escape the notice of the venerable Benedict, whose ear had heard the thoughts of the mind.

XXI On another occasion a famine struck that region of Campania,[46] and everyone was suffering as a result of a severe shortage of food. They had already run out of grain in Benedict's monastery and almost all the loaves of bread had been eaten – no more than five could be found for the brothers at dinner-time. When the venerable abbot saw them looking unhappy, he made an effort to correct their lack of faith by reproaching them a little, and to cheer them up by means of a promise. He said, 'Why is your mind saddened by a lack of bread? Today there is indeed little, but tomorrow you will have plenty.'

2 The following day two hundred measures of flour, sent by the almighty God, were found in sacks in front of the monastery gates although even now no one knows who brought it there. When the brothers saw it, they gave thanks to the Lord for they had now learned not to lose faith in God's generosity, even in times of shortage.

3 PETER: Tell me, please: are we to believe that this servant of God always possessed the spirit of prophecy or was it only occasionally that the spirit of prophecy filled his mind?

GREGORY: The spirit of prophecy, Peter, does not always illumine the minds of the prophets because, just as it says of the Holy Spirit, *it breathes where it wills;*[47] so we must also understand that it inspires when it wills. That is why when Nathan was asked by the king if he could build the temple, he first agreed and later refused.[48] That is why Elisha, seeing the woman crying and not knowing why, said to the boy who was trying to make her stop, *Leave her alone. Her soul is bitterly distressed and the Lord has concealed it from me and has not revealed it to me.*[49]

4 The almighty God arranges it in this way according to the dispensation of His great love, for by sometimes granting the spirit of

prophecy and sometimes taking it away, He raises the minds of those who prophesy up to the heights and He also keeps them in humility. In this way, when they receive the spirit they discover what they are from God, and then when they no longer possess the spirit of prophecy, they learn what they are by themselves.

5 PETER: These are convincing arguments making it evident that things are as you claim. But please tell me anything else that occurs to you about the venerable abbot Benedict.

XXII GREGORY: On another occasion he was asked by a devout man to send some of his disciples to build a monastery on this man's estate near the town of Terracino.[50] Benedict agreed to his request: he chose some brothers, appointed an abbot and decided who would be their prior. As they departed, he gave them a promise, saying, 'Go now, and on such and such a day I will come and show you where you ought to build your chapel, the brothers' refectory, the guest-house and all the necessary buildings.' As soon as they had received this blessing they set off, and waiting impatiently for the appointed day, they made all the necessary preparations for those who might come with this wonderful abbot.

2 On the very night before the appointed day dawned, the man of the Lord appeared in a dream both to that servant of God whom he had appointed as abbot in that place, and to his prior, giving them a detailed description of all the different places where they were supposed to build something. When the two of them rose from their sleep, they told each other what they had seen, but because they did not entirely trust the vision, they awaited the arrival of the man of God in accordance with his promise.

3 When the man of God failed to arrive on the appointed day, they were very upset. They went back to him, saying, 'Father, we waited for you to come as you promised, and to show us where we ought to build, but you did not come.' He said to them, 'Brothers, why do you say this? Did I not come as I promised?' When they asked him, 'When did you come?' he answered, 'Did I not appear to both of you while you were asleep and describe all the places? Go and build all the monastery buildings just as you heard them described in the vision.' They were utterly amazed when they heard this, and returning

to the estate I mentioned earlier, they constructed all the buildings exactly as they had been told in the vision.

4 PETER: I would like to know how it could have happened that he went a long way to give them a reply which they heard and understood in a vision while they were asleep.

GREGORY: What is it, Peter, that you hope to gain by examining the order of events? It is obvious that the spirit is of a more mobile nature than the body. Moreover, we certainly know from Scripture that the prophet[51] who was lifted up in Judea was suddenly put down in Chaldea together with his meal. When he had given the prophet Daniel the meal, Habakkuk suddenly found himself back in Judea.[52] If Habakkuk, then, was able in one moment to travel so far in his body to transport a meal, is it surprising that father Benedict managed to move in the spirit to bring the necessary information to the spirits of the sleeping monks? Just as Habakkuk moved in the body in order to bring food for the body, so Benedict moved spiritually in order to promote the spiritual life.

PETER: The hand of your speech has, I admit, wiped away the doubts from my mind. But I would like to know what kind of man he was in his everyday speech.

XXIII GREGORY: Even his everyday speech was not devoid of miraculous power, for if a man's heart is fixed on the things above, the words that issue from his mouth are in no way worthless. If in fact he ever said anything not decisively but as a threat, his words had such power that it seemed as if he had pronounced them not in a hesitant or conditional manner but as if he were giving an official judgement.

2 Let me give you an example: not far from his monastery there were two religious women, born of noble families, living in their own house. A devout man offered these women his services to assist them in their daily chores. However, as often happens, nobility of family brings with it inferiority of soul: those who are conscious that they have been more important than others, are less likely to consider themselves of little value in this world. These religious women had not been completely successful in using the bridle of their way of life to restrain their tongue and so their careless speech frequently pro-

voked to anger this devout man who was offering his services for the daily chores.

3 After putting up with this for a long time he went to the man of God and told him all the insults he was having to endure. When the man of God heard about these women's behaviour, he immediately sent them a message, saying, 'Curb your tongues, for if you do not change, I will excommunicate you.' He did not actually impose this sentence of excommunication, but threatened it.

4 However, those women did not change their old habits and a few days later they died and were buried in the church. While the solemn mass was being celebrated in this church and the deacon was calling out, 'If anyone is not in communion, let him withdraw,' as was the custom, the women's nurse, who had been in the habit of bringing an offering to the Lord on their behalf, saw them come out of their tombs and leave the church. When she noticed on several occasions that they went outside at the sound of the deacon's announcement, and that they were unable to stay inside the church, she remembered the message that the man of God had sent them while they were still alive. Had he not said that he would bar them from communion if they did not improve their manners and their language?

5 Deeply upset, she told this to the servant of God, who immediately gave her an offering with his own hand, saying, 'Go and present this offering to the Lord on their behalf, and afterwards they will no longer be excommunicated.' When the offering had been presented on their behalf and the deacon called out as usual that those who were not in communion should leave the church, these women were no longer seen to leave the church. From this it was evident that as they no longer withdrew with those who were barred from communion, they had received communion from the Lord through the servant of the Lord.

6 PETER: I find it quite extraordinary that a man, even one who is venerable and very holy, could, while still living in this corruptible flesh, release souls which had already been brought before that invisible judge.

GREGORY: Peter, was he who was told, *Whatever you bind on earth will be bound in heaven and what you release on earth will also be released in heaven*[53] not still in this flesh? Saint Peter's power to bind and release is now in the hands of those who, on account of their faith and good character, are his representatives in holy government. But in order that man on earth might have such power, the Creator of heaven and earth came down to earth from heaven; so that the flesh might even be able to judge the spirits, God in His humble generosity was made flesh for mankind. Our weakness was able to rise above itself because the strength of God had become weak beneath itself.[54]

7 PETER: Your reasoning is consistent with the miracles performed.

XXIV GREGORY: One day one of his monks, a little boy who loved his parents more than he should have, left the monastery without a blessing[55] and set off for their house. On that same day, as soon as he reached them, he died. The day after he had been buried, his body was found thrown out of the grave. They buried the body carefully once more but the following day they found it thrown out again, unburied as before.

2 Then they ran in panic to the feet of father Benedict and begged him amid much weeping to be kind enough to bestow his grace on the boy. At once the man of God gave them, with his own hand, the communion of the Lord's body, saying, 'Go and place the Lord's body on his chest and bury him like that.' As soon as this was done, the earth retained the boy's body and did not throw it out again. You can appreciate, Peter, what merit this man possessed in the eyes of our Lord Jesus Christ, seeing that the earth itself threw out the body of someone who did not have Benedict's grace.

PETER: I certainly can! I am utterly amazed.

XXV GREGORY: One of his monks became obsessed with moving and did not want to remain in the monastery. The man of God rebuked him constantly and admonished him frequently but he absolutely refused to stay in the community and insisted relentlessly on being released. So one day the venerable father, worn out by this man's nagging, angrily told him to leave.

2 Hardly had he left the monastery when he came upon a dragon confronting him on the road with gaping jaws. When this dragon that had appeared looked as if it were going to devour him, the monk

began to shout in a loud voice, trembling and shaking, saying, 'Help, help, a dragon is going to eat me!' When the brothers came running they could see no dragon but they led the trembling and shaking monk back to the monastery. He immediately promised that he would never leave the monastery and from that moment on he kept his promise. It was as a result of the holy man's prayers that the monk had been able to see in front of him a dragon that had earlier been leading him without him seeing it.

XXVI I think I ought also to mention what I learnt from the illustrious Aptonius. He told me that his father's slave boy was stricken with elephantiasis, causing his hair to fall out and his skin to become swollen; and he was unable to conceal the increasing amount of pus. Aptonius' father sent the boy to the man of God who instantly restored him to his former health.

XXVII I should also mention what his disciple, by the name of Peregrinus, told me. One day a man of faith, driven by the difficulty of repaying a debt, came to believe that there was but one remedy for him, namely to go to the man of God and tell him of the difficulties caused by the debt oppressing him. So he went to the monastery, found the servant of God almighty and revealed to him that he was being hard pressed by his creditor for the sum of twelve gold pieces. The venerable abbot replied that he certainly did not have twelve gold pieces, but he reassured him in his financial difficulties with kind words, saying, 'Go away and come back in two days, for today I have nothing to give you.'

2 During these two days Benedict spent his time praying as usual. On the third day when the debtor returned, thirteen gold pieces were suddenly found on top of the monastery's chest which was filled with grain. The man of God gave the order for the money to be removed and given to the unfortunate petitioner, telling him to use twelve of them to pay his debt and to keep one for personal expenses.

3 But now let me return to the things I learnt from the account of those of his disciples whom I mentioned at the beginning of the book. A man was suffering from severe jealousy of his enemy: his hatred had reached the point where, unbeknown to the enemy, he put poison in his drink. Although this did not kill him, it did change the

colour of his skin in such a way that blotches, resembling leprosy, spread over his body. But when this man was brought to the man of God, he quickly recovered his former health, for as soon as Benedict touched him all the blotches on his skin disappeared.

XXVIII During the same period also when a famine was seriously affecting Campania, the man of God had given everything from his own monastery to a number of poor people, and there was hardly anything left in the cellar apart from a little bit of oil in a glass flask. Then a subdeacon called Agapitus arrived, demanding insistently that he should be given a bit of oil. The man of God, who had decided to give away everything on earth so that all things would be laid up for him in heaven,[56] ordered the small amount of oil that was left to be given to the man who was asking for it. But the monk who was in charge of the cellar, although he heard the order, refused to carry it out.

2 A little later when Benedict inquired whether the oil had been given as ordered, the monk replied that he had certainly not given anything because, if he were to give this away, there would be nothing at all left for the brothers. Then Benedict angrily told the others to throw the glass flask, in which there appeared to be a little oil left, out of the window so that nothing should remain in the monastery as a result of disobedience. This was done. Beneath this window there gaped a huge abyss, bristling with huge rocks. When the glass flask was thrown out, it landed on the rocks but it remained unbroken, as if it had not been thrown out at all: it did not break nor did the oil spill. The man of God told them to pick it up and as it was not broken, he gave it to the man who had asked for it. Then he called the brothers together and in front of them all he rebuked the disobedient monk for his lack of faith and for his arrogance.

XXIX His rebuke finished, he devoted himself to prayer together with these brothers. In the place where he was praying with the brothers there stood an empty oil jar with a lid on. As the holy man continued to pray, the lid of the jar was lifted up as the jar filled with oil: the lid moved and was lifted up as the increasing amount of oil spilled over the edge of the jar on to the stone floor of the room where they had knelt to pray. As soon as the servant of God noticed this he immediately brought his prayer to an end and the oil ceased to flow out over the stone floor.

2 He then admonished the brother at even greater length for his lack of faith and his disobedience, so that he might learn to have faith and humility. This brother blushed at the rebuke which was given for his own good, because by these miracles the venerable father manifested that power of the almighty Lord which he had referred to in his admonition. There was now no way that anyone could doubt His promises, seeing that in one moment He had replaced a nearly empty glass flask with a jar full of oil.

XXX One day while Benedict was on his way to the chapel of St John, which was situated at the very top of the mountain, the old enemy came to meet him disguised as a horse doctor, carrying a funnel made of horn and a shackle. Benedict asked him, 'Where are you going?', to which he replied, 'I am going to the brothers to give them some medicine.' Then the venerable Benedict went on his way to pray and when he had finished he returned in haste. The evil spirit had found an elderly monk drinking water, and entering him at once, threw him to the ground, tormenting him violently. As soon as the man of God returned from his prayer, he saw this man being cruelly tormented. He merely gave him a slap and this immediately drove the evil spirit out of him and it never again dared to return to him.

2 PETER: I should like to know whether he always performed these great miracles by virtue of his prayers or whether he sometimes produced them solely by means of his will?

GREGORY: Those who cling to God with devotion usually produce miracles in two ways, as circumstances demand. Sometimes they perform wonderful things by means of prayer, at other times by means of their own power. Seeing that according to St John, *All those who have received Him, to them He has given the power to become the sons of God,*[57] why is it surprising if those who are sons of God can use their power to perform miracles?

3 Peter witnesses to the fact that miracles may be performed in two ways, for he awakened Tabitha from the dead by praying,[58] but when Ananias and Sapphira lied he gave them over to death simply by rebuking them[59] (for we do not read that he prayed to bring about

their death but merely rebuked them for the wrong they had done). And so it is clear that they sometimes perform these things by their own power, and sometimes by praying, since Peter deprived them of their life by means of rebuke and restored life to Tabitha by means of prayer.

4 I am now going to describe two things done by Benedict, that faithful servant of God, which show clearly that sometimes his ability derived from divinely inspired power, at other times from prayer.[60]

XXXI At the time when Totila was king of the Goths, a Goth by the name of Zalla, who was an Arian heretic, burned with an intensely cruel passion against the religious men of the Catholic church. If a cleric or a monk came face to face with him, he would certainly not escape alive from Zalla's hands. One day, inflamed with the fire of his greed, his mouth agape with the desire to steal, he attacked a peasant with his cruel torments and tore him to pieces using a number of different tortures. Overcome by the pain the peasant confessed that he had handed over his things to Benedict, the servant of God, hoping that if the torturer believed this, his cruelty might be suspended for a while and a few hours of life might be gained.

2 So this man Zalla stopped torturing the peasant but tied his arms with strong cords and began to drive him in front of his horse so that the peasant might show him who this Benedict was to whom he had handed over his possessions. The peasant, his arms bound, walked in front as he led Zalla to the holy man's monastery where he found Benedict sitting alone in front of the entrance to his cell, reading. The peasant said to the infuriated Zalla who was right behind him, 'Here he is, the one I was talking about. This is father Benedict.' Zalla, fuming with anger, looked at him in the madness of his deranged mind, and thinking that he would use his usual terror tactics, he began to shout in a loud voice, saying, 'Get up, get up! Give back this peasant's belongings which he handed over to you.'

3 At the sound of his voice the man of God immediately raised his eyes from his reading, looked at him and then noticed the peasant whom he was holding captive. As he turned his eyes to the peasant's arms, the cords miraculously came undone and began to fall from his arms with such speed that they could not have been untied as quickly

by any man, however much he hurried. The man who had arrived tied up suddenly stood there unbound. Zalla, shocked by the strength of such power, fell to the ground at Benedict's feet and, bending his neck, rigid with cruelty, he commended himself to his prayers. The holy man did not even get up from his reading but called the brothers and told them to take Zalla indoors so that he might receive a meal.[61] When Zalla was brought back to him Benedict warned him that he must give up this mad and cruel behaviour. He went away a broken man, and did not dare to demand anything further from the peasant whom the man of God had set free not by touching him but simply by looking at him.

4 This, Peter, is what I said: those who serve the almighty God most faithfully are sometimes able to perform miracles merely by means of their power. For Benedict had managed, while seated, to subdue the fierceness of a terrifying Goth, and to undo with a look the knotted cords binding the arms of an innocent man. The very speed of the miracle reveals to us that he had been allowed to do what he did by his power. Now I must also describe the remarkable kind of miracle he was able to perform by means of prayer.

XXXII One day he went out to work in the fields with the brothers. A peasant, carrying the body of his dead son in his arms and wild with grief at his bereavement, came to the monastery to ask for father Benedict. When he was told that the abbot had gone out for a while in the fields with the brothers, he immediately put the body of his dead son down in front of the monastery door and, distraught with grief, ran as fast as he could to find the venerable abbot.

2 At that moment the man of God was returning with the brothers from his work in the fields. As soon as the bereaved peasant saw him, he began to shout, 'Give me back my son, give me back my son!' Hearing these words the man of God stopped, saying, 'Surely I did not take your son from you?', to which the man replied, 'He is dead. Come and bring him back to life.' As soon as the servant of God heard this, he was very distressed and said, 'Go away, brothers, go away. It is not up to us to deal with this, it is for the holy apostles. Why do you want to impose unbearable burdens on us?' But the man, driven by excessive grief, persisted in his plea, swearing that he

would not go away unless Benedict brought his son back to life. Then the servant of God inquired of him, saying, 'Where is he?', to which the man answered, 'Over there. His body is lying at the door of the monastery.'

3 When the man of God and the brothers reached the place, Benedict knelt down and lay on top of the little child's body;[62] then lifting himself up he raised his hands to heaven, saying, 'Lord, do not look upon my sins but upon the faith of this man who asks that his son be brought back to life. Restore to this little body the soul which you have taken away.' Hardly had he finished the words of his prayer when the soul returned and the whole of the boy's little body shuddered so much that to the eyes of all those present it was clear that he had moved as a result of some miraculous tremor. Then Benedict took the boy's hand and gave him back to his father, alive and well.

4 It is clear, Peter, that he did not perform this miracle by means of his own power for he prayed to be able to perform it as he lay on the ground.

PETER: It is obvious that everything is as you claim because you have facts to prove the theories you put forward. But I ask you to tell me if holy men can do everything they want and if they obtain everything they desire.

XXXIII GREGORY: Will there ever be a more sublime person in this life than Paul? Yet he asked the Lord three times to be freed from the goad of this flesh but was unable to obtain what he desired. In this connection it is necessary for me to tell you about the venerable father Benedict because there was something which he wanted but which he was not able to accomplish.

2 His sister, whose name was Scolastica, had been dedicated to the almighty Lord since her very infancy. She used to come to see Benedict once a year and the man of God would come down to meet her at a property belonging to the monastery not far from the gate.[63] Now one day she came as usual and her venerable brother came down to meet her with his disciples. They spent the whole day praising God and in holy conversation, and when night's darkness fell, they ate a meal together. While they were seated at table, talking of holy matters, it began to get rather late and so this nun, Benedict's sister, made the

following request, 'I beg you not to leave me tonight, so that we might talk until morning about the joys of the heavenly life.' Benedict answered her, 'What are you saying, sister? I certainly cannot stay away from my monastery.'

3 The sky was so clear at the time that there was not a cloud to be seen. When the nun heard the words of her brother's refusal she put her hands together on the table and bent her head in her hands to pray to the almighty Lord. When she lifted her head from the table, such violent lightning and thunder burst forth, together with a great downpour of rain, that neither the venerable Benedict nor the brothers who were with him could set foot outside the door of the place where they were sitting. For the nun, as she bent her head in her hands, had poured forth rivers of tears on to the table, by means of which she had turned the clear sky to rain. That downpour began just as her prayer finished – in fact, the coincidence between the prayer and the downpour was so precise that she lifted her head from the table at the very moment when the thunder sounded and the rain came down at exactly the same moment that she raised her head.

4 Then the man of God realized that he could not return to his monastery in the midst of the thunder and lightning and the heavy downpour of rain. This upset him and he began to complain, saying, 'May the almighty God forgive you, sister. What have you done?' To which she replied, 'Look, I asked you and you refused to listen to me. I asked my Lord and He heard me. Go now, if you can. Leave me behind and return to your monastery.' But being unable to leave the building, he had to remain there against his will since he refused to stay there voluntarily. And so they spent the whole night awake, satisfying each other's hunger for holy conversation about the spiritual life.

5 I said that he wished for something but was totally unsuccessful in achieving it because, if we consider the thoughts of the venerable man, it is clear that he would have wanted the fine weather in which he had gone down from the monastery to continue. But contrary to his wishes, the power of the almighty God caused him to discover a miracle produced by a woman's heart. It is not surprising that a woman was able to achieve more than him at that time, seeing that she had

long desired to see her brother. For according to the words of John, *God is love*,[64] and so it was by a very just judgement that her power was greater because her love was stronger.[65]

PETER: I confess that I very much approve of what you say.

XXXIV GREGORY: The following day, this venerable woman returned to her own cell and the man of God went back to the monastery. After spending three days in his cell, he raised his eyes to heaven and saw the soul of his sister: it had departed from her body and penetrated the mysterious regions of heaven in the form of a dove. Rejoicing in her great glory Benedict gave thanks to the almighty God in hymns of praise and then announced her death to the brothers.

2 At once he sent them to bring her body to his monastery and place it in the tomb which he had prepared for himself. By this means it happened that the bodies of those whose mind had always been united in God were not separated even in the grave.[66]

XXXV On another occasion the deacon Servandus, the abbot of the monastery that had earlier been built in Campania by the patrician Liberius,[67] came on a visit to Benedict, as was his wont. Like Benedict he, too, was a man of deep spiritual understanding and he used to visit Benedict's monastery so that they might pour into one another the sweet words of life. Although they could not yet enjoy it fully, they might at least, by sighing with longing, have a taste of the delicious food of the heavenly homeland.

2 But when the time for sleep demanded, Benedict took his place in the upper part of his tower while the deacon Servandus took his place in the lower part, where a staircase allowed easy communication between the lower and upper parts. In front of the tower there was a large building in which the disciples of both men slept. While the brothers were still asleep, Benedict the man of the Lord was awake, standing at the window. Anticipating the time of the night office he was praying to the almighty Lord when, suddenly, in the dead of night, he saw a light pouring down from above that dispelled all the darkness of the night, shining so brightly that the light casting its rays amid the darkness surpassed the daylight.

3 Then, while he watched, a most remarkable thing happened. As he himself reported later, the whole world was brought before his eyes,

apparently drawn together beneath a single ray of sunlight. While the venerable abbot kept his eyes fixed on the bright blazing light, he saw the soul of Germanus, the bishop of Capua, being carried up to heaven by the angels in a fiery sphere.

4 Wishing to find someone else to witness this great miracle, he called the deacon Servandus, repeating his name two or three times in a loud voice. Disturbed by the unusual shouting of the great man, Servandus went up and had a look but saw only a small bit of light. When the man of God told him exactly what had happened, Servandus was stunned by such a great miracle. At once Benedict ordered the devout Theopropus[68] at the fort at Casinum to send someone that very night to the city of Capua to find out what was happening to bishop Germanus, and to come and tell him. When the messenger did this he found that bishop Germanus, that most reverent man, was already dead, and on making detailed inquiries he learned that his death had occurred at the very moment when the man of the Lord witnessed his ascent.

5 PETER: This is quite amazing – utterly astounding, in fact. But what you said, namely that the whole world was brought before his eyes, apparently drawn together beneath a single ray of sunlight, this is something I have never experienced and which I cannot even imagine. How can it possibly happen that the whole world is seen by one man?

6 GREGORY: Hold on tight to what I am saying, Peter: the whole of creation is small to the soul that sees the Creator. Although it has seen only a tiny part of the Creator's light, all that has been created becomes small to him because in the light of the vision the folds of the innermost mind are relaxed and it expands in God to such an extent that it becomes larger than the world. The soul of the one who sees rises up above itself. In the light of God it is drawn up above itself and its innermost parts expand. As it looks down below itself from above, it understands how small everything is which it was unable to grasp from down below. The man who saw the fiery globe and the angels returning to heaven could not possibly have seen this except in the light of God. Is it surprising, then, if he saw the world drawn together before him after he had been lifted up outside the world in the light of the mind?

7 The fact that the world is said to be drawn together before his eyes does not mean that heaven and earth had contracted but that the mind of the observer had expanded. Caught up into God he could easily see everything that is beneath God. To that outer light, then, shining before his eyes, there corresponded an inner light in his mind which swept the soul of the observer up to the higher regions and showed it how insignificant everything below was.

8 PETER: I think it was a good thing that I did not understand what you said, seeing that your explanation developed as a result of my obtuseness. But now that you have made these things clear to my understanding, I ask you to return to the order of the narrative.

XXXVI GREGORY: Peter, I would like to tell you many more things about this venerable abbot but I must pass over some things on purpose because I am keen to give an account of other people's deeds. However, I do not wish you to be unaware that amidst all the miracles which made him famous throughout the world the man of God was no less outstanding for the wisdom of his teaching. For he wrote a Rule for the brothers which is remarkable for its discretion and the clarity of its language. If anyone should wish to know about his character or his way of life in greater detail, he can discover in the teaching of that Rule a complete account of Benedict's practice: for the holy man was incapable of teaching anything that was contrary to the way he lived.

XXXVII In the same year that he was going to depart from this life, he announced the day of his most holy death to some of the disciples who were living with him and to some who lived far away. To those who were with him he said that they should remain silent about what they had heard, while to those who were far away he indicated what kind of sign they would receive when his soul departed from his body.

2 Six days before his death he ordered that his tomb should be opened for him. Then he was gripped by a fever: he had a high temperature and began to grow weak. The illness grew worse every day, and on the sixth day he made his disciples carry him into the chapel and there he armed himself for death by partaking of the Lord's body and blood. While his disciples' hands supported his weakened body, he stood

with his hands raised to heaven and breathed his last in the middle of a prayer.

3 On that day one and the same vision appeared to two of his brothers, to one in his monastery and to another who lived at some distance. They both saw a road spread with cloaks and shining with innumerable lights, stretching eastwards from Benedict's monastery to heaven. Above it stood a man of majestic appearance, shining brightly, who asked them whose road it was they were looking at. They admitted that they did not know and so he said to them, 'This is the road along which Benedict, beloved by the Lord, is going up to heaven.' Then just as those who were with Benedict witnessed the holy man's death, so those who were far away learnt of it by means of this sign.

4 He was buried in the chapel of St John the Baptist that he had himself built on the site of the altar of Apollo he had destroyed.

XXXVIII In the cave of Subiaco where he had lived earlier, to this day dazzling miracles still occur if the faith of those who ask demands it. Recently something happened which I shall tell you about: a madwoman had lost her senses completely and was wandering night and day over mountains and through valleys, forests and fields. She would only rest where exhaustion forced her to do so. One day when she was wandering without stopping, she came to the cave of that blessed man, father Benedict: she entered it and stayed there without realizing where she was. When morning came she departed, her mind restored to such perfect health that it was as if no madness had ever gripped her. For the rest of her life she continued in the same state of health which she had recovered there.

2 PETER: How is it that we often find the same thing happening in the case of the patronage of martyrs? They do not offer as much assistance through their bodily remains as through their relics and they perform greater miracles in those places where they are not actually buried?

3 GREGORY: It is certain, Peter, that the holy martyrs can perform many marvels in those places where they are buried, as indeed they do, and reveal innumerable miracles to those who seek with a pure mind. But because it is possible that weak minds might doubt whether the holy martyrs are present and listening in those places where they

are obviously not physically present, it is necessary for them to perform more impressive miracles in those places where a weak mind might doubt their presence. But those whose mind is fixed in God gain greater merit for their faith, for they know that the martyrs are listening even though their bodies are not buried there.

4 To increase the disciples' faith the Truth itself also said, *If I do not depart, the Comforter will not come to you.*[69] For since it is certain that the Comforter, the Spirit, always proceeds from the Father and from the Son, why does the Son say that He will depart so that He who never leaves the Son may come? But because the disciples, seeing the Lord in the flesh, thirsted to see Him always with their bodily eyes, it was right that they should be told, *If I do not depart, the Comforter will not come*, as if to say, 'If I do not withdraw physically, I will not show you what is the love of the spirit and unless you cease to see me physically, you will never learn to love me spiritually.'

5 PETER: What you say is quite right.

GREGORY: We must now stop talking for a while. If we wish to go on to recount the miracles of others, a period of silence will give us time to recover our powers of speech.

NOTES

Life of Antony by Athanasius

INTRODUCTION

1. There has been much debate over whether Athanasius really did write this work. See K. Heussi, *Der Ursprung des Mönchtums* (Tübingen 1936), chapter 3. It was certainly attributed to Athanasius by Gregory in his *Oration* on Athanasius (20.5), probably composed in 380, and by Jerome in his work *On Famous Men*, written in 392.

2. R. C. Gregg and D. E. Groh, *Early Arianism – a View of Salvation* (London 1981), p. 133.

3. D. Brakke, *Athanasius and the Politics of Asceticism* (Oxford 1995), p. 264.

4. See the remarks of R. C. Gregg in the introduction to his translation of Athanasius' *Life of Antony* (New York 1980), pp. 11–13.

5. J. Leclercq, *The Love of Learning and the Desire for God*, trans. C. Misrahi (2nd edition, New York 1974), p. 125.

6. Gregory of Nazianzus, *Oration* 20.5; Palladius, *Lausiac History*, 8; John Chrysostom, *Homily on Matthew*, 8; Jerome, *On Famous Men*, 88; Rufinus, *Ecclesiastical History*, 1.8; Augustine, *Confessions*, 8.6.15.

7. Eusebius had been sent into exile in 355 for his refusal to condemn Athanasius at the Synod of Milan.

8. See *Life of Martin*, VI.4.

9. It is possible that it was Evagrius who suggested that Jerome, after his unhappy time in the Syrian desert, might go to Rome and work as Pope Damasus' secretary. Since it was Damasus who in 382 asked Jerome to revise the Latin text of the Bible, it may be that we are ultimately indebted to Evagrius for the Vulgate.

10. Jerome, *Letter* 1.15, the earliest of Jerome's surviving compositions.

11. Cf. Jerome, *Life of Malchus*, 2.

12. Jerome, *Letter* 7.1.

13. This is not to be confused with the Melitian schism, referred to by Athanasius in the *Life of Antony*, which occurred earlier in the fourth century and centred on Egypt.

14. Jerome, *On Famous Men*, 125.

15. Many, including J. N. D. Kelly *Golden Mouth* (London 1995), take it that Evagrius died in 393.

16. Basil, *Letter* 156 is addressed to Evagrius after Evagrius had visited Basil at Caesarea on his way back from the west to Antioch.

17. Jerome, *Letter* 1.15.

LIFE OF ANTONY

1. Egypt.

2. The mss are divided between the two readings '*feci*' and '*fecit*'. I have chosen to accept the reading '*fecit*', given in PL 73, as it seems to make more sense here. The reading '*feci*' implies that Athanasius spent a long period with Antony but also makes Athanasius his own primary source; furthermore it does not provide a sufficiently strong contrast with the previous phrase, 'those things I myself know'.

3. Cf. Genesis 25:27.

4. Luke 5:11.

5. Acts of the Apostles 4:34−5.

6. Cf. Colossians 1:5.

7. Matthew 19:21−2. This quotation follows the usage of Athanasius and Evagrius. The same verse in the General Introduction follows the modern Bible text.

8. An *aroura* here is an Egyptian measure of land: it has been calculated that Antony was the owner of about 200 acres of fertile land.

9. Matthew 6:34.

10. 2 Thessalonians 3:10.

11. 1 Thessalonians 5:17.

12. Cf. Ephesians 6:12.

13. 1 Corinthians 15:10.

14. Mark 9:18; Acts of the Apostles 7:54.

15. Cf. Hosea 4:12.

16. Psalm 118:7.

17. Romans 8:4.

18. 1 Peter 5:8.

19. Ephesians 6:11.

20. Cf. 1 Corinthians 9:27.

21. 2 Corinthians 12:10.

22. St Paul in Philippians 3:13.

23. 1 Kings 18:15.

24. Romans 8:35.

25. Psalm 27:3.

26. The devil.

27. Psalm 68:1–2.

28. Psalm 118:10.

29. Cf. Colossians 4:6.

30. Cf. Romans 8:32.

31. In Athanasius' Greek version, it is specifically noted here that Antony spoke in the Egyptian, i.e., Coptic, language.

32. Psalm 90:10.

33. Romans 8:18.

34. This appears to be a paraphrase from *Ecclesiastes* rather than a specific quotation.

35. Cf. John 14:2–3. Athanasius, unlike Evagrius, makes no explicit allusion to a biblical passage at this point.

36. Cf. Luke 12:35–47.

37. Ezechiel 18:30, 33:20.

38. Romans 8:28.

39. 1 Corinthians 15:31.

40. Genesis 19:26.

41. Luke 9:62.

42. Luke 17:21.

43. Joshua 24:23.

44. These are the words of John the Baptist, as recorded in Matthew 3:3, Luke 3:4 and John 1:23, echoing Isaiah 40:3.

45. James 1:20.

46. James 1:15.

47. Cf. Proverbs 4:23.

48. Ephesians 6:12.

49. Cf. Cassian, *Conferences*, 7.17, 17.20, 17.32; Augustine, *The City of God*, 8:22.

50. Cf. 1 Corinthians 12:10.

51. 2 Corinthians 2:11.

52. Job 41:9–11 (41:18–21 in the Jerusalem Bible).

53. Cf. Job 41:27.

54. Exodus 15:9.

55. Isaiah 10:14.

56. Cf. Job 40:24.

57. Cf. Luke 10:19.

58. Habakkuk 2:15.

59. Cf. Luke 4:41.

60. Psalm 50:16.

61. Psalm 39:1–2 and Psalm 38:13–14.

62. John 8:44.

63. Ecclesiasticus 1:32 (some manuscripts).

64. 2 Kings 19:35.

65. Matthew 8:31.

66. Luke 10:19.

67. Cf. John 15:14–15.

68. Cf. Isaiah 42:2.

69. Luke 1:13.

70. Luke 2:10–11.

71. Matthew 28:5.

72. John 8:56.

73. The phrase in parentheses is Evagrius' paraphrase of the Greek term *Theotokos* applied to the Virgin Mary as the mother of God.

74. Luke 1:41.

75. Matthew 4:10; Deuteronomy 6:13.

76. Luke 10:20.

77. Matthew 7:22–3.

78. Cf. Psalm 1:6.

79. 1 John 4:1.

80. Psalm 20:7.

81. Romans 8:35.

82. Luke 10:18.

83. Cf. 1 Corinthians 4:6.

84. Psalm 9:6.

85. John 14:20.

86. Cf. Joshua 5:13.

87. Daniel and Susanna (chapter 13 of the Greek version of Daniel) 51–9.

88. Numbers 24:5–6.

89. Cf. John 14:2 and 14:23.

90. 2 Corinthians 12:2.

91. Matthew 6:31–3.

92. 'Maximin' is the reading given in PG 26 as opposed to 'Maximian' given in PL 73. It is likely that Antony's visit to Alexandria referred to here took place in 311 during the persecutions of Maximin Daia, who caused many Christians to be mutilated and sent from Egypt to the mines of Palestine and Cilicia, as well as to the porphyry quarries near the Red Sea.

93. Peter of Alexandria was beheaded in 311.

94. Matthew 7:7.

95. The Bucolia (pastures) seems to refer to a marshy district in the region of the Nile Delta close to Alexandria, inhabited by a wild tribe who kept sheep there (Cf. *Life of Hilarion*, 43), but this area is in the Lower Thebaid, not the Upper Thebaid which is where Antony says he intends to go.

96. This was the so-called Inner Mountain or Mount Colzim, about 160 kilometres south-east of present day Cairo, to which Antony withdrew after spending twenty years at the Outer Mountain beside the Nile.

97. Ephesians 6:12.

98. Psalm 125:1.

99. Cf. Job 5:23.

100. The author is referring to David and specifically to Psalm 37:12: *The wicked plots against the righteous, and gnashes his teeth at him.*

101. The Greek text is more specific, giving 'hyenas'.

102. Proverbs 24:15b.

103. Ephesians 4:26.

104. 2 Corinthians 13:5.

105. The teacher is again St Paul: 1 Corinthians 4:5.

106. Romans 2:16.

107. Proverbs 14:12 and 16:25.

108. Galatians 6:2.

109. Cf. note 92.

110. The historian Socrates (*Ecclesiastical History*, III.23) alludes to this, as well as mentioning the miracle of Ammon's crossing of the river.

111. Ammon, the founder of the semi-eremitic settlement at Nitria in Egypt, died in about 350. Cf. *The Lives of the Desert Fathers*, 22 and Palladius' *Lausiac History* for near contemporary accounts of Ammon; also D. Chitty, *The Desert a City* (Oxford 1966) *passim*.

112. Sozomen, *Ecclesiastical History*, I.14, calls it a canal.

113. Matthew 14:29.

114. Ephesians 6:12.

115. Ephesians 6:11.

116. Titus 2:8.

117. 2 Corinthians 12:2.

118. Cf. 2 Corinthians 12:4.

119. John 6:45, echoing Isaiah 54:13.

120. Cf. Philippians 3:13.

121. Proverbs 15:13.

122. Genesis 31:5.

123. Cf. 1 Samuel 16:12.

124. In the Greek text, these schismatics are specified as Meletians or Melitians, followers of Melitius of Lycopolis who organized a break-away church in Egypt and Palestine in the early years of the fourth century. See also *Life of Antony*, 89.

125. This is a term used by Athanasius for his Arian opponents.

126. This visit to Alexandria to denounce the Arians probably took place in 337 or 338.

127. 2 Corinthians 6:14.

128. Romans 1:25.

129. Romans 8:22.

130. Cf. Romans 11:36.

131. This is the only passage in this work where the author implies that he was himself present at the incident he is relating.

132. Cf. Colossians 4:6.

133. Reading *superatam* (the reading in PG 26) for *separatam* (PL 73).

134. Libera is more commonly known as Proserpina or Persephone.

135. The teacher is Paul and the passage Athanasius alludes to is probably 1 Corinthians 2:5.

136. Constantine was Caesar and Emperor from 306 to 337; Constantius was Constantine's second son: he was Emperor from his father's death until his own death in 361; Constans was Constantine's youngest son who became Emperor of the west from 337 until he was murdered in 350. Cf. *The Sayings of the Desert Fathers*, trans. B. Ward, p. 8, where Antony is said to have received a letter from the emperor Constantius asking him to go to Constantinople. Antony asks his disciple Paul whether he ought to go, to which Paul replies, 'If you go, you will be called Antony, but if you stay here, you will be called Abba Antony.'

137. Cf. Daniel 4:19 (4:16 in the Vulgate).

138. Serapion, bishop of Thmuis in the Nile Delta from 339.

139. Matthew 17:20.

140. John 16:23–4.

141. Matthew 10:8.

142. Cf. Gregory's *Life of Benedict* (XXX.4), in which a distinction is made between miracles accomplished by prayer and those brought about through power granted to Benedict by God.

143. Matthew 7:2.

144. Matthew 27:60.

145. Cf. Joshua 23:14, 1 Kings 2:2.

146. Luke 16:9.

147. Antony insists that his body should not be mummified in accordance with non-Christian Egyptian tradition.

148. Jerome in his *Life of Paul* (12) says that Paul asked Antony to bury him in the cloak Athanasius had given him. Hilarion wears a tunic given to him by Antony (*Life of Hilarion*, 4). For a similar gift of a cloak of camel's hair, the regular clothing of fourth-century monks, see Paulinus of Nola, *Letter* 29.1, in which he thanks his friend Sulpicius Severus for his gift.

149. Athanasius himself.

150. According to Gregory of Tours, *History of the Franks*, I.35, Antony died at the age of 105 in the nineteenth year of the reign of Constantius II, i.e., in 356.

Life of Paul of Thebes by Jerome

INTRODUCTION

1. An earlier date has also been suggested, based on the view that it was written while Jerome was still in the desert. See J. N. D. Kelly, *Jerome, His Life, Writings and Controversies*, pp. 60–61.

2. This means that the meeting between Antony and Paul, and Paul's death, occurred in 341.

3. This is apparently the same cloak which Antony is said to have bequeathed back to Athanasius when he died some fifteen years later! It may be Jerome's witty means of insisting on Paul's priority over Antony.

4. Jerome, *Letter* 10.

LIFE OF PAUL OF THEBES

1. Palladius (*Lausiac History*, 21.1) also mentions these disciples by name, perhaps using Jerome as his source. Athanasius had not given their names in his *Life of Antony*.

2. Jerome is presumably referring to Athanasius' Greek version and Evagrius' Latin translation.

3. Cyprian, *Letter* 33.

4. Tertullian in his *Apologeticum* refers to an unnamed Greek prostitute who bit off her tongue and spat it in the tyrant's face rather than be forced to reveal certain secrets.

5. Virgil, *Aeneid*, 3:57.

6. This sentence is an echo of Lucius Florus, *Epitome of Livy*, I.40.7.

7. Cf. Mark 9:23.

8. Cf. Psalm 19:4 and Romans 10:18.

9. 1 John 4:18.

10. Matthew 7:7 and Luke 11:9.

11. Virgil, *Aeneid*, 2:650.

12. Virgil, *Aeneid*, 6:672.

13. 1 Corinthians 13:7.

14. Elijah was also fed by ravens at God's command: 1 Kings 17:4–6.

15. Cf. Philippians 1:23.

16. Cf. 2 Timothy 4:7–8.

17. Cf. 1 Corinthians 13:5.

18. Ecclesiastes 3:7.

Life of Hilarion by Jerome

INTRODUCTION

1. Epiphanius himself founded a monastery at Eleutheropolis in Palestine.

2. A chapel was apparently also built on the site of his mountain retreat on Cyprus, near the coast north of Nicosia; later the Crusaders built a castle there, named after Hilarion.

3. By C. Mohrmann, in her introduction to an edition of the *Life of Hilarion* (A. Bastiaensen (ed.), Milan 1975), p. xxxi.

4. *Life of Hilarion*, 4.

LIFE OF HILARION

1. Sallust, *The Conspiracy of Catiline*, 8.

2. Daniel 8:3; 7:6; 8:5, 21.

3. Arrian, *Anabasis*, I.12.1; Plutarch, *Alexander*, 15.4; Cicero, *On behalf of Archias*, 10.24.

4. See D. Chitty, *The Desert a City*, for later monastic settlements, down to the sixth century, at Thabatha. Hilarion was born there in the last decade of the third century.

5. Cf. *The Sayings of the Desert Fathers* (trans. B. Ward), p. 111, where Antony and Hilarion are reported to have greeted each other thus: 'You are welcome,

NOTES

torch which awakens the day,' says Antony, to which Hilarion replies, 'Peace
to you, pillar of light, giving light to the world.'

6. Acts of the Apostles 5:1–11.

7. Luke 14:33.

8. Majuma was later accorded the status of a separate city by Constantine,
who renamed it Constantia, favouring it over Gaza because Majuma's population was predominantly Christian, unlike that of Gaza (Sozomen, *Ecclesiastical
History*, V.3).

9. Isaiah 14:14.

10. 2 Thessalonians 3:10.

11. Exodus 15:1.

12. Psalm 20:7.

13. Luke 5:31.

14. Marnas was a pagan divinity, worshipped chiefly at Gaza, Cf. *Life of
Hilarion*, 20.

15. Rhinocorura was a maritime city on the borders of Egypt and Palestine, apparently originally founded as a penal colony; now known as El
Arish.

16. Cf. Mark 8:23.

17. 2 Kings 5:20ff.

18. Acts of the Apostles 8:18ff.

19. Consus seems to have been an old Roman God whose festival, a type of
harvest festival, was traditionally celebrated with horse races. Cf. Cicero, *On
the Republic*, II.7.12; Ovid, *Fasti*, 3.199ff.; Tertullian, *On the Shows*, 5.

20. Gaza seems to have continued as a predominantly pagan city until at least
the end of the fourth century. See Ramsay Macmullen, *Paganism in the Roman
Empire*. (New Haven, Connecticut 1981), p. 134.

21. Memphis was the centre of the Egyptian cult of Aesculapius, the god of
medicine.

22. Matthew 8:28–33, Mark 5:1–16.

23. This implies that he was a pagan priest.

24. A city of Lower Egypt situated on the east bank of the Nile near the
Mediterranean.

25. Cf. *Life of Antony*, 50.

26. Cf. *Life of Antony*, 91.

27. The Oasis was a strip of habitable land surrounded by desert. Here Jerome
is presumably referring to the so-called Great Oasis which lay west of the
Nile. It had been a place of banishment for political offenders and later of refuge
for Christian fugitives. Gradually it filled with monasteries and churches. Cf.
Socrates, *Ecclesiastical History*, II.28. A nineteenth century visitor to the Great

Oasis (G. A. Hoskings, *A Visit to the Great Oasis* (London 1837)), described it thus:

Let the reader imagine a long and broad valley bounded nearly on every side by low, and I might say, horizontal ranges of mountains, and the whole surface of this enclosed space one immense down of light moving sand. In this fearful valley is a narrow broken chain, a verdant thread of little groves of date trees . . . appearing like little islands in this sea of barrenness.

28. The pagan Julian was emperor from 361 until he was killed in 363 when he was succeeded by Jovian.

29. Matthew 5:14.

30. In about 320 the emperor Constantine began to build a church on the site of the apostle Peter's martyrdom and/or burial. It seems to have been finished by 329 and parts of it survived until the seventeenth century.

31. Matthew 10:8.

32. This seems to be the modern Dubrovnik; as Epidaurus it is mentioned by Procopius, *The Gothic War* V.7.28,32.

33. '*Boa*' is connected with the Greek word *bous*.

34. Matthew 21:21.

35. Matthew 14:31.

36. These three cities were in the east, south and north of Cyprus; together with Paphos in the west, they here represent the whole island.

37. For this area of Egypt known as 'the pastures' cf. *Life of Antony*, 49 (n.95).

38. This may be the place referred to by Sozomen (*Ecclesiastical History*, V.10) as Charburis.

39. Embalmed.

Life of Malchus by Jerome

INTRODUCTION

1. See J. N. D. Kelly, *Jerome, His Life, Writings and Controversies*, pp. 182–9.

2. Cf. Jerome's *Letter* 22, addressed to the young girl Eustochium in 384 but destined to become one of Jerome's best-known works, in which the ideal of chastity is hammered home with more force and less charm.

LIFE OF MALCHUS

1. Evagrius of Antioch was a close friend of Jerome and the translator of Athanasius' *Life of Antony*.

2. Luke 1:5-6.

3. Nisibis was a town in northern Mesopotamia. It is now Nusaybin in south-east Turkey.

4. Beroea was a town in Syria between Antioch and Hierapolis. It is now Aleppo.

5. Proverbs 26:11, *Like a dog that returns to his vomit is a fool that repeats his folly*; cf. 2 Peter 2:22.

6. Cf. Luke 9:62.

7. A city in northern Mesopotamia.

8. Ephesians 6:5-8.

9. Cf. the decision of Ammon and his wife on their wedding night not to consummate their marriage. They lived together for eighteen years, but sleeping in separate beds, before his wife persuaded him to leave her so that he could devote himself to the ascetic life more perfectly. See Sozomen, *Ecclesiastical History*, I.14.

10. Proverbs 6:6.

11. The manuscripts are divided between the readings '*matutina*' and '*mature*', neither wholly satisfactory: I have chosen the latter.

12. Some texts give the reading Sabianus. The name Sabinianus occurs in the extant records in the form of a man who was '*magister equitum*' in the east in 359-60, but this man's career seems to be too late to be that of the man whom Malchus encountered as a young man. However, Reginald of Canterbury, in the twelfth century, wrote a verse life of Malchus, an expanded version of Jerome's biography, in which he uses the reading Sabinianus, which inclines me to consider this reading preferable.

Life of Martin of Tours by Sulpicius Severus

INTRODUCTION

1. For the events surrounding Martin's death, see Sulpicius Severus, *Letters* 2 and 3.

2. See, for example, the introduction to Adomnan, *Life of St Columba* (trans. R. Sharpe, Harmondsworth 1995), pp. 57-9.

3. Sulpicius Severus, *Dialogues*, I.23.

4. *Life of Martin*, XIX.3.

5. *Life of Martin*, XXV.

6. C. Stancliffe, *St Martin and his Hagiographer*, pp. 15–16.

7. It is not only the preface, but also the portrayal of Martin which contains echoes of classical literature, for the structure of the *Life of Martin* has much in common with Suetonius' *Life of the Caesars*.

8. Edward Gibbon, in his *Decline and Fall of the Roman Empire* (chapter 27), contrasted Sulpicius' literary style, which he commended as 'not unworthy of the Augustan age', with much of the content of the work, which he referred to as 'facts adapted to the grossest barbarism'.

LIFE OF MARTIN

1. Cf. Horace, *Epistles*, I.18.71, 'the word once let slip flies beyond recall,' and *Ars Poetica*, 389–90, 'you can delete what you have not published, but once the voice has been sent forth it cannot return.'

2. This preface bears similarities to that of Sallust at the beginning of his work on the conspiracy of Catiline.

3. Probably Szombathely in Hungary, about 100 kilometres south-east of Vienna, close to the border with Austria.

4. Constantius was Roman emperor in the east from 337 to 361; in 355 he made Julian Caesar in Gaul. Julian succeeded Constantius as emperor from 361 to 363.

5. A catechumen was a Christian convert who was being instructed in the faith prior to baptism.

6. Cf. Matthew 6:34.

7. Matthew 25:40.

8. Julian was sent to the Rhine frontier to repel barbarian raids after he had been nominated Caesar in 355. For a contemporary account of these campaigns, see Ammianus Marcellinus, *The Later Roman Empire*, 16.2–3. The incident at Worms, when Martin came up against the pagan authorities, probably took place in 356, the year of Antony's death in Egypt.

9. This was the city later known as Worms.

10. Hilary, one of the great Latin theologians, famous for his work *On the Trinity*, was born in Poitiers in about 315 and died there in about 367.

11. One of the minor orders of the church, below the diaconate.

12. i.e. Martin returned to Sabaria.

13. Psalms 118:6; cf. *Life of Antony*, 6, where Antony also answers the devil with a verse of this same psalm (118:7).

14. Hilary was sent into exile in Asia Minor in 356 for refusing to condemn Athanasius.

15. Auxentius was the Arian bishop of Milan from 355 to 374, when he was succeeded by Ambrose.

16. Gallinara is a tiny island opposite Albenga, 80 kilometres south-west of Genoa on the Italian coast.

17. Constantius sent Hilary back to Gaul in 360.

18. This was at Ligugé, outside Poitiers.

19. Psalm 8:2. The reading 'defensor' (defender) which plays on the name of Martin's principal opponent and is crucial to the point of this episode, is not found in the Latin Vulgate version, but only in the version of the Psalms known as the Psalterium Romanum.

20. Augustine also continued to live in a monastic community even after becoming bishop of Hippo: see Possidius, *Life of Augustine*, 5.4.

21. At Marmoutier outside Tours.

22. Cf. Acts of the Apostles 4:32, 4:35.

23. Martin visited Trier in the period 385–7 in connection with the Priscillianist controversy.

24. Paulinus of Nola, renowned for his renunciation of his great wealth and a close friend of Martin's biographer. Cf. *Life of Martin*, 25.4.

25. Magnus Maximus Maxentius, Roman emperor in the west, 383–8. This banquet was probably held at Trier at some point during the years 385–7.

26. As a result of Maximus' usurpation, Valentinian II was deprived of his imperial sovereignty in Gaul, while Gratian was murdered, allegedly at Maximus' orders.

27. Cf. Orosius, *History against the Pagans*, 7.34.

28. Clarus is mentioned by Paulinus of Nola in *Letter* 23.3.

29. Sulpicius may here be alluding to Jerome's preface to the *Life of Hilarion*, where Jerome mentions Homer in similar terms.

Life of Benedict by Gregory the Great

INTRODUCTION

1. While the first three books recount the miracles of various saints (the account of Benedict's miracles being by far the longest), the fourth book of the *Dialogues* deals with death, heaven and hell.

2. Paulinus of Nola, the friend of Sulpicius Severus, is included among these saints: although he came from Gaul he spent most of his life in Italy at the shrine of St Felix of Nola in Campania.

3. Gregory wrote the *Moralia*, which uses the text of the book of Job as a starting point for spiritual and theological discussions, homilies on Ezechiel and the Gospel, as well as the *Pastoral Rule*.

4. The earliest example of this apologetic use of the genre is probably the *Octavius* of Minucius Felix, dating from the early third century.

LIFE OF BENEDICT

1. In the Latin there is a pun here on the name Benedict which means blessed.

2. Nursia, now Norcia, lies some 100 kilometres north-east of Rome. Benedict was born there in about 480.

3. i.e. at Subiaco.

4. Cf. Matthew 5:15.

5. Numbers 8:24–5.

6. This was the monastery of Vicovaro.

7. Luke 15:11–17.

8. Acts of the Apostles 12:11.

9. St Paul.

10. Philippians 1:21, 1:23.

11. Acts of the Apostles 9:24–5; 2 Corinthians 11:32–3.

12. Gregory interprets this episode in a similar way in his *Moralia in Job* 31:58.

13. It is from this disciple of Benedict that the Maurists, the members of the French Benedictine congregation founded in 1621 and known for its scholarship, took their name.

14. Cf. *Life of Antony*, 6.

15. humble; Cf. Matthew 5:3.

16. Cf. Matthew 11:30.

17. Exodus 17:1–7; Numbers 20:2–13.

18. 2 Kings 6:4–7.

19. Matthew 14:28–9.

20. 1 Kings 17:6.

21. 2 Samuel 1:11–12, 18:33.

22. John 1:9.

23. John 1:16.

24. Matthew 12:39–40.

25. At Monte Cassino.

26. Cf. Paulus Diaconus, *History of the Lombards,* 1.26. In Benedict's day St Martin was widely venerated in Italy.

27. The devil calls Benedict 'Maledictus' (cursed), playing on the meaning of his name (blessed).

28. Prologue, 2.

29. Cf. 2 Kings 5:25−6 where Elisha reveals that he knows of Gehazi's conversation with Naaman.

30. The meeting between Totila and Benedict seems to have taken place in 546.

31. Totila died in 552.

32. In south-east Italy. The bishop's name was Sabinus.

33. In 546.

34. Cf. Prologue, 2.

35. Aquinum lay about ten kilometres west of Monte Cassino.

36. Until the man died.

37. 1 Corinthians 6:17.

38. St Paul at Romans 11:34.

39. 1 Corinthians 2:11.

40. 1 Corinthians 2:12.

41. 1 Corinthians 2:9−10.

42. Romans 11:33; Peter quotes Romans 11:34 in section XVI.4.

43. Psalm 119:13.

44. The destruction by the Lombards probably occurred in 577. The monks fled and the buildings remained ruinous for the next 140 years.

45. Acts of the Apostles 27:22−4.

46. Probably in 537−8.

47. John 3:8.

48. 2 Samuel 7:1−17.

49. 2 Kings 4:27.

50. Terracino lay some fifty kilometres south-west of Monte Cassino.

51. Habakkuk.

52. *Bel and the Dragon* (chapter 14 of the Greek version of Daniel), 33−9.

53. Matthew 16:19.

54. In the Incarnation.

55. According to the *Rule of Benedict* (67.7) monks were not allowed to leave the monastery without their abbot's permission.

56. Cf. Matthew 6:19−20.

57. John 1:12.

58. Acts of the Apostles 9:40.

59. Acts of the Apostles 5:1−10.

60. Cf. *Life of Antony*, 84, on the performing of miracles.

61. The word '*benedictio*', usually meaning a blessing, here bears one of its rarer meanings, being used of a free meal which is blessed and given to visitors.

62. Cf. Elisha and the Shunammite's son: 2 Kings 4:34–5.

63. This was because women, even close relatives, were not allowed to enter the monastery.

64. 1 John 4:16.

65. Cf. Luke 7:47.

66. This recalls the account of Saul and Jonathan in 2 Samuel 1:23: *in their death they were not divided*.

67. Liberius' illustrious career spanned the years 484–554 approximately. He is mentioned by, amongst others, Cassiodorus, Ennodius and Procopius.

68. Cf. *Life of Benedict*, 17.1.

69. John 16:7.

READ MORE IN PENGUIN